The Italian Renaissance
Part III

Professor Kenneth Bartlett

THE TEACHING COMPANY ®

PUBLISHED BY:

THE TEACHING COMPANY
4151 Lafayette Center Drive, Suite 100
Chantilly, Virginia 20151-1232
1-800-TEACH-12
Fax—703-378-3819
www.teach12.com

ISBN 1-59803-061-2

Kenneth Bartlett, Ph.D.
Professor of History and Renaissance Studies, University of Toronto

Kenneth Bartlett, Professor of History and Renaissance Studies at the University of Toronto, received his Ph.D. from the University of Toronto in 1978. He served as editor of *Renaissance and Reformation/Renaissance et Réforme* and president of the Canadian Society for Renaissance Studies. He was founding director of the University of Toronto Art Centre and remains coordinator of faculty programs in Arts and Science.

Much of Professor Bartlett's career has been devoted to bringing Renaissance culture into the undergraduate and graduate classroom. He has taught regularly in the University of Toronto Program in Siena, Italy, as well as in the Oxford Program. In 2002, he was appointed the first director of the Office of Teaching Advancement for the University of Toronto. He has been the recipient of the Victoria University Excellence in Teaching Award, the Students Administrative Council and Association of Part-Time University Students Teaching Award, and the Faculty of Arts and Science Teaching Excellence Award. In 2005 he was awarded a prestigious national 3M Teaching Fellowship.

Dr. Bartlett is the author of *The English in Italy, 1525–1558: A Study in Culture and Politics* (1991); *The Civilization of the Italian Renaissance* (1992); and *Humanism and the Northern Renaissance* (with M. McGlynn, 2000). He was co-editor or translator of four other books and the author of more than 35 articles and chapters on Renaissance history and culture. In 2003, Dr. Bartlett was co-curator of the exhibition *Gods, Saints and Heroes: Italian Renaissance Maiolica from the Metropolitan Museum of Art* at the Gardiner Museum of Ceramic Art. In addition, he has been the academic consultant on the Illuminated Filmworks videos on the Vatican Library, *The Halls of Virtuous Learning*, *The Galleries of Sixtus V*, *and Pages of Light*, as well as for the international exhibitions *Raphael and His Circle: Drawings from the Royal Collection at Windsor* and *Angels from the Vatican* at the Art Gallery of Ontario.

Dr. Bartlett lives in Toronto with his wife, Gillian.

Table of Contents
The Italian Renaissance
Part III

The Italian Renaissance

Scope:

This course on the Italian Renaissance will attempt to answer the question: Why was there such an explosion of creative culture, human ingenuity, economic development, and social experimentation in Italy beginning in the 14th century? It will also address the question of why the Renaissance ended in the middle years of the 16th century.

In order to investigate the phenomenon of the Renaissance in Italy, it is necessary to look at every facet of human endeavor. Thus, this series will not be a discussion of major political, military, or economic events, although these will appear, as appropriate. Rather, the course will follow the model of writing Renaissance history designed by its first great practitioner, Jacob Burckhardt, whose 1860 book-length "essay," *The Civilization of the Renaissance in Italy*, initiated the model of cultural history, that is, looking at a period in the past from several perspectives simultaneously to produce a sophisticated, multidimensional image. Just as each tessera in a mosaic contributes to the whole, so each element in social, political, economic, cultural, intellectual, and religious history contributes to the composite picture of life in Italy in the years between the birth of Petrarch in 1304 and the terrible events of the 1520s–1540s that extinguished the flame that the poet first lit.

Several elements must first be assessed before the question of cultural development can be answered. We must investigate why the Italian peninsula was so different from the rest of Europe in the 13th and 14th centuries. How did the city-states of Italy manage to develop such sophisticated societies based on various forms of government, with social mobility and secular education, and amass such enormous wealth, when most of the rest of the continent still lived under feudal regimes, largely local economies, and clerically dominated culture? To what extent was the very lack of unity in the peninsula an advantage? And why did such states as Florence choose to invest so much of their surplus capital in art and learning? What was Humanism and why was it a peculiarly Italian phenomenon in the 14th century? And why do we begin our study of the culture of the Renaissance with Francesco Petrarca (1304–1374), or Petrarch, a poet and thinker who believed he had the misfortune to have been born outside his age? These are complex parts of a complex story, but one worth telling because the Renaissance gave us so many of the tools by which we still interpret our lives and the world around us.

In discussing these aspects of the culture of the Renaissance, we will see that many of the fundamental perspectives of the modern world were formed at that time. It has been argued that Petrarch invented the contemporary concept of the individual, writing in his *Secret Book*, the first psychological autobiography since Augustine's *Confessions*. Such artists as Donatello and Brunelleschi developed the principles of linear perspective, which permitted the creation of a three-dimensional image on a two-dimensional plane. In so doing, not only did they open the way for Naturalism in art—reproducing what the eye sees—but they set the intellectual stage for modern cartography and, hence, the voyages of discovery, because objects could be put in correctly calibrated relative space and distances could be precisely mapped. The desire of Renaissance thinkers to know themselves and others drove artists to perfect the reproduction of correct anatomy in painting and sculpture, with Donatello's *David* the first freestanding male nude figure since antiquity. Portraiture allowed viewers to identify their fellow citizens or famous men and women through their appearances and, soon after, through the skill of the painter, acquire an insight into their characters. All of this was the product of the Italian Renaissance mind.

In addition, Renaissance writers, in their desire to know the world around them and make correct observations about that world and the variety of its inhabitants, extended the importance of individual experience and privileged it. In other words, life became less a vale of tears on the part of faithful servants of God acting out a role he had determined for them with little sense of personal agency. Rather, individuals, acting either alone or in concert with their fellow citizens, could assume some responsibility for creating art, ideas, and even social experiments that benefited our lives on Earth. Secular knowledge, practical skills, political involvement, marriage, family, and even the paying of taxes became instruments for human fulfillment and the means of constructing a more pleasant and meaningful life. The human perspective changed from the theocentric world of the Middle Ages to the anthropocentric world of the Renaissance. This shift emphasized the ideal of the creation of an individual life as a work of art and the building of cities that were equally things of beauty and commodity. It celebrated human achievement, including social mobility and social responsibility. This is not to say that the Renaissance was pagan or any less Christian—it was not—but it shifted the balance in the role of human free will and unleashed the creative spirit of thousands of individuals. Fame and history became important to Italians, who saw themselves as part of the human continuum; the ancient pagan classics could be applied to contemporary situations in art, learning, and even ethics, because it could be shown that the ancient Greeks and Romans were good men with good advice concerning the human condition. Salvation remained a matter of faith and religious communion, but the complexity of human experience on Earth had been recognized and validated.

The Renaissance manifested itself differently in different places in Italy. The great republics, such as Florence and Venice, enjoyed a form of government that permitted a different kind of social and economic organization. These, especially Florence, have often been identified as the primary theaters of Renaissance culture. However, this is both unfair and incorrect. As we will see, small, petty principalities, such as 15th-century Urbino, contributed greatly to the Renaissance ideal, as did the enormously complex but equally influential city of Rome. Rome was at once the center of Western Christianity, with its bishop the head of the Church, and the city, the head of the Roman Empire, the living memory of a time when Italy ruled the known world and created so many of its fundamental institutions and ideas. Humanism, Renaissance culture, and the desire for fame and personal power infected the Church just as much as it did the republican magistracies in Florence or the courtly societies of monarchical regimes. We will need to look severally at the major centers of Renaissance culture to trace the flexibility of its dominant ideals and see how competition and patronage in different environments added to the rich growth of Italian culture.

Many of the principles of Renaissance Italian Humanism and ideals remain with us today, and not just the appreciation for Naturalism in art and the validity of individual experience, without which we could not have experimental science, for example. The principles of Renaissance education, based on knowledge of the Greek and Roman classics, remained the foundation for elite education well into the

20th century. Philosophical ideas, such as the dignity of man (a precursor of the principle of basic human rights) and the belief in ideal worlds, still inform our discourse. Italian commercial inventions still drive the engines of any capitalist society, and acceptance of the unique responsibility of the individual to construct himself or herself into the best model of achievement and civic engagement continues to go straight to the heart of a free society. These principles might have developed in the seemingly distant world of Renaissance Italy, but their attraction to the essence of human nature and the multiplicity of human experience make them as valid now as they were then.

Finally, we will discuss why these heroic ideals and institutions collapsed. Here, too, there might be lessons to learn for our own world. I will suggest that the conditions that gave rise to such noble practices and principles were crushed by the terror of war, occasioned by the French invasions of Italy in 1494, which turned the peninsula into the battleground of Europe for almost 60 years. I will argue that unspeakable events, such as the 1527 sack of Rome, made it difficult to sustain such ideals as the dignity of man. And the repressive reaction of the Church and many Italian states to the challenge of the Reformation introduced mechanisms that crushed the imagination, freedom of speech, and freedom of action. The introduction of the Roman Inquisition in the 1540s, the Index of Prohibited Books in the 1550s and 1560s, and the growing authoritarianism in the monarchies that ruled Italy snuffed out the light that Petrarch and those of his generation had lit. Of course, there were external forces, such as the capture of Constantinople by the Turks in 1453 and the consequent shift of the European economy to the Atlantic seaboard from the Mediterranean (the *Media Terra*, the center of the world since the beginning of recorded European history). But challenges had been met previously; now they appeared insurmountable. There was a failure of will, imagination, and belief. For example, Italians were still among the greatest of seafarers, but they sailed for Spain, England, and France; Italians remained great shipbuilders, but they continued to construct shallow- draft, wide-beamed galleys that were suited to the Mediterranean—where trade was being strangled by the Turkish advance—and completely useless on the open ocean, where new opportunities lay.

In many ways, the Renaissance was an attitude and a quality of mind, a belief that "Man is the measure of all things," that "Man can do anything that he but wills." It was a failure of will and a loss of belief in the capacity and creativity of the human mind that ended the Renaissance, because it put an end to the principles that had driven its creation and expansion.

Lecture Twenty-Five
The Crisis—The French Invasion of 1494

Scope:

The Italian Renaissance had flourished so richly in part because of the protected space of the peninsula. Surrounded on three sides by water and the Alps to the north, Italy had not suffered from foreign invasion on a large scale since the barbarian incursions after the collapse of Rome. However, at the end of the 15th century, the situation changed. The creation of dynastic territorial monarchies in the north, such as France, permitted the concentration of huge resources for foreign adventures. Also, the competing state system and the ambition of many of the ruling houses of Italy resulted in northern monarchies, such as France, Spain, and the Holy Roman Empire, having dynastic or sovereign claims on various states. In 1494, King Charles VIII of France decided to invade Italy with the largest army then amassed and with sophisticated materiel, such as mobile artillery, in order to assert his claim to the Kingdom of Naples. Initially aided by the Milanese, who thought to manipulate the French into destroying the threat posed to Lodovico il Moro's rule by the Neapolitans, the French army was virtually unopposed and the conquest of Naples was an easy victory. Although the Milanese realized their error and joined with the other Italian states to hurry the French out of Italy, Charles had shown that the rich cities of the peninsula were vulnerable and that the peninsula would never again enjoy its unmolested independence.

Outline

I. In previous lectures, we have alluded to the events of the French invasion of 1494, particularly its role in ending the Sforza rule in Milan (Lecture Twenty-One).

   A. In fact, this cataclysmic event can be interpreted as the crisis of the Renaissance in all of Italy: the beginning of the end of this remarkable historical period.

       1. As you will recall, the Peace of Lodi (1454) and the Italian League (1455) negotiated between Cosimo de'Medici and Francesco Sforza had created spheres of influence on the peninsula.

2. The league had allowed for collective security, encouraging all the other major Italian states to come to the assistance of any one of them attacked from without.

3. The consequence had been a significant reduction of the endemic warfare of the peninsula.

B. Contributing to this sense of security was the situation north of the Alps in the 15th century.

1. The potentially powerful dynastic monarchies in the north were, at the same time, divided.

2. France only became a centralized dynastic monarchy under Louis XI (d. 1483) following the end of the Hundred Years' War.

3. The Iberian peninsula similarly was not united until the dynastic union of Isabel of Castile and Ferdinand of Aragon in 1469.

4. Thereafter, the energy of Isabel and Ferdinand remained directed toward the conquest of Granada and the expulsion of the Moors, not accomplished until 1492.

5. The Holy Roman Empire remained weak, because the emperor was elected and required the cooperation of the German princes for any coherent policy.

C. There were, however, growing threats to the economy and stability of the Italian peninsula.

1. The capture of Constantinople by the Turks in 1453 ended the virtual Italian monopoly on the luxury trade with the East, a source of great wealth, especially for Venice.

2. This also led to increased warfare in the Mediterranean with the Turks, who began to encroach on Italian territory, capturing previously safe harbors.

3. The dangers in the Mediterranean led to the exploration and opening of other routes to the East that further sapped Italian control of trade.

4. The economic center of Europe shifted away from the Mediterranean to the Atlantic seaboard, slowly reducing Italy to an economic backwater.

5. As peace was restored in Europe after the Hundred Years' War, Florence lost many of its markets for wool.

6. Italian bankers also suffered, because England and France no longer came to them for huge loans with which to wage war.

II. The young, ambitious, and delusional king of France, Charles VIII (r. 1483–1498), had planned from the time of achieving his majority to take Naples, believing that he had a divine mission to take a crown he judged to have belonged to his family but had been usurped.

    A. The House of Aragon (co-ruling Spain with the House of Castile) had historic claims on not only Naples and Sicily but Milan, as well.

        1. It was also rich in zealous, battle-hardened soldiers, whom the Spanish king wished to keep occupied in warfare outside of the kingdom rather than within.

        2. Spain, then, would soon challenge France for hegemony in the peninsula.

    B. Events within the individual Italian states also contributed to the instability of the situation.

    C. Lorenzo de'Medici, one of the key proponents of the Peace of Lodi, died in 1492, leaving control of the city of Florence to his incompetent son Piero.

        1. Piero was no match for the ascetic Dominican monk Girolamo Savonarola (about whom we will hear in the next lecture), who not only polarized and destabilized Florence but also added an atmosphere of apocalyptic fatalism.

        2. Savonarola was a millennial preacher, prophesying that the judgment of God was at hand.

        3. His working of the old Italian prophetic tradition helped create a mood of doom and inevitability that sapped Florentine resolve.

    D. In the same year that Florence lost its leader, the pope, Innocent VIII, died in Rome.

        1. Although morally suspect, Innocent had at least been a peaceful pope who had married his son to a daughter of Lorenzo de'Medici and had actively cooperated in the period of stability in Italy.

2. Elected in his place was the ambitious Borgia pope Alexander VI, who plotted to establish a Borgia kingdom in Italy based on the states of the Church.

3. Alexander was also willing to cooperate with northern powers to weaken opposition in Italy and aid his cause.

4. Thus, the Borgia campaigns exploded the Peace of Lodi and brought a deep vein of instability and danger back into Italian diplomacy and politics.

E. The situation reached its head in 1494, when King Ferrante of Naples died, leaving the crown to his ambitious son Alfonso.

1. The House of Aragon had already separated Sicily from Naples.

2. As you will recall, Lodovico il Moro and Beatrice d'Este of Milan had a son whom they were afraid would be murdered by the rightful Sforza duke, Lodovico's nephew Giangaleazzo II, should he ever assume active rule.

3. Giangaleazzo II was married to the sister of Alfonso, king of Naples, who plotted with the legitimate duke to take control away from the regent Lodovico and set Giangaleazzo in power.

4. To preempt this danger and destroy the threat from Naples, Lodovico encouraged the French to invade the peninsula and take the crown of Naples.

III. When Charles VIII crossed the Alps into Italy in 1494, he led the largest force Italy had seen since the barbarian invasions of the 5th century.

A. The military campaign proved to be easier than anyone in France could have predicted, with virtually no resistance offered against Charles.

1. The Milanese welcomed his troops.

2. The Venetians could mount no opposition, because they were occupied in the Mediterranean against the Turks.

3. Florence, under the foolish leadership of Piero de'Medici, tried to broker a peace with the French.

4. Piero achieved only a humiliating arrangement, through which Florence lost control of Pisa, the republic's prized port on the Arno, as well as fortresses on the republic's perimeter.

5. The pope, Alexander VI, was interested only in his own family ambitions and was willing to bargain away the security of Italy rather than alienate the French.

6. Naples could not, then, hold out against this invincible force.

7. It capitulated in 1495, and Charles entered the capital as king.

B. With Naples captured, France had to find a way of keeping the kingdom and neutralizing the forces that were becoming alarmed at Charles's easy victory.

1. Unable to stay indefinitely in Naples, Charles began his return to France in 1495.

2. In the intervening months, however, the other states of Europe and Italy realized the extent of the danger.

3. Spain and the Holy Roman Empire saw the political implications of French control of Italy: the extinction of Aragonese claims to Naples and the ability of France to attack the Holy Roman Empire on two fronts.

4. Venice joined them, followed by Milan, as Lodovico il Moro realized his mistake in inviting the French to intervene: Milan, too, could be claimed by the French royal house.

5. The French were harried on their retreat, one inconclusive battle being fought at Fornovo.

6. In the end, Charles lost control of Naples, and the House of Aragon returned to reassert its authority.

IV. Charles may have lost, but he had illustrated the weakness and division of the Italian peninsula and rich prizes available for the taking.

A. Charles died without issue from an accident in 1498 while planning his second campaign in Italy.

B. He left as his heir his cousin, the duke of Anjou, who as Louis XII, intended to pursue Charles's claim on both Naples and Milan.

C. Italy's history for the next 350 years would be one of foreign occupation and control.

Primary Source Texts:

Alessandro Benedetti, *Diaria de Bello Carolino* (*Diary of the Caroline War*).

Francesco Guicciardini, *The History of Italy*.

Secondary Sources:

Denys Hay and John Law, *Italy in the Age of the Renaissance, 1380–1530*.

Questions to Consider:

1. Consider why the Italians were so slow to anticipate the danger posed by the northern European monarchies. Do you think Renaissance cultural ideals had anything to do with their complacency?

2. Petrarch, Machiavelli, and other Renaissance Italians believed that the northerners were barbarians. Was their assessment fair?

Lecture Twenty-Five—Transcript

The Crisis—The French Invasion of 1494

In previous lectures, we've alluded to the events of the French invasion of 1494—particularly when we discussed in Milan the desire of Lodovico Sforza to maintain his rule, and the circumstances that gave rise to his welcoming the French.

But we also must know that these invasions of 1494, represented amongst the most cataclysmic moments in all Italian history, began a period that would ultimately end in the subjection of the peninsula for more than 350 years to foreign rulers. It was also the crisis of the Italian Renaissance. It was the moment when all of the values that we've been investigating were challenged—challenged by forces from without, forces that the Italians themselves were really unable to sustain.

As you'll recall, the Peace of Lodi of 1454 and the Italian League (which followed the subsequent year), which were negotiated between Cosimo de'Medici and Francesco Sforza, created a period of remarkable peace in the Italian peninsula. Italy began to see a period of at least a serious reduction of the endemic warfare that had characterized Italian life. The League allowed for collective security. It allowed for an opportunity for the five major states of the peninsula to work together in order to limit war, and also to provide a kind of collective security against external aggression. And in many ways, it worked.

There were also other factors that allowed Italy to develop independently—things again outside of Italian control, but that benefited the Italians so greatly that the Renaissance could take place; these were things that had economic implications, but for the moment of this lecture, they were things that had very, very significant political and military implications as well.

First of all, the great dynastic monarchies north of the Alps were themselves divided. The feudal kingdoms of France and the Iberian peninsula hadn't yet coalesced into powerful centralized states. But that was beginning to change, especially in the second half of the 15th century.

France became a centralized territorial monarchy under Louis XI, known appropriately as the "Spider," who died in 1483. And this was the consequence of the end of the Hundred Years War in part, when the French kings could concentrate on building their own power internally, as opposed to trying to keep the English out.

The Iberian peninsula, at about the same time, was coming together as a result of a dynastic union. The kingdoms of the Iberian peninsula—that is, that territory that contains Spain and Portugal and the remnants of the Moorish kingdoms in Europe—the Iberian peninsula came together as a result of the marriage of Isabel of Castile and Ferdinand of Aragon. This united, then, all of the Spanish-speaking territories into a single state. And the intention was not just to create this dynastic union, which ultimately give rise to the Kingdom of Spain, but also to use this as a foundation for the driving of the moors—that is, the Islamic kingdoms from Grenada—and also, ultimately, the expulsion of the Jews, both of which took place in 1492.

The Holy Roman Empire—that is, the German-speaking lands on the other side of the Rhine—remained weak. The Holy Roman Emperor was, after all, an elective office. The power base of each individual emperor depended almost completely on the degree to which the electing princes and the other princes of Germany would provide support. Consequently, in the 15th century, there was a sense of weakness without a sense of general purpose to the empire. But all of these things changed.

First of all, there was that other event of the second half of the 15th century that changed European history so dramatically for such a long time. In 1453, the Turks, under Mohammed the Conqueror, took the city of Constantinople, the capital of the Byzantine Empire, that empire founded by the Emperor Constantine—that empire that was a continued, unbroken succession of emperors from the time of the first Christian emperor of Rome—fell to the Turks, seen in Europe as the infidel.

The effect of this, then, was not only psychological, but it was also military and economic. In particular, it meant that the luxury trade, largely managed by the Venetians with huge profit, was challenged. And, in fact, that Venetian monopoly, that Italian monopoly, on long-distance luxury trade evaporated. The Turks had no interest in sustaining the benefits that the Venetians had received after the Fourth Crusade. To them, all of the Italians, all Christians, were merely infidels to pay higher taxes, bribes, and fees.

Also, the victory of the Muslims in the eastern Mediterranean resulted in constant warfare. As the Turks began to expand into the Aegean, into the Mediterranean, and then ultimately into Europe itself, there was need for constant warfare. The previously safe harbors, the protected trade routes, were then gone. The Venetians and the other Italians, then, had to turn their trading galleys into war galleys, and the amount of trade was limited. It became much more expensive and dangerous, and it naturally declined.

The effect of this on Italy was also felt through forces, again, outside of Italian control. It was clear to the Portuguese that there had to be another way around the continent of Africa in order to get to the rich cities of the east. If the Mediterranean had become too expensive and too dangerous to trade in with any kind of security and comfort, then perhaps there was an end to the African continent. Then maybe what the Romans did not know could be proved by the contemporary Portuguese, who every year went a little bit farther down the coast of that continent until, ultimately, Vasco da Gama sailed around it, proving not only that it had an end, but also that you could sail from the cities of the Atlantic seaboard, from the cities of Portugal and Spain, and later, from the cities of Holland, and England, and France, and reach the rich trading cities of the east—of India and, ultimately, China.

The result was that the monopoly that the Italians had enjoyed in the Mediterranean ended. No longer was the Mediterranean Sea the *media terra*, the center of the earth, as it had been almost from anthropological times. Now for Europe, the new center of economic authority was the Atlantic seaboard, where ships could be loaded and sailed directly to the east, and return full of rich treasure. This began the decline of Italy economically, a decline that ultimately, by the 17th century, would turn Italy into an economic backwater, just looking at its past glory with nostalgia.

Similarly, the end of the Hundred Years War had an enormous effect on Italy. First of all, it meant that the dynastic kingdoms could unite. Secondly, it meant that the French and the English were no longer in need of huge amounts of money borrowed from Italian bankers to fight their continuous wars. The Italian bankers suffered, and consequently the Italian economy suffered, with less and less of the accumulated wealth of Europe being funneled into their coffers.

Equally, the coming of peace, especially to the Low Countries, meant that their indigenous woolen industry, those great cities like Ypres that had produced high-quality woolen cloth, could now once more challenge the Florentines. This cloth—so much more easily available, costing less to transport—could then clothe the rich merchants and nobles of the north. The Italian industry, especially that of Florence, then, began to suffer as well.

Much of this came to a head in the personality of a very, very curious young man—the young, extremely ambitious, delusional Charles VIII of France. From the time he reached his age of majority, this young king believed that he had a divine mission. He believed that the figure who was going, ultimately, to put together a great Crusade and drive the infidel from the Holy Lands, defeat the Turks, and unite the world under a single Christian monarch, would, of course, be himself, Charles.

He also believed that the first stage was to undo one of the misfortunes of history, and that is keeping his family away from the crown of Naples. He believed that the crown of Naples was his by dynastic right and that it had been usurped, and it was his intent to undo this terrible event that took place as a consequence of the madness of Queen Joanna of Naples, and thereby make history right once more so his Crusade could begin.

The House of Aragon, which of course co-ruled the Iberian peninsula with the House of Castile as a result of the marriage of Ferdinand and Isabella, had not only claims on Sicily and Naples, but also on the duchy of Milan. It was also, this Kingdom of Spain, as it was becoming, rich in zealous, battled-hardened soldiers—those soldiers who had fought in the re-conquest of the Iberian peninsula, who had fought in the Crusades against the moors. These professional, very experienced soldiers were, in fact, a danger to any force that controlled them. And the King of Spain realized the best thing to do was have them fight outside his kingdom, fighting someone else, rather than fight within the kingdom, fighting him.

Spain, then, would soon be a force that would challenge French hegemony. The Kingdom of France—one of the largest, most centralized, richest in natural resources, and most fertile kingdoms—was clearly a force to be reckoned with. The Spanish, though, were beginning to realize that they had conflicting claims and conflicting rights, and these would be fought out in Italy.

Moreover, within the Italian states themselves, there were problems that gave rise to this kind of crisis. In 1492, Lorenzo de'Medici died. Lorenzo, the grandson of Cosimo, was very much a proponent of the Peace of Lodi, of the Italian League. He helped to make it work through his personal skillful diplomacy.

When he died, he left the rule of the city to his eldest, totally incompetent son, Piero. Piero was no match for the forces at work. He was no match internally for the ascetic Dominican monk, Girolamo Savonarola (about whom we will hear much in the next two lectures). Savonarola polarized Florence, and those that were opposed to the Medici were the supporters of the monk. There was also, as a result of the preaching of this apocalyptic Dominican, a sense of fatalism that began to almost engulf the Florentine people. There was a sense that something terrible was about to happen and they had little control over it. The mood, then, of Florence was not one of standing firm, but rather a fear.

Savonarola, the millennial preacher, believed, then, that the judgment of God was at hand, and it was a judgment that would necessarily be harsh. The Florentines needed to recognize this, and the Florentines needed to repent—when, in fact, the Florentines needed to be decisive and fight.

Savonarola, moreover, worked on the old Italian prophetic tradition. There was in Italy, from the Middle Ages, a long history of prophecies about foreigners who had come and cleansed the church and restored God's intent for man. Joachim of Fiore, those in the Franciscan movement who prophesized a new need to cleanse man of sin—all of these prophesies Savonarola knew and used brilliantly. And this, too, sapped some of the energy, and it also made, in his reading of the Book of Daniel, for example, the belief that the final seals were about to be opened, but the apocalypse was, in fact, at hand.

In Rome, there was another crisis. The death of Pope Innocent VIII—at the same time almost of that of Lorenzo de'Medici—took away an irenic pope. Innocent was not a person of high moral standards, to say the least, but he had been peaceful, and he wanted peace and quiet. He had married his son to one of the daughters of Lorenzo de'Medici, and there was, then, a sense of shared responsibility for the peace of the peninsula.

Innocent worked hard, then, to ensure that there would be nothing that would interrupt his enjoyment of the papacy. The result was stability. Elected in his place, though, was someone of a very different personality and a different set of ambitions—Rodrigo Borgia, who became Pope Alexander VI. The Borgia intention from the beginning was to establish a Borgia kingdom using, as a base, the states of the church. Their ambitions were huge. The intention, then, was to use the papacy as an instrument for Borgia aggression. The idea of peace really wasn't part of it.

Alexander, moreover, would do anything to achieve his goal, and he was even willing to compromise with foreign powers in the north in order to ensure that the Borgias would rule something in Italy while he was still pope.

The Borgia campaigns, then, in many ways, exploded the Peace of Lodi and brought a deep vein of instability and danger back into Italian diplomacy and politics. All of this reached a head, that moment of crisis, in 1494 when King Ferrante of Naples died, leaving the crown to his extremely ambitious, energetic son, Alfonso.

The House of Aragon had already succeeded in separating Sicily from Naples, and the situation of the dynasty in the peninsula was very much challenged by the circumstances, as we've seen, of Lodovico Il Moro as regent of Milan. Lodovico Il Moro had married Beatrice d'Este, and they had produced a son. And, as I said earlier, the danger was that if the real duke, Giangaleazzo II Sforza, should ever achieve rule, then, in fact, the danger to Lodovico and his family would be extreme. Moreover, Giangaleazzo II was married to the sister of Alfonso, and, consequently, the Neapolitans had a direct interest in overthrowing Lodovico's regency and establishing Giangaleazzo II as the reigning Duke of Milan.

Something, then, had to be done, and as we've seen, Lodovico very cleverly manipulated the situation so that the French would not only be invited into the peninsula to claim the Kingdom of Naples, thereby helping secure Lodovico's rule, but also would do so with the cooperation of the Milanese. The crown of Naples, then, was offered, in effect, to Charles by the Milanese, and Charles, that delusional young man who truly believed that he was God's instrument in the new Charlemagne, crossed the Alps to claim it.

When Charles VIII of France crossed the Alps in 1494, he led the largest army to enter Italy since the barbarian invasions of the 5th century. Moreover, it was an army the like of which the Italians had not seen—a raid with differentiated weapons, bringing mobile field artillery, cannons mounted on wheels, huge in numbers. These were not the sorts of armies that the Italians had been experienced to fight. What they saw, then, was a national dynastic feudal army confronting the mercenary forces—those tiny, highly professional groups of mercenary soldiers that fought the Italian Wars. There was no contest. There couldn't be. There was no way the Italians could stand up to the French.

The Milanese, as we've seen, helped pay for Charles's expedition and welcomed him. The Venetians couldn't do anything because they were busy fighting the Turks. Florence, under the foolish leadership of Piero de'Medici, simply wanted peace—wanted some kind of security. And Piero, in his own delusion, believed he had his father's diplomatic skills and went to Charles, and Piero tried to broker a deal in which Florence would end up ahead. Instead, he achieved only total humiliation, an arrangement through which Florence lost its port of Pisa at the head of the Arno, a city that Florence had fought so hard to achieve—a city that was necessary for Florentine long-distance trade and access to the sea. Also, Florence gave up the fortresses on the perimeter of its territory. Fortresses like Sarzana that were built in order to protect the territory of the Florentine people were now turned over to French garrisons.

The pope, Alexander VI, was interested only in his family ambitions, and he was willing to bargain away Italian liberty and freedom to further those things. So, when the French army entered Italy—Naples, in fact, already had its fate sealed. There was nothing that could, in fact, stop the French. In 1495, Naples capitulated. Charles entered the city as a conqueror, claimed its crown, and spent his time enjoying his victory.

With Naples captured, France then had to find a way of keeping the kingdom, of trying to neutralize the forces that were then coalescing around the opposition, recognizing how dangerous this moment had become. Initially, these were events that seemed to be driven by a kind of mad logic. Everything seemed to be working in its favor. But, as soon as the ease of the victory of Charles VIII was known—not only in Italy, but in the rest of Europe—a great sense of fear, a sense of unease about the future, began to inhabit the capitals of the continent.

Everything was too easy. Charles's advance was too easy. It was more like a military parade than a military campaign. And Charles knew that he, ultimately, would have to leave Naples and return to his own kingdom, which he began in 1495. In the intervening months, though, that sense of unease, that general recognition of the serious danger that this circumstance had given rise to, galvanized the other kings and princes of Italy and Europe to do something.

It became clear, then, that the French extinction of Aragonese claims in Naples was a great danger to the empire, for example, and a great danger to the dynastically united Spanish peninsula. It would be easy, then, for France to attack the empire, for example, on two fronts: from below, and also from the west. It was also clear, then, that the same circumstance could arise in the Spanish peninsula. France had to be humbled. France had to be controlled.

Moreover, Lodovico Il Moro very, very quickly saw the danger of his desperate gamble. He realized what a mistake it had been, because he also knew perfectly well that the Royal House of France had legitimate dynastic claims on the duchy of Milan. He knew very well that he was seen as, in some ways, a usurper. He was seen as someone who owed his crown to the emperor. The French, then, would have no compunction whatsoever of doing what they had done to the Florentines: essentially, treacherously abandoning their interests and taking advantage of the circumstances, and giving rise to a new sense of French hegemony on the continent.

Lodovico, then, joined the opposition. He helped hurry Charles VIII and his army out of Italy. And, in fact, the Milanese were largely responsible for the one inconclusive battle, that at Fornovo, which technically the Italian forces won, but really was a kind of draw. In the end, Charles lost control of Naples. It was too far. His supply lines were too long. He had too many enemies in between. But it was very clear that a new order, in fact, had been created as a result of his military experiment.

The Aragonese reclaimed the Kingdom of Naples, and they were determined that they weren't going to give it up. Something, in fact, had to be done, and the Italians knew it. They began to think amongst themselves about how to achieve some form of protection. But the days of the Peace of Lodi, and the days of Francesco Sforza, and Lorenzo de'Medici, and Cosimo de'Medici, were long passed. A time when the states could work together for common purpose had passed. What was seen now was a new world, one in which individual self-interest on the part of Italian princes began to play a desperate role in trying to further their interests at the expense of those of their neighbors.

The Borgia pope had clear ambitions. Piero de'Medici had his own ambitions, and he was, on top of that, stupid, foolish, and incompetent. He had bargained away the good will that his father had established, and now he was left in the situation of being allied to the kingdom that threatened his rule the most. The same was true with the Milanese. Lodovico Il Moro still ruled a brilliant court, but he also ruled it in fear, knowing that the next French invasion could very well be directed at Milan, as well as Naples.

Charles, then, had succeeded in completely and totally fragmenting the Italian peninsula—politically, militarily, and even kind of psychologically. The Italians, then, stopped thinking the way that they had after the Peace of Lodi, being able to consider themselves Italians. They now saw themselves, rather, as desperate Florentines, desperate Milanese, of the papal ambitious ruler of the Holy See, or the desperately nervous King of Naples.

Also, it was clear to anyone who watched that this *promenade militare* over the Alps, that easy victory that Charles VIII had achieved, meant that the entire Italian peninsula, with its incredibly rich prizes, its concentrated wealth, its wonderful cities, its art—all of these things were available for the taking. Whoever had the ability to cross those mountains and simply march and claim some form of victory over the disunited states of the peninsula could, in fact, take whatever he wanted.

The death of Charles VIII, by accident, in 1498 focused much of this fear in another way. Charles, as I said, was an extraordinarily improbable conqueror. He was small, top-heavy, not completely capable of closing his mouth, foolish looking—in fact, the object of some ridicule when he wasn't watching. The means of his death reflected this. He was scurrying along a parapet at his chateau at Amboise. He saw a tennis match in one of the courtyards below; it captured his interest and attention, and he stared at it intently while he continued to scurry along the parapet. He didn't notice a very low lintel, hit his head, and knocked his brains out and died.

His death at the age of 28 without any legitimate issue, focused the crisis because it turned the crown of France to his cousin. His cousin was the Duke of Anjou, who then took the regal title of Louis XII. The Duke of Anjou was the grandson of a daughter of Giangaleazzo Visconti.

Earlier, I said that one of the dangers of the Milanese and the attempt to create some form of dynastic equality with the great powers of the north was to marry their daughters to their sons. The marriage of the children of Giangaleazzo Visconti into the Royal House of France resulted in a direct claim through the Visconti line of the House of Anjou to Milan. This, of course, Louis XII saw with delight. He saw the opportunity, and he had every intention of acting on it.

Louis XII was a very different kind of ruler from Charles VIII. Louis was an extremely careful, organized, brilliant king. He knew that if he was going to maintain his singular rule of his rather fractious dynastic monarchy, if he was going to succeed in maintaining it united and centralized, what he had to do was keep his fractious and violent feudal nobles fighting elsewhere. And his decision was for them to fight in Italy. It didn't take much for Louis to claim Milan. We've seen from the perspective of Lodovico Il Moro and Beatrice d'Este the tragic events that gave rise to the French conquest of the duchy and the terrible effect that it had on, not only Lodovico himself and on his son, but also on Italian history altogether.

When that campaign of 1500 began, it began the way Charles VIII had—an enormous feudal army with the kinds of weapons and organization the Italians couldn't imagine assembling, marching into the Italian peninsula across the flat Lombard plain towards the great city of St. Ambrose. Its fall, and the ultimate capture of Lodovico Il Moro and the establishment of a French ruler in Milan, would have disastrous effects.

First of all, it meant that the French would have a power base within Italy, one that they could use in order to challenge the Aragonese in Naples, because the French continued to claim that crown of Naples. The circumstance, then, is that Italy was not just fragmented amongst the various states of the peninsula, but there was superimposed a division of two great northern dynastic powers: that of Aragon in the south, and that of France in the north. Their wars would bring in all of the Italian states, devastate the peninsula, and cause 60 years of the most terrible bloodshed the peninsula had seen.

It was a situation that then became intolerable because there was nothing the Italians could do. It began a period of not just fragmentation, but a period of internecine and civil war—a time when each of the Italian states tried, in their own way, to confront what all of them called "the barbarians."

It's not an accident that Machiavelli and his prince, and almost every other writer that was Machiavelli's contemporary, called the French, Spanish, and the Imperials "barbarians." They saw them as the heirs of those same tribes that had destroyed Rome. They saw the effect that these invasions had on the Roman Empire, and they feared the same effect at their own time.

The result then: Italy began a decline, a fragmentation—indeed, disintegration. What we will look at now is the effects that gave rise to not just that tragic moment which would result in Italy being ruled by foreigners for the next 350 years and more, until the Risorgimento of the second half of the 19th century—not just the loss of Italian liberty, but also the terrible events that each of the Italian states experienced, as each one tried to confront and deal with, and ultimately try to solve, this crisis. And, of course, they couldn't.

Machiavelli, as we'll see, was quite right when he said the great failure of the Italians was the inability to work together against a common enemy. They, rather, in fact, fought the enemies they knew. Those enemies were often inside their own walls, as we'll see in the next lecture with Savonarola and the opposing factions—occasionally amongst their own fellow Italians, as in the issues between the various Italian states.

Similarly, we see that in this period of crisis on the peninsula, the larger period of crisis of the Turkish expansion, the threat to Christianity altogether that the Turks caused with their invasion of the heartland from the Balkans in the 16th century—all of this then came to a kind of focus, into a time of crisis.

When Savonarola said the last days were at hand and prophesized the end of the world and the second coming, it was easy, then, for people to believe him. They simply had to look about, and there seemed to be evidence everywhere. Savonarola seemed to be simply saying what everybody saw to be true: the seventh seal was about to be opened, and the period of Armageddon had begun.

Lecture Twenty-Six
Florence in Turmoil

Scope:

One of the casualties of the French invasions of 1494 was the Medici hegemony in Florence. Lorenzo de'Medici had died in 1492, succeeded by his incompetent eldest son, Piero. The French invasions caused Piero to panic in 1494, driving him to yield to all of the French king's demands, including the payment of a huge indemnity and the loss of the port at Pisa and the fortresses protecting the Florentine perimeter. On hearing of his capitulation, the Florentines drove him and his family from the city and declared the pristine republic restored. But 60 years of Medici rule had so weakened the opposition that a power vacuum ensued. The only force sufficiently organized to fill the void was led by a millenarian Dominican monk, Girolamo Savonarola (d. 1498). He had come to Florence to preach, soon becoming prior of San Marco, from which his sermons on Florence's divine mission attracted large crowds. In particular, he attacked Lorenzo de'Medici, claiming he had stolen the people's liberty, assuming spiritual leadership of a faction of republicans, and demanding a harsh puritanical regime.

Outline

I. Girolamo Savonarola, a zealous political and social reformer, came to Florence as a result of his early career as a millenarian preacher.

    A. Savonarola was born in Ferrara in 1452 into a family of celebrated physicians with good court connections.

        1. In 1474, he entered the Dominican order, initially without the knowledge of his family.

        2. He began his religious life in Bologna and developed a reputation for great asceticism and learning, writing scholastic materials and poetry against what he saw as the decadence and depravity of his age.

        3. In 1481, he entered Florence for the first time, sent there by the Dominican order.

4. However, he was not a success: His gloomy, apocalyptic sermons and their rough delivery alienated the Florentines, who were familiar with Humanist culture and more accustomed to rhetorically elegant preachers.

5. Savonarola left in 1485 and traveled about Italy, perfecting his style and becoming increasingly influenced, particularly as the century drew to a close, by the Book of Revelation and the Italian prophetic tradition of the apocalypse.

6. At the instigation of Pico della Mirandola, Lorenzo de'Medici invited Savonarola back to Florence in 1489 to the monastery of San Marco, founded by his grandfather, Cosimo.

B. This second period in Florence was, for Savonarola, much more successful than the first.

1. From 1490, he began his fiery sermons, describing the last days and the anger of God: He claimed that the judgment of God was at hand and would be harsh.

2. The Florentines this time responded enthusiastically, attending in such large numbers that the sermons had to be moved from San Marco to the cathedral of Florence itself.

3. In 1491, Savonarola was appointed prior of San Marco.

4. Despite his refusal to offer Lorenzo de'Medici the customary allegiance, Lorenzo graciously continued his generous support of the monastery.

C. Savonarola began to assert his growing ambition and independence, separating San Marco from the control of the Dominican order and demanding the strictest adherence to monastic discipline.

1. He himself grew even more ascetic, practicing constant vigils and mortifications and wearing a hair shirt.

2. His sermons also grew more radical, castigating the Florentines in general for their immoral lives and Lorenzo in particular for his "pagan" tendencies.

3. Nevertheless, when dying in 1492, Lorenzo sent for Savonarola for extreme unction, given that it was common for the Medici to rely spiritually on the prior of San Marco.

II. The death of Lorenzo in many ways focused Savonarola's attacks on the Medici and their circle more sharply, because he recognized the incompetence and immorality of Lorenzo's heir, Piero.

   A. The crisis of the French invasions of 1494 also played perfectly into Savonarola's hands.

      1. Savonarola began preaching that Charles VIII of France was the new Charlemagne, foretold in prophecy as sent by God to chastise Italy, cleanse the Church, and vanquish the infidels by reclaiming the Holy Land in preparation for the second coming of Christ.

      2. He also declared that Florence was the chosen city and Florentines were the instruments selected by God to bring about the cleansing of the Church and the moral regeneration of Italy.

      3. In so doing, Savonarola capitalized on the Humanist belief in Florence as the new Athens, or new Rome, but now interpreted as the new Jerusalem.

      4. This message appealed to those in Florence who were more influenced by radical religion than classical Humanism, those who were troubled by the secular, almost pagan element of much of Laurentian culture.

      5. There was also a deep apocalyptic strain of prophetic tradition in Italy, and Savonarola built successfully on these old beliefs.

   B. The coming of Charles VIII to Florence revealed the stupidity and cowardice of Piero; he yielded to all of Charles's demands, such as posting French garrisons in the Florentine perimeter fortresses and the port of Pisa.

      1. When the Florentines learned of this capitulation, they rioted and drove the Medici out of the city.

      2. The palaces of the Medici supporters were looted, including the great Palazzo Medici itself, which was stripped of its wonderful collections of art.

3. The small anti-Medici faction was strongly supported by the puritanical followers of Savonarola, who saw an opportunity to turn Florence into a theocratic image of the Dominican's message.

III. The political conditions in Florence were extremely unstable after the expulsion of the Medici.

   A. Charles paraded through the streets as a conqueror, and he failed to honor his commitments to Piero.

      1. Pisa was not returned to Florence but permitted to declare its renewed independence, eliminating Florence's only access to the sea.

      2. An embassy that included Savonarola was sent to Charles VIII, but Savonarola's intentions were not to restore Florence's dignity or possessions.

      3. Rather, the Dominican wished to cement Florence to the French in the belief that the king would cleanse the Church and, in particular, depose Pope Alexander VI, whom Savonarola increasingly saw as the Antichrist.

   B. In the previous 60 years, the Medici had so weakened any of the forces of opposition that once the anger over Piero's policies of appeasement had subsided, there was no single group in the city able to fill the vacuum left by the Medici.

      1. The only constitutional mechanism was a *parlamento*, that is, a summoning of the heads of household to the piazza by ringing the bell in the Palazzo della Signoria.

      2. The *parlamento* granted authority for 20 citizens to appoint a new *Signoria* and fill vacant magistracies for one year.

      3. Thereafter, all offices would again be filled by the usual electoral means of lot and voting from all eligible citizens.

      4. The council then abolished all the means of Medici control of the city.

   C. The power vacuum left by the Medici became very apparent as factions returned full force.

      1. Some wanted a return to narrow oligarchic rule, as before 1434.

2. Others wanted a theocracy guided by Savonarola.

   3. Others wanted a broadly based participatory republic, as after 1343.

   4. Many wanted the Medici to return.

   5. Moreover, personal, family, and factional strife appeared once more, making clear the success of the Medici hegemony in controlling such special interests and personal grudges.

   6. It appeared that the republic would break down and that the crisis in government was becoming extreme.

IV. At this point, it was agreed that Savonarola be admitted to address the council.

   A. This was done despite Florentine law and tradition that barred clerics from any political role.

   1. The situation was dire.

   2. Savonarola had the greatest respect in the city.

   3. The ascetic also seemed to be above factionalism.

   B. In his address to the council, Savonarola proposed a radical new model of political, moral, and economic reform: a political vision expressed in his Constitution of 1495.

   1. Savonarola took as his model the Venetian Republic, which was widely seen as the ideal stable, successful mercantile republic.

   2. Like Venice, Florence was to have a Great Council in which sovereignty would be vested and that would be composed of representatives from old political families, that is, any who had held office for at least three generations.

   3. But to avoid the closed oligarchy in effect in Venice, the Florentine Great Council was to elect 28 new members each year to replace those who died or left the city.

   4. The Great Council would then elect the executive, the nine priors, again to serve, as before, for two months.

   5. In addition, various committees were formed to deal with specific policies, such as taxation and war.

C. It was a dramatic compromise of aristocratic and democratic traditions: Never before had so many citizens been able to serve the state.

    1. There was no room in Florence large enough to hold the Great Council.

    2. The artist/architect Cronaca designed the huge Room of the Five Hundred in the Palazzo della Signoria.

    3. The great artists Michelangelo and Leonardo da Vinci were commissioned to decorate it.

D. On June 10, 1495, the new constitution came into force, with the full support of Savonarola and his followers.

Primary Source Texts:

Kenneth R. Bartlett, "Girolamo Savonarola," pp. 329–336, in *The Civilization of the Italian Renaissance*.

Secondary Sources:

Lorenzo Polizzotto, *The Elect Nation: The Savonarolan Movement in Florence, 1494–1545*.

Supplementary Reading:

Donald Weinstein, *Savonarola and Florence: Prophesy and Patriotism in the Renaissance*.

Questions to Consider:

1. How did the expulsion of the Medici after 60 years of rule help illustrate the dangers implicit in one family or faction controlling a republic for too long?

2. Savonarola's appeal to the Florentines was the repudiation of everything Humanism stood for. In times of crisis, why does such a message resonate?

Lecture Twenty-Six—Transcript

Florence in Turmoil

The story of Savonarola in Florence is one of the strangest in Italian Renaissance history. It's very difficult to explain why the city of Lorenzo de'Medici, the city of Humanism, the city of the recovery of ancient wisdom and reason, should succumb to an apocalyptic Dominican preacher.

But in the context that we've seen of the French invasions, it was, in fact, almost the fulfillment of, if not a prophecy of, at least a set of circumstances that could allow this curious event to occur. Savonarola was a zealous political and social reformer, but he was not even a Florentine by birth. He was from Ferrara, born into a family of physicians that had served the Este court for generations.

In 1474, he entered the Dominican order without really the knowledge of his family. He gave two reasons why this happened: one, highly unlikely, an unsuccessful love affair; the other, a moment of religious revelation, much more convincing. He began his religious life in Bologna and developed a reputation for great asceticism, as well as learning. He wrote scholastic material. He had a very medieval mind from that perspective, seeing the scholastic application of divine inspiration as, in fact, his understanding of the world as he knew it. He also saw the world as fallen. He wrote poetry against the decadence and the depravity of his age. He yearned for a pure faith, and what he saw around him did not give him much cause for hope.

In 1481, he entered Florence for the first time. He was sent there by the Dominican order in order to preach in the great Dominican church of Santa Maria Novella, but he was a failure. His first trip to Florence, in fact, was characterized by lack of interest on the part of the Florentines, and a lack of connection with Florentine culture. His gloomy, apocalyptic sermons and their extremely rough delivery didn't suit the Florentines of this age immediately following the War of the Pazzi Conspiracy, when there was still that sense that the Florentines were the center of a cultural world, where Lorenzo de'Medici still had that glow of his early rule about him.

Florence was self-confident. Florence was still full of the energy and imagination of Humanism and Neoplatonism, and the sad, apocalyptic, very negative view of life that Savonarola offered in his sermons simply did not attract the Florentines; nor did that rough style, which was so alien to the Florentines with their love of rhetoric and elegant speech. So, Savonarola failed and left.

Leaving Florence in 1485, he traveled about Italy, perfecting his style and becoming increasingly influenced, moreover, by messianic visions. He began to draw very, very powerfully from the Book of Revelation. And he began seeing the prophetic tradition of Italy and its apocalyptic tradition as part of his own. He began to see, in fact, that there was a kind of coherence in his message and what he saw around him—what he saw as the depravity of his age.

He was invited back to Florence ironically by that extremely close friend of Lorenzo de'Medici, Count Pico della Mirandola. Pico, that Neoplatonic philosopher who believed in the unity of truth, saw in this Dominican someone who had a spiritual gift, someone who Pico thought could regenerate and revitalize Christianity.

Pico, himself, was slipping into a kind of deep religious observance that ultimately would see him embracing Savonarola and, in fact, taking the robes of a Dominican tertiary at the time of his death. He convinced, then, Lorenzo de'Medici to invite Savonarola to enter the Dominican monastery of San Marco. San Marco was a foundation of Lorenzo's grandfather, Cosimo de'Medici, so the Medici had some right of appointment, and Savonarola entered Florence then as a client of the Medici.

The second period of residence in Florence was much more effective than the first. From 1490, he began to sermonize increasingly about the last days, about the anger of God, and about how he believed the judgment of God upon people who were then alive would have to be particularly harsh, because they were living a pagan, unchristian life that was in no way suitable to the sort of perfection that God had promised—you only obeyed him in the strictest of ways.

The Florentines this time responded enthusiastically. They came to hear his sermons in such numbers that they had to move them from the church of San Marco into the cathedral itself. Only that huge expanse of the cathedral could hold the crowds that Savonarola's millenarian prophecies were attracting.

Moreover, the church itself wasn't large enough. The huge square in front of Santa Maria del Fiore, the cathedral of Florence, began to fill. And in something worthy almost of Albert Speer, the Dominicans suggested that those who couldn't hear—in this world before loud speakers—those who could hear, should repeat to those behind what the sermon said. The result was an echoing through the crowd—a sense that almost the voice of doom and judgment was being heard, as one group repeated the sermon to those behind.

In 1491, Savonarola became the Prior of San Marco; he became the head of this monastery founded by the Medici. Despite the fact that he refused to offer the customary allegiance to the Medici family that had founded the monastery, Lorenzo de'Medici very graciously continued his support, continued to give large sums of money, and continued to try and make Savonarola a little more tractable—at least in his sermons regarding political freedom and in sermons about the character and rule of the Medici themselves.

Savonarola, though, began to assert his growing ambition—that is, independence. He, first of all, separated the monastery of San Marco from the Dominican congregation itself, so that he was, in many ways, responsible only for his own house. He then began to impose the strictest of monastic discipline on the monks, making them follow his extremely ascetic life, which was becoming more and more rigorous as every day passed.

He practiced constant vigils, mortifications of the flesh, and began wearing a hair shirt that can be seen to this day in the museum of the monastery of San Marco. There, in a case, in what was his cell, the shirt that Savonarola wore everyday of his life, including the day of his execution, can be seen hanging on the wall.

His sermons also grew more radical. He began to castigate the Florentines in particular—attacking the very people who came out in thousands to hear him—for their immoral lies. And he also began directing much of his invective against the person of Lorenzo de'Medici and against the Medici faction's rule in the city. He called Lorenzo and his friends "pagan," interested more in ancient philosophy than in Christian teaching. He saw their commitment to ideas, and reason, and beauty, and art as taking away from this world, which he still saw as a veil of tears to be gotten through so that there could be some form of divine reward.

Nevertheless, in 1492, as he lay dying, Lorenzo still summoned Savonarola to his bedside. This was the Medici tradition—that the Prior of San Marco would give absolution to the dying Medici, and so he did. But, as we saw earlier, there are two versions of the story: one in which absolution was simply granted; the other in which Savonarola refused because Lorenzo refused, himself, to acknowledge that he had taken the liberty of his people and would not return it.

The death of Lorenzo, in many ways, focused Savonarola's invective; focused his anger against the Medici and against what he saw as the sins of his world, against Lorenzo's son, Piero. Piero, in many ways, was guilty of most of the things that Savonarola accused him of, but not, of course, to the level that the rhetoric of the friar indicated. He was incompetent; he was immoral in his personal life; and he did represent that taking of the freedom of his people that Savonarola saw as part of the failure of his own time.

As we'll see, Savonarola's prophetic tradition was to raise Florence to the chosen city—to the new Jerusalem—one that required freedom in order to fulfill God's plan for it. And he saw the Medici as in the way.

Then the French Invasions of 1494—these played perfectly into Savonarola's hands—indeed, to the point where it seemed as though his prophecies were being fulfilled. Those terribly dark, bleak prophecies that had no relation to his first visit to Florence in 1481, now, in 1494, all seemed to be coming true—a time of the second coming; a time when God's Church would have to be cleansed; a time of divine chastisement; a time when the Book of Revelation had, in fact, foretold where the apocalypse was now.

Savonarola began preaching that Charles VIII of France was the new Charlemagne—the one foretold in ancient prophecy as sent by God to cleanse the Church of all of its abuses so that all of Christianity could be united and led in a great Crusade against the infidels to free the Holy Land, and to unite the world behind Christ, who is about to return for the second coming.

Savonarola, then, took what he knew of the political and military situation in Italy and simply used it in the traditions that were very deeply established in the Italian mental geography. They were waiting for the new Charlemagne. They were waiting for this scourge that would come and cleanse the Church. And Savonarola said, "He's here."

Also, Savonarola played on the vanity of the Florentines, which was very, very deep. He said that Florence was chosen by God as the city that would be the instrument of cleansing and the moral regeneration of Italy. He said that Florence was the new Jerusalem. Here, too, not only is there an example of the Florentines' vanity being used by Savonarola to twist his message in order to attract more to his cause, but also he's, in fact, working brilliantly on what he knew to be true, on a tradition of Florentine intellectual life that went right back to the days of Leonardo Bruni.

Bruni in his history, and Bruni in his panegyric on the city of Florence, talked about Florence as the new Athens, the new Rome. Florence was a city chosen, not by God, but by history and its commitment to republic and freedom, in order to be that beacon of freedom and liberty that would then cleanse all of Italy of tyrants; be the model of freedom and republican government; be the example of the exercise of free reason amongst free people.

This, of course, was very deep in the Florentine mentality—a very, very long tradition, now a century old, that associated Florence with great deeds and an almost universal responsibility of reclamation. Savonarola simply changed the vocabulary. He changed the vocabulary of Leonard Bruni and the other humanist apologists away from the creation of the new secular ideal state—a new Rome or new Athens—to being the new Jerusalem, chosen not by freedom, but by God, and not to be a beacon of liberty only, but to be a beacon of morality, and goodness, and complete and total obedience.

The pagan element, then, of Laurentian culture, those things that we saw associated with Neoplatonism in the circle of Lorenzo de'Medici, and Ficino, and the Villa Careggi, these things were for a small elite of humanists; a small number of highly educated, well–placed, polished individuals who wanted to practice their knowledge, read their classical texts, and believe that they were part of a small coterie who could understand the complexities of life as revealed in philosophy, literature, art, and religion.

Savonarola attracted the others: those who felt left out; those who felt marginalized by a Neoplatonic world they couldn't completely understand; those who didn't have access to the court environment of Laurentian Florence; those whose traditions were Christian; and those whose beliefs was obedience to a divine will. These were the ones that Savonarola initially attracted. They weren't necessarily stupid people. Stupid people are not simple people. Simple people are those who, really, simply believe that they want to do good and need someone to help them get there, and they saw Savonarola as their instrument.

This deep apocalyptic strain that attracted those who felt marginalized by the high culture of Laurentian Florence began to spread because Savonarola seemed to be telling the world what they were experiencing before they experienced it. His prophecy seemed to be exactly what was happening. He seemed to have some kind of divine knowledge and inspiration. He said, and many believed, that God spoke directly to him and through him.

The coming of Charles VIII revealed the stupidity of Piero de'Medici; revealed that some of the things that Savonarola had said about the treacherous, incompetent, evil nature of the Medici were, in fact, coming to pass—because when Piero returned from his negotiations with Charles VIII, he didn't, as his father had done in the War of the Pazzi Conspiracy when he went to the court of Naples to speak to King Ferranti, come with a great liberation of Florence. Piero returned with a humiliation of Florence. Piero returned without the port of Pisa, without the fortresses, and with the complete subjection of Florence to the French king's will.

Piero, then, lost his credibility. When word was received about what he'd agreed to at his conference with the French king, the people of Florence gathered in the streets and threw mud upon him and his followers, and the Medici ultimately were expelled from Florence. They were expelled, in part, because of the stupidity of Piero, but they were also expelled, in part, because of Savonarola's preaching. He identified the Medici—and Piero in particular—as the source of the problem, a problem that had to be solved, the first stage of which was the recovery of Florentine freedom and the traditions that the

Florentines had not been obeying because of the Medici hegemony. The expulsion of Piero, then, was, with the invasion of Charles VIII, another fulfillment of the Savonarola prophecy. He did, in fact, seem to have a direct line to God.

The rioting in the city following the expulsion of Piero and his party was intense. The palaces of the Medici faction were looted. The great palace on the Via Larga built by Michelazzo for Cosimo de'Medici, that wonderful Palazzo Medici, with its great art collection, was looted as well, and the collection was disbursed throughout the city.

The anti-Medici faction, though, was small. The Medici had been so successful in the previous 60 years at containing and co-opting all opposition, that there were very, very few individuals who were willing to stand up against them. Consequently, there were very few who had the political power base, who had the authority, to actually become the political leaders of the city against the Medici—despite the fact of the power vacuum that emerged with the expulsion of Piero and his family.

The Dominican, though, had enormous power. Savonarola was seen as the voice of God, as the prophet, as the one who seemed to know what was going to happen—the one who, in fact, had the ability to do something that was good, and to fulfill the Florentine promise.

The political conditions, then, in Florence were extremely unstable. Charles paraded through the streets of the city as a conqueror. He openly humiliated the Florentines through that military parade that he required down the main streets of the city. He humiliated the Gonfaloniere, the great Gonfaloniere Caponi.

When Charles arrived in the city and effectively said hotly to the government that he could do whatever he willed merely by blowing on his horn, Caponi looked him straight in the eye and said, "You blow upon your horn, I shall ring upon our bells," indicating that Florence would withstand him.

There was, then, this tension. There was this terrible sense of unstable government. There was a sense of power vacuum. There was a sense of crisis. The crisis continued because of Piero's stupidity and because the Florentines had lost all of their bargaining power. Pisa was not returned to Florence as was promised, but, in fact, was permitted to reassert its independence, taking away Florentine access to the sea.

An embassy, led in part by Savonarola and members of this new provisional government, went to Charles VIII in order to try and salvage some of the situation. But it became clear that those who wanted a political solution really were separated from Savonarola, who wanted a kind of divine solution. Savonarola was not terribly interested in undoing the disasters of Piero's decisions. Rather, he was interested not in restoring the dignity of Florence, but in establishing a new kind of authority, a divine power—something that would raise Florence above even the King of France, the city that would be chosen for the second coming.

Consequently, the intention of Savonarola in these discussions would be to bind Florence even more closely to France, because Savonarola truly believed, I think, that Charles VIII was God's instrument, and one of the reasons God sent him into Italy was to cleanse the Church, to overthrow the pope, Alexander VI, whom, increasingly, Savonarola was labeling the anti-Christ. The Borgia pope was not a particularly holy man, not particularly interested in things of the spirit, but he wasn't very pleased about being called the anti-Christ, even though it, again, played somewhat into the hands of the French.

It also was clear that the only person with enough authority, enough respect within the city, to have any voice that would be listened to by all classes was Savonarola. That power vacuum that resulted from 60 years of Medici rule and the careful destruction of any possible opposition meant that none of the opposing factions could, in fact, do anything without Savonarola's approval. He seemed to speak at least for the city, and so he gained an enormous amount of influence, despite the fact, again, that Florentine legislation and tradition meant that members of religious orders or priests could have no role in politics.

A *Parlamento* was held by the ringing of the bell in the tower of the Palazzo della Signoria. This brought the heads of all households together in order to choose a Balìa, to choose a special committee that would, then, for one year, act as a government. Twenty citizens were appointed to fill vacant magistracies, and all offices subsequently would be filled by the usual constitutional measures of lot and election. All means of Medici control—the Council of

Seventy, the *accoppiatori* —were abolished, and in their place were put instruments that reflected the well being of the republic, guided in many ways by Savonarola.

The power vacuum left by the Medici became apparent also in the recovery of faction. Faction, the great danger of all Italian republic regimes in Florence, had been a terrible problem, as we've seen earlier in this series. It came back in full force, indicating how well the Medici had managed this endemic problem—how well the Medici regime had managed to control faction, and make as many as possible work together for the well being of the state.

The factions were the obvious ones: those great patricians—those in the oligarchy who wanted to return to the form of rule that the Albizi regime had enjoyed before 1434, an extremely narrow oligarchy of great rich families who had used the city for their own best interest. There were those who wanted a theocracy guided by Savonarola, who had become a kind of Ayatollah, who would speak for God, and then the legislators would listen to his guidance and then enact laws following what Savonarola said was God's plan.

There were those who wanted a very broadly based republic as the kind that had existed in 1343; those who wanted all eligible citizens to have as much access to political power as possible. And then, of course, there were the Medicians, of whom there were many still who wanted a return of the Medici—perhaps not Piero, but maybe his bright, younger brother Giovanni, who was a cardinal in Rome.

On top of this, there was the usual experience of personal grudge, of economic interest, of neighborhood and family struggle for influence. This division of the city into factions, both ideological and economic, personal and local, all of this turned Florentine politics back into that chaotic mixture that we saw before the Medici arrived. It seemed as though civil government would simply collapse, and that Florence would descend into a kind of chaos.

Seeing the danger—knowing that the only person in the city with enough personal authority and with enough influence amongst all classes of citizens to have any kind of positive influence on this chaos was Savonarola—Savonarola was invited to address the Council.

Again, this was against Florentine law, but the argument was there was no other alternative. It was only Savonarola who could address and solve the problem, so give him a chance. The situation was, indeed, desperate. Savonarola was the only person who seemed to be able to have a plan that people would listen to, and, most importantly, he seemed to be above faction. With the exception of his hostility to the Medici, he didn't seem to be part of any group, any economic or family gathering, any class group. He seemed to be speaking the word of God for all Florentines.

His address to the Council and the subsequent actions that he and his followers took were revolutionary. He proposed a radical new model of political, moral, and economic reform. He promised a political vision and put it in place through a draft constitution for the Republic of Florence that he promulgated in 1495.

This republican model was based heavily upon the model of Venice, which then seemed to be the ideal, stable, perfect republican government. It was to be based, as the Venetian Republic was, on a Great Council, which was the source of sovereignty in which all of the great families would be represented by birth. Those families who had provided three generations of magistrates would have immediate access to this Great Council. But Savonarola was hostile to the idea of oligarchy, and he decided there had to be an instrument for regeneration. And so 28 new members would be elected each year in order to replace those members of the Great Council who died or who had to leave the city for business reasons.

The Great Council would then elect the executive, the nine priors, again sustaining the idea of a collective executive—those individuals who had to, through consensus, rule the city in the best interest of all. And in addition, there would be the usual councils and committees to deal with specific policies, such as war, taxation, and internal affairs.

This was a dramatic compromise. It was a dramatic document. It was something quite out of the context of Florentine tradition, and it was clearly inspired by the success of Venice and the almost religious awe in which the world saw that stable constitution of the maritime republic.

Borrowing heavily from Venice, but adding to it that sense of popular sovereignty that the Venetian constitution lacked,

Savonarola had, in fact, created a remarkable piece of legislation—a kind of constitution that had brought appeal. It was, in fact, a compromise that suited the Florentines perfectly—a comprise between aristocratic traditions represented by the great oligarchs, and the democratic tradition represented by those experiments of the 1340s in which even the lesser guildsmen could hold a plurality of seats in the executive committees.

There wasn't a room large enough to hold this Great Council when it met for the first time. The Palazzo della Signoria had to be restructured. The artist/architect, Cronaca, was asked to build a room, which he did: the *Sala dei Cinquecento*, the Room of the Five Hundred, that huge room that exists to this day on the ground floor of the Palazzo, which was to be decorated by the greatest artists in the city, Michelangelo and Leonardo da Vinci, painting a wall each, representing the great victories of the Florentine Republic and the battles against their enemies.

On June 10, 1495, the new constitution came into force. Savonarola and his followers, of course, celebrated it. All in the city saw that this was an opportunity for some kind of regeneration. It was an opportunity for the Florentines to come together and to try and supersede faction, to overcome what they saw as the burden of the Medici hegemony, to create a new Florence. But as we'll see in the next lecture, their intentions, really, were not the same—even though one constitution, and one council, and one room held them all.

The theocracy that was wanted by Savonarola and those of his closest followers was quite at odds with those who wanted to create a dynamic republic to serve their political and, in particular, economic interests. Those who wanted Florentine territorial integrity restored were at odds with those who were willing to sacrifice anything to sustain the French alliance. And there were those who also saw the dangers in Savonarola's increasingly powerful attacks on the Church. They realized that the danger was that ultimately Alexander VI Borgia and his son Cesare were not men to trifle with.

The result was a new kind of stasis and a new kind of danger. Savonarola may have created on paper a brilliant, compromised document, but he had also created a circumstance in which the powerful groups within the city would be able to fight amongst one another for the prize—which was the city of Florence itself, and the future of that most remarkable republic.

Lecture Twenty-Seven
Savonarola and the Republic

Scope:

The regime established by Savonarola was a puritanical theocracy. Although the institutions of the republic continued, Savonarola had become the guiding force in the city and directed a potent faction that supported his policies. Simple pleasures, such as cards and carnival, were banned; bands of boys collected "vanities," parading them through the streets and setting bonfires in the Piazza della Signoria. A broadly based republican constitution was written by Savonarola and instituted by his followers. The monk began to preach against the Borgia pope, Alexander VI, resulting in his excommunication. Believing the French to be God's scourge for a decadent Church and a "pagan" Italy, Savonarola also refused to abandon the French alliance, despite the hostility of Italians to the foreign invaders. Diplomatic and natural disasters, however, began to alienate moderate Florentines, who in 1498, arrested Savonarola and tried and burned him as a heretic, yet his faction and his constitution for Florence survived him.

Outline

I. The restored republic of 1495 attempted at first to return to its most liberal roots, opening the *Signoria* to as many eligible citizens as possible.

    A. The new regime began well and moderately, granting amnesty to all previous supporters of the Medici.

        1. A new bank, the *Monte di pietà*, was established, largely through Savonarola's demands, to lend money to the poor at low interest.

        2. As compensation to the bankers, who protested this competition in lending, the Great Council abolished all taxes except the tax on land.

        3. Unfortunately, this move alienated large landowners in the countryside and led to a rise in rents and food prices that disadvantaged the poor.

B. But it was Savonarola's moral legislation that caused the greatest divisions and disharmony.

    1. Entertainments, such as horse races, dice, cards, dancing, and carnival, were outlawed.

    2. The state brothels were closed, and homosexuality was cruelly punished as a capital crime.

    3. Torture was encouraged to foment a fear of wrongdoing and sin: Blasphemers, for example, had their tongues cut out.

C. Young boys, offered by their parents, were gathered into Bands of Hope.

    1. These boys were sworn to attend sermons regularly and to avoid all sinful activities, including most childhood pastimes.

    2. Their education was to be purely religious, and they were required by law to inform on their teachers if they saw sinfulness.

    3. They roved the streets in bands that became increasingly thuggish, breaking up card games and dances and ripping immodest clothes from women in the street.

    4. They went from door to door demanding sinful possessions, such as mirrors, cosmetics, art depicting non-religious subjects, ancient literature, and popular authors, including Boccaccio.

II. During his period of control, Savonarola continued to preach and prophesize, intensifying his attack on the Church and its leaders.

A. He preached that Christ was the true and only ruler of the city; hence, all laws and all behavior had to reflect his teachings, interpreted, of course, by his prophet, Savonarola, who spoke to God directly.

    1. This "Invisible King," in Savonarola's own terminology, was about to return to Earth and chastise the sinful, and Florence must be prepared to receive him.

    2. Pope Alexander VI was the Antichrist and Christians were to ignore or depose him.

    3. The institution of the visible Church was corrupt and had to be cleansed.

B. Some Florentines listened with rapture and pride to these prophecies, wishing to become the new Jerusalem and the chosen people.

    1. Many others, however, remained silent from fear of the Bands of Hope and Savonarola's threats to denounce the sinful and punish them accordingly.

    2. A spiritual repression descended bleakly on the city.

III. The opposition to Savonarola's influence began to grow rapidly.

  A. Savonarola had made many enemies, especially among secular Florentines.

    1. The patriciate resented its loss of power, while the bankers remained angered over the *Monte di pietà*.

    2. Many Humanists and educated believers in secular governments were alarmed by the theocratic nature of Savonarola's policies and believed them to be unsound.

    3. They also resented the breach of traditional Florentine policy forbidding those in religious orders from having any role in politics.

  B. There was also powerful religious opposition to the Dominican.

    1. Franciscans and other religious orders were jealous of the success of the Dominicans and the consequent increase in their share of the city's religious donations.

    2. Traditional Catholics disliked Savonarola's extreme attacks on the papacy and his sermons against the decadence of the Church.

    3. And there were sincere Catholics who simply did not believe that Savonarola was God's prophet and that God spoke through him

  C. The division of Florence into factions supporting and opposed to Savonarola resulted in bitter civic discord and political and religious instability.

    1. The opposition to Savonarola came together into a group called the *Arrabbiati*, or the "Hotheads."

    2. They, in turn, named Savonarola's faction the *Piagnoni*, or "Snivelers," because of their tendency to cry and sob during the monk's sermons.

3. The *Arrabbiati* viewed the *Piagnoni* as theocratic fanatics following a false prophet against the established Church, Florentine tradition, and the law.

IV. Savonarola's influence began to decline because of his inflexibility in foreign and economic affairs.

    A. Savonarola adhered absolutely to his alliance with France, because he had prophesized that the French king was the instrument of Christian regeneration.

        1. But Charles VIII repaid Savonarola's loyalty by selling the Florentine fortresses to her enemies, Genoa and Lucca, and permitting the subject cities of Arezzo and Volterra to rise in revolt against Florentine hegemony.

        2. France also permitted Pisa, Florence's only seaport, to declare its independence.

        3. The Florentine state was disintegrating, and Savonarola's response was only the renewal of hymns and prayers.

    B. These losses proved to be a significant economic blow.

        1. The loss of Pisa played havoc with Florentine trade.

        2. The loss of the rich cities of the *contado* meant a great reduction in taxes that resulted in fiscal crisis.

        3. The treasury was empty and the city was approaching bankruptcy.

        4. The *Monte* shares collapsed, selling for just 10% of their face value, wiping out the capital of small traders and rich merchants alike.

        5. A desperate gesture was to illegally borrow the funds of the state dowry, the *Monte delle doti*.

        6. This panicked fathers of many daughters, who feared that the fund's collapse would mean their girls would not have dowries and, hence, would be unmarriageable.

V. The mood in the city was growing powerfully against Savonarola and his faction, particularly after the *Piagnoni* attempted a political coup.

    A. Manmade disaster was augmented by nature.

1. In what seemed to the *Arrabbiati*—and to some *Piagnoni*—as God's answer to Savonarola, rain came in 1496–1497 for 11 straight months.

2. Crops were destroyed and famine claimed the city.

3. Plague followed soon after; by early 1497, people were dying in the streets.

4. In an attempt to aid the situation, the *Piagnoni Signoria* ordered the communal granaries opened.

5. But thousands of desperate women rushed the storehouses and hundreds were trampled to death in the riot that ensued.

B. Soon after, five patricians of the noblest families were accused of plotting against Savonarola and in favor of the return of the Medici.

1. They were summarily executed without a fair trial and in contravention of all Florentine law and procedure.

2. A powerful pro-Medici faction formed.

3. Riots between factions broke out regularly in front of San Marco.

4. An attempt was made on Savonarola's life during a sermon, resulting in a bloody pitched battle between enemies and supporters within and outside the cathedral.

5. Florence had descended into desperate anarchy.

VI. The Church had also had enough of the chiliastic Dominican.

A. Pope Alexander VI was getting increasingly angry over Savonarola's attacks on his authority and the Church.

1. Further, Savonarola's allegiance to France threatened the stability of the peninsula when it was clear that another invasion was imminent.

2. Savonarola made both situations worse by writing to Charles VIII and requesting him to call a general council of the Church to depose the pope as an infidel and a heretic.

3. The monk also answered the pope's offer of a cardinal's hat by giving a vitriolic, vicious sermon, which he then had printed and sent around Europe—even to the sultan of Turkey!

B. With the city in crisis and Savonarola's only response to burn vanities and insult the pope, the *Arrabbiati* moved, gaining control of the *Signoria* in April 1497.

  1. Savonarola was excommunicated by the pope but promised leniency if he would come to Rome.

  2. The *Signoria* encouraged Savonarola to leave the city, but he refused, showing his contempt for the pope by saying mass publicly.

  3. The *Arrabbiati* began to fear that a papal army might be ordered to Florence to silence Savonarola.

C. The Franciscans responded to Savonarola's claims of prophetic status by challenging him to an ordeal by fire: A Franciscan and Savonarola were to walk through flames to see which one God protected.

  1. Savonarola could not refuse, but on the appointed day, he made so many demands of the challenge that many hours passed while the entire city gathered to watch the ordeal.

  2. Then, at last, it rained and the fires were extinguished.

  3. This infuriated the mob, which lost faith in Savonarola and followed the *Arrabbiati* leadership to San Marco, where they arrested him and brought him to prison.

  4. Tortured and condemned as a heretic and traitor, Savonarola and two of his followers were burned on the Piazza della Signoria on May 23, 1498.

Secondary Sources:

Gene A. Brucker, *Renaissance Florence*.

Supplementary Reading:

Lorenzo Polizzotto, *The Elect Nation: The Savonarolan Movement in Florence, 1494–1545*.

Donald Weinstein, *Savonarola and Florence: Prophesy and Patriotism in the Renaissance*.

Questions to Consider:

1. Why did the Florentine Republic have a policy to exclude those in religious life from political power?

2. Can you see any connection between the Civic Humanism of Bruni (see Lecture Eight) and the message of Savonarola?

Lecture Twenty-Seven—Transcript
Savonarola and the Republic

The restored republic of 1495 functioned under the imaginative constitution of Savonarola, a constitution that tried to compromise the traditions of oligarchic rule with those of broad republican representation. And it was, in fact, an interesting document, and one that might actually have worked.

Moreover, the new regime began well. It began moderately. It began reasonably. Amnesty was granted to all supporters of the Medici, those who had been villianized initially as supporters of a corrupt regime. Now there was a sense to bring them back within the pale of the constitution, and to allow Florence to come together again as the chosen city that the prophet said that it was. Moreover, Savonarola arranged for the establishment of a new bank in order to specifically help the poor, those disenfranchised citizens who had no political rights, but who often suffered terribly, economically, in hard times by having to borrow at a high interest because of their lack of collateral.

Savonarola established the *Monte di pietà*. This was a bank that leant small amounts to the poor at very low rates of interest. It was, in fact, a very good idea, at least for the poor. But it also alienated the great bankers who were used to making large profits from the high interest rates that the poor previously had to pay.

The Florentines, then, decided that they had to have a compensatory operation in place, so then they abolished all of the taxes, except the tax on land. This, too, was supposed to benefit the bankers, indicating that they understood there was a loss of profit, so, consequently, there would be a loss of taxation for the city. But the only effect of this was, really, to raise the rent of the poor peasants in the countryside, and to alienate the great landowners who were still powerful socially, and often closely intermarried with the great patricians—and then, also, and obviously, raised the price of food considerably. The poor, then, perhaps paid less interest, but then they paid more for food.

Savonarola's moral legislation, though, began in earnest, and it was this that completely alienated large sections of the Florentine population. Entertainments like horse races, dice, cards, dancing, and even carnival itself—a long Florentine tradition—were all outlawed. The state brothels were closed, and the argument in the Council was that the brothels existed under the patronage of the state in order to discourage homosexuality. Savonarola, then, replied, "I will stop homosexuality by making the punishment so severe that no one will even think of doing it." It became a capital crime and was punished. Torture became encouraged.

Savonarola argued that fear of torture was like fear of sin, and if you wanted to avoid sin you would also, then, want to avoid torture. Consequently, he put in place a regime that encouraged and practiced torture—to the point that those who were convicted of blaspheming had their tongues cut out.

Then, there was the movement called the Bands of Hope. The supporters of Savonarola pledged their young sons, when quite young, to the prophet, who would then be their leader. They would take their guidance from him. They would cut their hair short, in contrast to the Florentine youthful tradition of wearing long hair. They would often dress as angels. They would parade through the city in their bands, calling for moral regeneration, singing hymns. They agreed that they would not only go to mass regularly, but avoid all childhood pastimes that may be even considered, or lead to, sinful behavior. Their education was to be purely religious, and they were also required by their oaths to inform on their teachers, their servants, and even members of their family if they witnessed evil behavior.

It's often said that only the most horrific of totalitarian regimes gives power to children. And here is an instance where, in fact, that proves to be true once more. These Bands of Hope roamed the streets. They became increasingly thuggish. They broke up card games when they saw them. They interrupted dancing. And in a most curious behavior, they ripped the clothes from women they believed to be dressed immodestly. It, of course, made the situation momentarily worse, but at least it's something that only happened once.

They also went from door to door in the city, demanding sinful possessions, and sinful possessions were very, very broadly defined: mirrors, cosmetics, false hair, art that did not depict religious subjects, ancient literature. The poets like Ovid or Catullus, authors such as Boccaccio, were all demanded so that they could be taken to the Piazza della Signoria—and there, in ritual activity, burned in the famous bonfire of the "vanities."

This huge pyre of musical instruments, and books, and manuscripts, and pictures—including the pictures of Botticelli, who had become a follower of Savonarola—were all piled. There's a story that may be apocryphal that the Venetian ambassador looked upon this, and quickly ran to Savonarola trying to do a deal, and purchased the lot to take them out of the city, realizing he could sell them for high profit. Savonarola, of course, refused—thinking these things were intrinsically sinful; and not to be exported, bought, and sold; and the propaganda effect of their burning was just too attractive.

Also, Savonarola began concentrating his attacks on the Church, and in these attacks he became more and more powerfully invective, in particular against the person of the Borgia pope. He preached that Christ was the true and only ruler of the city; he was the invisible king who ruled through, of course, Savonarola. All behavior, then, had to reflect Christian teachings—and these teachings, again, were interpreted by Savonarola, who spoke to God directly.

This "Invisible King," and this is Savonarola's own terminology, "The invisible King of Florence was Christ, and he's about to come back. It's momentarily expected that the second coming would then allow for Christ to judge the sinful and the good, to allow the sinful to be chastised, and Florence must be prepared to receive him. The city must be sufficiently holy and good so that Christ would feel comfortable when he arrived."

The papacy under Alexander VI, then, became the anti-Christ. Christians should either ignore him or depose him. The institution of the visible Church, then, had become, in Savonarola's sermons, corrupt and evil. The structure of the Church, the very institution of the Church militant, was part of the problem, no longer part of the solution—and this is a subject to which Savonarola returned regularly.

Many of those in the congregation listening to the sermons of the prophet said that this is word of God—that clearly they were listening with rapture to these prophecies, pride that they were amongst the chosen who were going to institute the second coming and the new rule of Christ on earth. Many others, though, thought that Savonarola was becoming increasingly irresponsible—perhaps even to the point of delusional madness; these people, though, generally remained silent. Unless they were truly driven by a powerful sense of mission, they feared the Bands of Hope. They feared the kinds of recognition of sinful behavior that they and the other of Savonarola's thugs could, in fact, accuse them of. The punishments were severe. It was easier just to be silent and to try and avoid the sermons.

A spiritual repression descended on the city. It was a time of bleakness, and it was a time when Florence—so full always by tradition and by practice of intellectual debate and imagination—had become a dark and serious place. It became a place that reflected Savonarola's dark vision of the human condition and his belief that atonement required very serious compromise.

The opposition to Savonarola, though, began to grow. More and more citizens became alienated by his increasingly powerful invective. He made enemies, in particular amongst the secular Florentines. The patriciate, the great bankers, had lost a great deal of power, influence, political authority, and money. The *Monte di pietà* had sapped their wealth. The introduction of a broadly based republic had foreclosed their hope that the expulsion of the Medici would result in an oligarchic republic.

Many humanists and educated believers in secular government were alarmed at the clear theocracy of Savonarola's message. They felt that there was no argument to be made against God if Savonarola is the only person who can hear him speak. They saw the republic of which they were so proud being taken by what they saw as a madman—who was speaking in the name of God, but, in fact, exercising a repressive regime that was strangling not only open discussion and the free exchange of ideas, but also threatening the very political liberty of Florence and its economic foundation.

The traditional Florentine policy, they thought, of keeping Church and state separate, to the point that clerics could not exercise political power, was a good one. Why, then, change it? Why allow Savonarola the influence and power he had? There was something wrong. Florentine tradition had developed for a reason, and Savonarola was illustrating why that reason was just.

But not just secular Florentines, the other religious groups in the city became increasingly annoyed and distanced by Savonarola's preaching. The Franciscans and the other religious orders were jealous of the Dominican success. The Franciscans, in particular, who previously had been the voice of the poor, who had been the voice of prophecy, now saw the Dominicans taking their role. And what was more of a concern, at least in the short term, they saw the contributions of the faithful going into the Dominican coffers, and those of the Franciscans remaining empty.

The Franciscans and the other religious orders, then, felt that the Dominicans were going too far, and that Savonarola, in his attack on the institutionalized Church, was also attacking them. If the Dominican had the only direct line to God, what was their role? What were they to do? How were they to play some part in this new Jerusalem? Savonarola really couldn't care what they thought.

The factions, then, began to divide the city. And the factions became ever, ever more polarized. The opposition to Savonarola began to coalesce into a group that represented many perspectives: the secular; other religious groups; those who felt that their economic interests were challenged; young men who were simply upset that the brothels and the gaming tables were closed; those who enjoyed carnival; those who saw the Bands of Hope as threats to the usual kind of liberty that the city had always enjoyed. They were named by the followers of Savonarola as the *Arrabbiati*, the "hot heads," those who were stirred by hatred and maddened by anger.

They, in turn, identified the followers of Savonarola as the *Piagnoni*, the "snivelers." They were called snivelers because of their tendency to cry and sob as the friar spoke to them. When he preached, they would slip into a kind of religious ecstasy, or into a kind of despair, hoping that they could be sufficiently pure to receive Christ when he arrived. And he was expected, according to Savonarola, momentarily.

The *Arrabbiati* and the *Piagnoni* were divided to the point that they represented factions, mutually exclusive. They hated one another. They distrusted one another. As far as the *Piagnoni* were concerned, the *Arrabbiati* were secular anti-Christians. As far as the *Arrabbiati* were concerned, the *Piagnoni* were theocratic madmen—fanatics following a false prophet and leading their city into destruction and doom.

Savonarola's influence began to decline, not so much because of the polarization of the city internally, but because of his complete failure in foreign economic affairs. The city was not only exposed, the city was in a dangerous position. The wealth of the city—established for so many generations, upon which the Italian Renaissance and its Florentine model was built—began to be dissipated by the teachings of this millenarian, this chiliastic preacher.

Savonarola adhered absolutely to the alliance with France. He would hear nothing against it because he had preached and prophesized that the King of France was the new Charlemagne, was the instrument of Christian regeneration. Also, Savonarola's real intent was not to benefit Florence as much as to follow his true belief that the Church needed cleansing, and it required a secular ruler like the King of France to do it. He was, in fact, willing to sacrifice Florence for this higher purpose, and the Florentines became increasingly aware of it.

Charles VIII, though, humiliated Florence and showed his respect for Savonarola by his treachery. Savonarola's loyalty had yielded no benefit whatsoever except for the total and complete humiliation and exposing of Florence to its enemies. The Florentine fortresses that had been yielded to Charles VIII, those that had been filled with French garrisons under the arrangement made with Piero de'Medici, were sold to the enemies of Florence, to Genoa and Lucca.

The subject cities of the Florentine territories, the rich cities of Arezzo and Volterra, rose in revolt against Florentine hegemony, and the French did nothing to return them. Moreover, these cities, the rich cities of the Florentine *contado*, paid a much higher rate of tax. With the abolition of the internal taxes, there was so much dependent upon the tax of the subject cities that Florence began a serious economic collapse.

This was exacerbated by the situation of Pisa, Florence's access to the sea. When Pisa returned to its independent status, when the French garrisons simply left and allowed the Pisans to recover their freedom, it meant that Florence no longer could be part of the Mediterranean economy, as it had become after the city was conquered. The economic blow was enormous. This was so obvious, both as an element of pride and as an element of economic reality, that even those supporters of Savonarola went to him and said, "We have to do something about Pisa." Savonarola's response was cryptic and, in many ways, simply untrue. He said that God told him that he held Pisa in his hands. Those of his enemies said those hands should be opened and Pisa should be delivered. But Savonarola did nothing, and Pisa remained independent.

The economic blow, then, was serious, and it became increasingly debilitating. The loss of taxation from the subject territories, the loss of trade, resulted in the effective collapse of the Florentine economy. The treasury was virtually empty. The city would be in a stage of bankruptcy in a very short period of time. Nothing illustrated this more clearly than the collapse of the value of *Monte* shares. That funded state debt, or *Monte*, had—since the 14th century—been a barometer of the well being of the Florentine Republic. In these years under Savonarola, the *Monte* shares collapsed to just 10% of their face value. The result was that the paper fortunes of rich merchants and small shopkeepers alike were completely and totally wiped out. Their sense of the future was being compromised.

Some said it really didn't matter because the second coming was at hand. Those were the *Piagnoni*. Others, who were concerned about paying their rents and caring for their families, thought otherwise. And Savonarola's enemies were growing.

A desperate measure on the part of the *Piagnoni signoria* resulted in the alienation of another important group in the city, regardless of allegiance. These were the fathers of daughters. In order to try and get a quick infusion of cash, Savonarola agreed to heavy borrowing from the state dowry fund—that is, the *Monte delle doti*. This was not only illegal, but it was extremely dangerous. And the fathers of daughters were terrified that when their daughters reached the marriageable age of 15 when their shares matured, there would be no money to provide the dowry that would allow their daughters to marry.

Fathers began to fear that they would have large numbers of unmarriageable daughters in a collapsed economy, where they were rendered poor because of the economic experiments of Savonarola and by the alienation of Florence from the rest of the peninsula.

These panicked individuals began to move away from their sympathy for Savonarola's mission.

Savonarola's sermons had always been telling the Florentines that they were the elect, the chosen people, the instrument that God had chosen. What they were seeing increasingly was the humiliation and impoverishing of the city, the dividing of the city into polarized factions. It seemed as though Savonarola's prophecies were no longer true, and that his promises were not, in fact, reflecting the reality that they were experiencing.

The mood in the city, then, began to shift—began to move away from Savonarola. There was a recognition on the part of the political leaders of the *Piagnoni*, some of whom were cynical politicians, manipulating this group in order to get advantage over their enemies to be sure; but, there were others who truly believed that Savonarola had to remain in power, had to exercise his moral leadership, otherwise a second coming would not happen.

There was an attempt on the part of the *Piagnoni*, then, to affect a coup d'état, to take over the constitution that their own spiritual leader had largely written. It failed, but it indicated again that there was more at work than simply the unfolding of God's plan, as interpreted by Savonarola.

Then the signs began to become clearer and clearer that maybe God was not on Savonarola's side—that perhaps Savonarola did not speak for the Divine: the manmade disasters, the cause of so much of the alienation of the population from Savonarola, and which in large part were the result of Savonarola's own incompetence—fragmented by an angry, vengeful nature.

In what seemed to the *Arrabbiati*—and even increasing numbers of *Piagnoni*—as God's answer to Savonarola's promises, it rained in 1496-1497 for 11 straight months. The crops in the fields were ruined. There was no food to be purchased. Famine began to claim the city. After famine came plague—so that by early 1497, people were literally falling dead in the street from starvation and the effect of plague, so weakened were they by lack of food.

The *Piagnoni signoria* realized that they had to do something in order to shore the support for Savonarola—so they opened the communal granaries, but the word was put out simultaneously throughout the city, resulting in thousands of women who rushed into the state granary in order to get their share of the food. There was a riot. Hundreds of women were trampled to death, and, again, the lustrous Savonarola began seriously to dim.

Soon after this, fear on the part of the *Piagnoni* of a Medici return resulted in the execution of five young men of the greatest families in the city. These five patricians had formed a group trying to arrange for the Medici return—to try and arrange for the Medici to try and overcome some of the misery in which the city found itself, an attempt to try and undo some of the desperate measures that seemed to be reducing Florence to a state of complete chaos. Rather than follow Florentine law of due process and trial, all five were summarily executed. This, too, alienated those among the citizens who believed strongly in Florentine law and in Florentine tradition.

Also, their death had the effect that Savonarola most feared. It reinforced the pro-Medici faction. Here were young men willing to die for a cause, and maybe the *Piagnoni* didn't have the monopoly on this kind of divine approbation. Riots began to break out increasingly between the *Piagnoni* and *Arrabbiati*, or between just neighbors who either believed or refused to accept any longer Savonarola's place.

An attempt was made on Savonarola's life during one of his sermons. This resulted in what really amounts to a pitched battle in front of the Church. Those who wanted the prophet to be taken so that some order could be restored were fought physically by those who were trying to protect the prophet, so that his work could be done and Christ could return. In short, Florence, by 1497, had been reduced to a state of anarchy. The Church, moreover, had had enough of Savonarola. No pope likes to be called the anti-Christ, and if the pope is a Borgia pope, like Alexander VI, he likes it even less.

Alexander VI grew increasingly furious as Savonarola's attacks on him and his family grew more and more flagrant and direct. Moreover, Savonarola's attacks on the institution of the Church questioned the very role of the pope as a successor to St. Peter. And if Savonarola spoke to Christ, what role did the pope play in this Church? So, Savonarola's allegiance to France, moreover, completely and totally undermined any opportunity that there would be for the peninsula to cooperate against the invaders. Something, again, had to be done.

It was obvious that another invasion was imminent. Charles VIII, before his death, was planning on exactly that and, as we know, with his death in 1498, the successor Louis XII had an even greater claim on Italian territory. Something had to happen. And Savonarola's response to the claims of the Church was to then call upon the King of France, to call upon Charles VIII, to fulfill his divine responsibility—call a council of the Church to depose Alexander VI as an infidel and a heretic.

The pope, then, said that Savonarola must be silenced, and he initially tried to be conciliatory. Alexander said, "Look, we clearly have disagreements, but, nevertheless, let's settle these as churchmen." He offered Savonarola a cardinal's hat if he would come to Rome. Now, knowing the Borgia, this was a ploy to simply get Savonarola under their control so he could be tried and executed. But Savonarola's response was exactly what we might anticipate. He unleashed an invective sermon against the person of the pope, so powerful that he had it printed. And this printed version of this personal attack on Alexander VI—and his morality and his unbelief, according to Savonarola—then spread amongst all of the princes of Europe. This printed version was sent everywhere, including a copy that was delivered to the sultan of Turkey, who mischievously sent it back to the pope and said, "I think this is yours."

Within the city, the crisis got worse. Savonarola's response, then, was what it had always been—more prayer, more hymns, burn more vanities. The *Arrabbiati* began to take over the city, and, in 1497, in April, they managed to control the *signoria*. This was a critical moment. Savonarola, as a result of his sermon, had been excommunicated by the pope. Savonarola's response to his excommunication was to say mass publicly.

Now the people of Florence, led by the *Arrabbiati*, knew that the danger to the city wasn't just famine and plague, wasn't just economic collapse, but the danger of a Borgia army besieging the city in order to silence this person who was claiming that he spoke to God, dividing the Church and calling upon a council to depose the pope, and perhaps leading the Church back into Schism. The possibility of a papal army investing Florence was real.

The Franciscans, then, responded in a way that only the Franciscans could. Seeing that they had an opening, they finally challenged Savonarola in a way that he could not refuse. Savonarola was challenged to an ordeal by fire. The city of Florence—the city of Humanism, the city of reason, the city of art—was reduced to a medieval battle where one Franciscan and one Dominican would walk through flames to see which one God would protect. Savonarola had no choice but to agree, otherwise he'd be admitting that God wouldn't protect him.

On the appointed day, it was decided that three Dominicans and three Franciscans would walk through the fire. The pyres were laid out in the Piazza della Signoria. The entire city gathered to watch the event. Before anything could happen, though, there were the disputes, the negotiations. The Franciscans said they didn't like what the Dominicans were wearing, perhaps fireproof. They had to reduce to shifts. Who would go first? They debated and argued so long that ultimately, in this time of rain, the sky opened. There was a great deluge and the fires were extinguished. For the whole population gathered to watch the event, this was God's judgment, and Savonarola clearly was on the wrong side of it.

The mob, led by the *Arrabbiati*, rioted. They walked to the monastery of San Marco, where they found Savonarola and his followers in his cell, and they arrested him. He was taken to the Piazza della Signoria—where he was charged, brought into the Palazzo, and tortured. Under torture, he admitted that he had made everything up: that he didn't speak to God, he wasn't God's instrument, that he did this for his own vanity.

He was charged first for breaking the laws of Florence by being a priest involved in politics. He was then charged by the Church with heresy. There was no question but that he was guilty of both of these things from the perspective of Florentine law, and the law of the Church, and the judgment of the pope.

On May 23, 1498, Savonarola and two of his followers were led into the Piazza della Signoria, and there they were hanged and burned—executed publicly. They were, though, not the end of their movement. The *Piagnoni* continued, and to this day, on the spot where Savonarola was burned, you often find red roses to mark it. Indeed, there's a movement in the Church now to have Savonarola beatified, a move to try and reverse this excommunication and this decision.

Savonarola is a curious function of Florentine history and tradition—a moment of history, but one that seems to be so alien of Florentine culture that he must be looked at as a consequence of those terrible years of the 1490s.

Lecture Twenty-Eight
The Medici Restored

Scope:

The broadly based republic established by Savonarola survived, but the factional disputes within the large Council of Five Hundred resulted in instability. To ensure continuity of policy, a new office, standard bearer of justice for life, was created, but it was not sufficient to preserve the city's liberty in a European environment of war and expansion. In 1512, the Medici were returned, with the head of the family, Cardinal Giovanni de'Medici (d. 1520), taking control and turning the clock back to the days of his father, Lorenzo the Magnificent. Just months later, Giovanni was elected pope as Leo X; thereafter, the fate of Florence and the papacy became inseparable, as Leo was succeeded in 1521 by his cousin Giulio as Clement VII (d. 1534). With the leaders of the Medici now in Rome, Florence was governed either by papal representatives or by young or lesser members of the family, who often were incompetent or insensitive to Florentine traditions.

Outline

I. Despite the fall of Savonarola, the broadly based republican constitution centered on the Council of Five Hundred remained in place in Florence.

   A. The execution of Savonarola resulted in quick political maneuvering by all those opposed to his rule.
   1. The Medici began serious plotting to return, led by the clever second son of Lorenzo, Cardinal Giovanni, in Rome.
   2. The various factions among the great patricians, all wishing a return to some form of oligarchic rule, also conspired to destroy the broad republic.
   3. However, the *Piagnoni* still had significant influence and wished to continue the moral reform of the city and the French alliance.

   B. A renewed foreign threat was also becoming increasingly visible.

1. The death of Charles VIII of France in 1498 had left as his heir Louis XII, a claimant to the Kingdom of Naples and the duchy of Milan.
2. In 1500, Louis continued Charles's ambitions in Italy by marshaling a huge army to press his claims to Milan.
3. Venice was bought off.
4. And the papacy was made an ally when Louis gave the pope's son, Cesare Borgia, the French duchy of Valence and a French princess for a wife.

C. Florence remained connected to its French alliance, but the factional turmoil in the republic made it difficult to follow any consistent policy.

D. As a result, Piero Soderini (1450–1513) was elected *gonfaloniere* for life in 1502, a fundamental change to the Florentine Republic's principle of sharing executive power through a committee.
1. Soderini was committed to the republic and a good leader, but he relied altogether on the French alliance for his foreign policy.
2. He tried to galvanize the republic by letting Machiavelli create a citizens' army and tried other means of revitalizing the chaotic political situation in Florence.
3. But his election for life also introduced the principle of monarchical control, absent from Florence for centuries.

II. The French conquered Milan as planned, but a treacherous move against Naples renewed the warfare in the peninsula between the French and the Spanish.

A. In a complicated series of maneuvers, including treacherous arrangements with Ferdinand of Aragon against his own cousin, Frederick, Louis moved against Naples.
1. The Spanish armies of Ferdinand the Catholic smashed the Neapolitans.
2. But immediately Louis and Ferdinand fell out over the division of the spoils.
3. In 1503, Ferdinand's great general Gonzalo da Cordoba defeated the French and drove them from the south, leaving all of Italy south of the states of the Church to Aragonese rule.

3. Florence, then, was tranquil until the death of Leo X in December of 1521, at which time Cardinal Giulio returned to Rome in hopes of succeeding Leo.
4. The machinations of Piero Soderini's brother in the Sacred College ensured that the papal election went to the Dutchman Adrian VI.
5. However, he died within months, leaving the papal throne open to the election of Giulio as Clement VII in 1523.

V. The transfer of Medici power back to Rome again left Florence subject to papal governors.

A. Clement was unable to control the city through members of his family, because there were none appropriate to do so.
1. Rather, he appointed foreign cardinals to rule in his name.
2. Most of these were seen as outsiders with little sympathy for Florentine traditions.
3. Although they were unpopular, the cardinals were not despised as much as two young Medici bastards sent by Clement to prepare them for the future rule of the city.
4. In particular, Alessandro, who was certainly an illegitimate son of the pope by a Moorish slave, was already showing signs of the mental imbalance that was to characterize his future regime.

B. But before Alessandro would assume rule of Florence, terrible events were to occur: the disaster known as the sack of Rome.

Secondary Sources:

J. R. Hale, *Florence and the Medici: The Pattern of Control.*

Supplementary Reading:

Christopher Hibbert, *The House of Medici: Its Rise and Fall.*

Questions to Consider:

1. By establishing the position of *gonfaloniere* for life, were Florentines already compromising the republic?

2. Was the election of Giovanni de'Medici a benefit or a disaster for Florence?

Lecture Twenty-Eight—Transcript
The Medici Restored

The fall of Savonarola and his execution didn't end the constitutional experiment that he had largely crafted. The idea of a Great Council, the Great Council of Five Hundred, representing a compromise between the aristocratic, oligarchic traditions of Florence and the republican traditions of broad engagement in government on the part of all property holders was, in some ways, just too good to simply let die.

Moreover, there were those groups that saw it as an instrument by which they might be able to take some measure of power back, and to re-create a city that would give them the kind of context that would allow their own ambitions to be realized.

The execution of Savonarola, though, did, in fact, create another kind of power vacuum. There were so many groups opposed to his rule that the only one completely and totally knocked out of any kind of political ambition was the *Piagnoni*. The followers of Savonarola had, to a degree, been discredited. They were still large in number. They still represented some of the political parties in the state, but mostly they represented those who were not part of the political scene: the poor and many women.

Nevertheless, the end of Savonarola did not, in fact, solve the political crisis. Every group opposed to Savonarola was united simply by the desire to rid the city of the prophet. They were not, in fact, following the same principle. They did not, in fact, have a singular vision for how the republic was to function with him gone. They all had their own agendas. They all had their own interests. And with Savonarola gone—the thing that united them—their own factional squabbles began anew.

Of these, perhaps the most influential was the pro-Medici group. The Medicians had strong supporters in Florence, those who had long memories and remembered the glory days of Laurentian Florence, a time of Cosimo de'Medici, the time when Florence was at its greatest authority, ruled by a family that seemed to be above faction. Moreover, they had a strong supporter and a great leader in the extremely clever, younger son of Lorenzo de'Medici, Giovanni, who was a cardinal in Rome. He worked with the pro-Medician group within the city to build the Medici faction that would be ready, if the time should be right, to take the city back for the family that had ruled it so well in the 15th century.

The various factions among the great patricians, then, all had their own perspective, and most of them were mutually exclusive. They all were working towards their own self-interest, and this did not bode well for the security and stability of the republic, even with Savonarola gone.

Moreover, the context in Europe and the Italian peninsula did not support any kind of experimentation, or did not provide the peace and quiet that would allow these factional groups to work out their problems within Florence without any reference to what was happening in the rest of the world. The death of Charles VIII of France, as we saw in 1498, left as his heir Louis XII, with his claims not just to Naples, but also to Milan—and his desire to ensure that France would remain united and centralized by keeping his nobles fighting elsewhere, and establishing a French position on the continent as a kind of counterweight to the growth of the power of a united Iberian peninsula under Ferdinand and Isabella, and the danger that could always arise should there be unity in the empire.

Louis fulfilled his ambitions in 1500 by crossing the Alps, as his cousin had, and pressing his claims to Milan. The Republic of Venice was, in effect, bought off and given a large sum of money to stay out of the fight. The papacy was bought off in a very imaginative way. Louis gave the pope a princess for his son to marry. Cesare Borgia was given, as a wife, a French princess, and while the king was at it, threw in the duchy of the area around Valence, the Valentinois.

Cesare Borgia became a French duke with a French princess. The Borgia family, and hence the papacy, became part of the ambitions of the King of France in Italy. It was, for this reason, by the way, that in *The Prince* by Machiavelli, Cesare Borgia is always referred to as Duke Valentino, because of this title of the territory of Valence given to him as this arrangement between Louis XII and his father.

Florence, moreover, remained committed to the French alliance. There were historical reasons for this, but also there was a simple, practical situation—it was a policy that was intact, a policy that although had not yielded many benefits to Florence, at least seemed at this point to be backing the strongest party. From anyone's perspective in 1500, it looked as though the French were going to prevail. So, to remain pro-French was, as far as the Florentine Republic was concerned, a kind of insurance policy that they would remain secure regardless of what happened to the other states of the peninsula.

This was, in fact, the policy of the person who had become the *gonfaloniere*, Piero Soderini. Soderini was a committed republican. He was an idealistic ruler. He was an imaginative, intelligent person. He was a very close friend of Machiavelli. In fact, he was Machiavelli's patron. He learned from his own experience, and he also learned from what Machiavelli told him from his service at the court of Louis XII, as an ambassador—that Florence suffered terribly by not having some kind of consistent policy, particularly foreign policy. The tradition of the Florentine Republic to change the executive every two months—so that power would be broadly distributed, and so no one faction could get sufficient authority to overthrow the state and establish itself in a position of continuing authority—had resulted in diminution of Florentine's power.

The Florentines, in the eyes of the French and the other states north of the Alps, were a vacillating group who were interested only in their internal self-interest. There wasn't any sense that the Florentine Republic could make foreign policy that would withstand the pressures that the world seemed to bear. There was, then, a change under these circumstances that altered the Ordinances of Justice, those fundamental laws that had given rise to the Florentine Republic at the end of the 13th century.

In 1502, it was decided that Piero Soderini would be *gonfaloniere* for life; that the exchange of office, that distribution of power, that need of consensus, that idea of collective executive shared amongst nine men, now was sacrificed in favor of a principle that, again, reflected the Venetian constitution. This was the model everyone thought of, that the Venetians elected the doge for life. He was one of them, chosen from amongst the political class. The Soderini were a patrician mercantile family—so it was only reasonable.

But, this was a major departure from Florentine tradition, and it introduced something that had always been an anathema to the Florentine political classes—the idea of monarchy. In fact, Soderini can be seen not just as a doge, but as a kind of surrogate prince, someone who was forced to do, through constitutional means, what the Medici had succeeded in doing for 60 years through extra constitutional means: that is manipulate the republic, give it coherence and consistency, establish policy that could withstand the terrible attacks and the experience of a dangerous period.

Soderini was committed to the republic—there is no doubt. He, himself, was an excellent choice. He was a very good leader. He was shrewd. He also was committed to France. He tried to galvanize the republic and change its traditions and character—and he tried to change its traditions and character by allowing Machiavelli to engage in his formation of a citizen militia, for example. He saw that the only way that Florence would be able to withstand the assaults of the northern armies was to have a group to fight them, based on the same principle of commitment—not professional soldiers fighting for pay, but citizen soldiers fighting to protect their homes and their families.

But his election for life also was a threat to the other patricians. They saw, then, Soderini as being something that they could never be. He represented a set of principles that they saw as not part of Florentine tradition. Soderini, then, had enemies. The problem of the republic, the problem of faction, the problem with disunity, was not solved by this. In many ways, it was focused and exacerbated.

The situation in Europe brought all of this to a head. The French succeeded in conquering Milan, and they then moved in concert with the Aragonese to try and move against Naples in a way that would allow the King of France and the King of Aragon to share the spoils in such a way as to perhaps bring some measure of compromise to a peninsula that had seen too much war in the previous decade.

A very complicated set of maneuvers resulted in treachery on the part of Ferdinand of Aragon. Ferdinand of Aragon threw in his lot briefly with Louis XII in order to take his own cousin, Frederick, from the throne. Ferdinand of Aragon realized that his claim to Naples could be consolidated if he worked with the French, and they would then together separate the spoils of the Kingdom of Naples so that both might inhabit the peninsula with some measure of solidity.

The Spanish armies of Ferdinand the Catholic then entered Italy and smashed the armies of his cousin, Frederick, completely. But, as one might expect, the positions of Louis XII and Ferdinand of Aragon were not the same. They had very different ambitions, and they very quickly, almost immediately, fell out about distribution of spoils. Who was to get what from this treacherous arrangement? Who was to get the greater part of the southern part of the Italian peninsula? Who would get Sicily? Who would get Naples? Who would, then, get the most?

In 1503, Ferdinand's great general, again celebrated in Machiavelli's *The Prince*, Gonzalo da Cordoba, defeated the armies of Louis XII and drove the French from the south, leaving all of the territory south of the states of the Church in the hands of the Aragonese. The King of Aragon then united with the Queen of Castile, and the uniting of the Iberian peninsula into a single monarchy now had added to that, the monarchy of Naples. Ferdinand was amongst the most powerful princes on the continent. Louis had been humbled to a degree, and Florence found itself allied to Louis.

By 1503, that division that I mentioned in the Italian peninsula, a division that saw the Aragonese in the south and that saw the French in the north, divided Italy in such a way as to put the Florentines, who largely were in that north-central part in theory, dependent upon Milan, but really just as exposed to the Neapolitans in a very, very difficult set of circumstances. The Aragonese were in the south; the Florentines were allied to the French.

This situation made the Florentines extremely vulnerable and extremely nervous. Soderini felt that he had no choice but to sustain the French alliance. But the other states of Italy saw an opportunity to drive the French out of Milan, and perhaps solve the problem that had been instigated by the French invasions of 1494. The Holy League tried to drive Louis XII out altogether, and tried to reunite the peninsula in some kind of shared enterprise that would allow for Italian freedom. But, unfortunately, Florence remained allied to France.

Moreover, the most powerful cardinal in the Sacred College was Giovanni de'Medici. He was enormously rich. He was extremely intelligent. He was young—still in his 30s. He was full of ambition, not so much for the papacy at this point in his life, but for Florence.

He felt, as a son of Lorenzo de'Medici and as the head of his family—his elder brother Piero had died, in fact drowned, fleeing with the French army—it was his responsibility to reunite the Medici in Florence. And he used his influence in the Sacred College and every kind of political and diplomatic machination to work for that.

It became his policy to work with the pro-Medici patricians in Florence to try and undermine Soderini, to try and expose him so that there would be even more factional struggle, so the Medici could come as saviors and solve the problem. And, to some extent, the political circumstances in the peninsula played into the Medici hands. The vulnerability of Florence, the exposure of the city after the defeat of the French, allowed Cardinal de'Medici to work, using the papacy as a base, and leading a papal army of 1,500 soldiers towards Florence that ultimately made it clear that Soderini had lost his support.

In September of 1512, Piero Soderini fled into exile. He knew that he could not sustain his rule in Florence, and that the constitution that he had established in order to give some measure of stability to the policies of the Great Council came to nothing. Giovanni de'Medici, cardinal of the Roman Church, head of the Medici family, marched triumphantly into the city, leading his army and instantly going to the Palazzo Medici, where he took up residence. The very palace where he had been born and where he had lived as a child now became his, and once more it was that palace on the Via Larga that became the center for all political activity in the Florentine Republic. The Medici had returned.

Giovanni de'Medici was an extraordinary man—extremely well educated, very sensitive, intelligent, one of the great art patrons of all times; he was a close friend of Raphael; this was the Giovanni who helped the *stanza* of Raphael to be painted when Giovanni became pope, a man very shrewd. He was also very aware, having lived in Florence in his early life, just how sensitive the Florentines were to any kind of princely rule.

He knew that what he would have to do was connect his administration to that of his father. There was a sense of nostalgia now about the Medici under Lorenzo, a sense of nostalgia and melancholy about that golden age that seems to have passed. There was a sense of anger at the Medici having been thrown out in that period of Savonarola, introducing ideas so anathema to the political classes.

Giovanni played brilliantly upon all of these things. He not only manipulated the situation, he flattered those of the political classes whom he needed. He promised them office. He gave back the kinds of ceremonies and the kinds of delightful entertainments that the common people so loved and so associated with the Medici, with their jousts and carnival activities.

He then decided that the golden age would be back, and he would be his father's son. The power of the Church would provide stability. His influence in the Holy See could be, then, something that could guarantee the republican freedom of the city by linking the Church and Florence against all possible enemies. It was a brilliant plan, and it worked almost perfectly.

He needed to give legality to his position because, essentially, he returned to Florence as a conqueror. There was a price on his head. He marched into the city, leading an army. So, he needed some form of constitution, some form of constitutional legitimization. He called a *Parlamento*, one of those meetings of the heads of households summoned by the ringing of the great bell in the Palazzo della Signoria, everyone coming together in the piazza in order to give extra constitutional authority to a new law. And everyone duly did as they were informed that they must do—that is, to create a new Balìa, a new committee of 40 members, all of whom were, not surprisingly, strong noted Medici supporters.

The purpose of this group was to restore Medici hegemony, but to do it in a way that would not alienate public opinion, wouldn't alienate the great patricians, and wouldn't alienate any group in society. And Giovanni was almost theatrical in his restitution of Florentine tradition—traditions he knew so well, traditions that he realized his father had used so brilliantly in order to shore the rule of his family.

First, no symbols of monarchy whatsoever were tolerated. There were to be no symbols that associated the Medici with the conquering family. They weren't to be associated with any kind of papal, or royal, or princely rule. Republican dress was required for all the Medici supporters. Simple magisterial behaviour, as opposed to swaggering, was required. The faction then went back to the kinds of activity that had given so much strength and power to the Medici in the 60 years of their hegemony, following the success of Cosimo in 1434.

The moral repression of Savonarola was reversed. And here, again, the symbolism was wonderful. It was reversed, and that gave the freedom back to those patrician youths who wanted to gamble, who wanted to dance and play cards, who wanted carnival to be enjoyed, who wanted the state brothels to be reopened. These things were not only restored, but they were restored through the authority of a prince of the Church, a cardinal of the apostolic Church who says that he is speaking also with the authority of someone who might elect the next pope. In other words, the attacks of Savonarola on the institution of the Church were brilliantly undermined by Giovanni.

The idea of Florence being the new Jerusalem was, again, subtly shifted so that Florence once more became a kind of new Athens, or more particularly, a new Rome—but not just the pagan republican Rome of Leonardo Bruni, but a Rome that also had with it the apostolic authority of the see of St. Peter.

Giovanni, as a prince of the Church and as head of the Medici family, was a perfect compromise. And with his great personal skills and towering intelligence, he did well, indeed. To the people of Florence, it seemed that Laurentian Florence had returned, that the time of Lorenzo de'Medici was back in the shape of his son. There was happiness and rejoicing.

The rejoicing, though, was nothing compared to that moment in March of 1513 when Giovanni de'Medici was unexpectedly elected pope—unexpectedly because he was only 37 years old. He, in fact, was a compromised candidate, and he found that he had to rush back to Rome in order to be properly installed because he hadn't even made all of the necessary religious arrangements for his entry into the priesthood.

With the celebration of Giovanni de'Medici as Pope Leo X, the city of Florence felt that this was God acting. Savonarola was obviously a false prophet. Now, what Savonarola had preached against, in fact had come to pass. The role of the Church, the role of the papacy, the role of God's plan for man in an orderly fashion, the uniting of civil and religious authority, all seemed to be fulfilled. Florence was, in fact, both the new Jerusalem and the new Rome simultaneously.

The people of Florence celebrated the way they did best—they looted the houses of the known anti-Medician patricians, burning their furniture in the streets as bonfires; they made fun of the Piagnoni, who still gathered in San Marco in order to snivel with the memory of Savonarola; and they said that *Papa Leone*, Pope Leo X, was, in fact, their real ruler—that God ruled through the appropriate offices, through his vicar honour, who was the head of the Medici family.

From that time on, from March of 1513 until the death of Pope Clement VII de'Medici in 1534, the history of Florence is linked inextricably to that of the papacy. Real power in Florence was transferred to Rome. This was something the Florentines did not see at the time. It's something that we know because we can watch it happening in every form. The power that was concentrated in the Medici family while in the city was now being diffused, brought to Rome where it was being exercised by a pope who necessarily had to rule his ancestral city of Florence through representatives.

Giovanni as Leo X had a plan that would link the papal states with Tuscany by connecting the two contiguous territories through, perhaps, a Medici principality. It was a brilliant idea, one that he thought could be sufficiently powerful to actually restrain, or at least restrict, the barbarian invaders, and would be a buffer between the potential French in the north and the power of the Aragonese in the south.

Giovanni's younger brother, Giuliano, had been named as head of the family in Florence, and he, too, was a brilliant choice. He stage-managed the republic just the way his father and brother had. He was up to it. He understood the sensibilities. He also knew very well that he had to be careful and represent his brother very effectively, while still giving some kind of natural and intrinsic authority to the traditional political classes in the city. Sadly, the dynasty began to crumble when Giuliano died in 1516, leaving only a very young illegitimate son. It seemed as though the dynastic success of the Medici was being undone by the problems of the inability of the next generation to live to adulthood.

Replacing Giuliano in Florence was the pope's nephew, Lorenzo, who was then in his twenties. Lorenzo was very different from Giuliano, and even more different from Pope Leo X. Lorenzo had been raised as a prince and unfortunately he lacked the sensitivity to the vanity of the republican patriciate in Florence to actually serve them in a way that would have allowed him to rule without very much hostility. He offended the pride of the city's elites. He behaved in inappropriate ways. He took a title, the title of Captain General of the Republic; this seemed to make him a kind of military dictator, which no one much liked.

Then he began to stack the magistracies with his cronies. He took advice from his favorites, rather than listen to the advice of the republican leaders and the councils that they represented. Only his early death in 1519 from syphilis saved the city from yet another revolt and another expulsion of the city, because in that short period he had become extremely unpopular.

In his place was set Giulio. Giulio de'Medici, the illegitimate son of Lorenzo the Magnificent's well-loved brother, Giuliano, who had been murdered in the Pazzi Conspiracy of 1478. Despite his illegitimacy, Giulio had been made a cardinal and enjoyed, again, the authority that came from being part of the Sacred College and having his first cousin as the pope.

He was very much like his cousin, in fact. He was thoughtful, wise, sensitive, extremely well educated, and enormously popular in the city. He then managed to restore the Medici rule of the city as manipulators of the republic, not stepping on the sensibilities of the patricians and recognizing the need to provide bread and circuses, as well as good government.

Florence, then, was tranquil until the early death of Leo X in December of 1521. At that time, Giulio de'Medici rushed to Rome, hoping to be elected in succession to his cousin. This was not to be because of the machinations of Piero Soderini's brother, who was a cardinal, and who ensured that the anti-Medician candidate would be elected. But the choice was a bad one. The choice was an ascetic Dutchman, who became Pope Adrian VI, the last foreign pope until the election of John Paul II.

Adrian VI was a pope that the Romans and the Church largely hated because he tried to live an ascetic life and impose an ascetic life on the rest of the Church. The city languished, and when he died just a few months after being inaugurated as pope, his doctor was carried through the city on the shoulders of the population as a hero. And the doctor said he had no hand in his death, but the people believed otherwise.

After the death of Adrian VI, there was elected Giulio de'Medici as Pope Clement VII. The Medici had claimed, once more, not just the city—but the papal tiara. This, though, put Medici power back in Rome, and Giulio was the last adult member of his family. There was no one who could rule in his name. He appointed foreign cardinals to act as his spokesman, to be the papal governor of the city, to represent the Medici and the papal interests. Most of these had little sympathy for, or knowledge of, the traditions of the republic. They weren't that familiar with how they needed to behave so as not to offend the dignity of those patrician magistrates who always just tolerated the Medici because they did such a fine job, and at least they were all treated equally.

But, as unpopular as they were, they were seen as, at least, reasonable compromises. The real fear was of the two very young Medici bastards sent by Clement to prepare them for the future rule of the city—in particular, Alessandro de'Medici, who was certainly an illegitimate son of Clement VII by a Moorish slave. He was already beginning to show the signs of the mental imbalance that was to imperil his future regime and that was to ultimately thrust Florence into another period of chaos.

But before Alessandro could assume rule of Florence and exercise his incompetent and evil rule, other events were to occur—events that were to be disasters, not just for Florence, but for all of Italy and, indeed, for the civilized world. The sack of Rome was to be a moment that indicated that the belief and the dignity of man had been, if not totally destroyed, at least seriously compromised. It allowed an element of violence to creep into Italian politics and Italian life that would be very difficult to expunge, and Florence suffered, as the rest of the peninsula suffered from this terrible event.

Lecture Twenty-Nine
The Sack of Rome, 1527

Scope:

The struggle between the French and the Spanish-Imperial Habsburgs for domination of the continent often took place in Italy, where both crowns had competing dynastic claims. Led by a French traitor, the Constable of Bourbon, an imperial army, unpaid, undisciplined, hungry, and including many zealous German Protestant soldiers, arrived at the gates of Rome. On May 6, 1527, the walls were breached and the city was stormed by this savage army, left leaderless by the death of Bourbon in the first assault. His army then proceeded to spend the next almost eight months ravishing the city, murdering and torturing its inhabitants. The Medici pope, Clement VII, had taken refuge in Castel Sant'Angelo but was able to watch the destruction. Churches and private homes were despoiled, wealthy citizens were held for ransom, nuns were raped and murdered, and even the tombs of popes and bishops were opened in search of valuables. The last months of the sack saw the use of whatever was made of wood as fuel to keep warm. Those who could escape did, although many were killed by starving peasants outside the walls or captured by thugs for ransom. About 50,000 inhabitants either fled or were killed through the savagery, making this sack more brutal than even the barbarian incursions at the end of the Roman Empire. Rotting bodies, along with lack of sanitation, food, and clean water, then gave rise to disease that devastated the few left behind. The result was that the pope was, in effect, the creature of the emperor, and the Humanist belief in the dignity of man was seriously tarnished.

Outline

I. As we have already seen, the situation in Italy in the first decades of the 16th century was chaotic and desperate, with rival claims of France and Aragon threatening the stability of the peninsula.

    A. This situation was made worse by the Habsburg inheritance of the Spanish crown in the person of Charles V, who was subsequently elected Holy Roman Emperor.

1. Italy was the battleground between the French House of Valois and the Spanish-Imperial House of Habsburg for hegemony over the continent.
2. The succession of Francis I of France in 1515 renewed this struggle in a personal way, because the young man wanted military glory.
3. Francis immediately embarked on an Italian campaign in 1515 against Milan, which was protected by a formidable army of Swiss mercenaries.
4. At Marignano, Francis defeated the Swiss and took Milan
5. However, in an extraordinary change in fortune, in early 1525, at Pavia, just outside Milan, Charles V defeated the French and captured Francis.
6. The French were completely humiliated, and Charles became undisputed master of Europe.

B. Charles V made a French traitor, the Constable of Bourbon, and cousin of King Francis, governor of Milan, but Bourbon was given insufficient funds.
1. With no money to pay them, Bourbon began losing control of his troops by the late summer 1526.
2. He tried everything possible, even selling his own property to pay his army.
3. Ultimately, these brutal professional soldiers started to live off the land in northern Italy, savagely looting towns in Milanese territory.

C. This practice resulted in a decision to march south toward Rome, where the best looting might be found.
1. It is unlikely that Bourbon encouraged this, but he could not control his own soldiers.
2. The army had abandoned all discipline and order and continued down the peninsula as the barbarians had done a millennium before.
3. Florence escaped by bribing the soldiers to bypass the city, but this actually hastened their march.
4. Moving with unprecedented speed, the imperial army reached Rome at the beginning of May 1527.

II. The situation in Rome was confused, in part because of the general conditions of Europe and in part because of the pope's character.

    A. The pope was Clement VII, cousin of Leo X de'Medici and illegitimate son of the murdered Giuliano de'Medici.

        1. The pope's character was exactly the wrong mix of elements at a time of crisis: He was very learned, charming, civilized, and shrewd, but he was also vacillating, indecisive, and occasionally naïve.

        2. In the terrible struggle between Habsburg and Valois, Clement had tried to be neutral, which meant that he was despised by both sides, especially by Charles V, who saw himself as the sword of the Church and the defender of orthodoxy against the rising heresy of Luther.

        3. Charles felt betrayed, given that France was forming alliances with the Protestant powers and even encouraging the Turks to attack central Europe to relieve pressure on France.

        4. Clement, though, saw the threat to the independence of the Church and to Italy of a continent completely controlled by the Habsburgs: He tried to steer an independent course.

    B. Clement tried to stop the imperial army before it reached Rome, engaging a relative, Giovanni de'Medici, a *condottiere* general, and his famous mercenary force, the Black Bands.

        1. Unfortunately, Giovanni was killed in a skirmish with the imperials, and his mercenary band withdrew.

        2. Rome was now without any protection.

        3. When Clement called for all able-bodied men to rally for the defense of the city, fewer than 500 appeared.

III. The capture of the city took place almost immediately and seemingly without any kind of coordinated plan.

    A. The day following the arrival of the imperial army was so foggy that nothing could be seen beyond a few feet.

        1. Either sensing an opportunity or—more likely—unable to control the men, Bourbon led his troops in the scaling of the walls.

2. Within the city, there was complete surprise; no one expected so quick an attack.

3. Bourbon himself was killed in the first assault.

4. Thus, the imperial army lost its last instrument of some kind of control: Leaderless, it became a band of murderers, looters, and rapists.

5. Because the attack was a surprise, the bridges over the Tiber had not been severed; thus, the entire city lay open to the thousands of soldiers as they streamed over the walls.

6. The pope and some fortunate members of his *Curia* managed to find safety in Castel Sant'Angelo, from which they watched the destruction of the city.

B. Working in small groups, the soldiers fanned out throughout the city, looting churches, taking wealthy citizens as hostages to be redeemed by their families, and slaughtering the poor on the spot.

1. Protestant Germans hanged bishops and cardinals by their hair from ceilings until they told where they had hidden Church treasures and their possessions. Sometimes, Church officials were ransomed; sometimes, killed.

2. All women, young and old, were repeatedly raped, and when they passed out or were no longer of interest, they were killed.

3. Companies of Protestant Germans played dice for whole convents of nuns, for the pleasure of raping these virgins first.

4. After the nuns had been brutalized for more than a week, they were slaughtered.

5. The dead did not escape, as the soldiers pried open the tombs of popes, cardinals, and bishops to steal their vestments, rings, and miters, throwing the bodies onto the floors of churches or in the street.

C. There was no escape and no help to be had.

1. The great Roman nobles who lived outside Rome, such as the Orsini, were not disposed to come to the pope's rescue.

2. They had long simmered in anger at their loss of power under such popes as Julius II.
3. As people fled the city, the Orsini abbot of Farfa sent thugs to rob those fleeing with their possessions.
4. In this atmosphere of total anarchy, peasants set up roadblocks around the city to rob and kill all of those they stopped.

D. The initial, most brutal period of the sack lasted just over a week, but Europe had seen nothing on this scale of savagery for a thousand years.
1. At least 40,000 people were killed; this total increases if those killed outside the city by the Orsini and the local peasants are included.
2. Not more than about 15,000 inhabitants remained, including the several hundred surrounded in Castel Sant'Angelo with the pope and the *Curia*.

IV. After the first frenzy of slaughter and destruction, the invaders settled down in the city in an occupation that was to last for eight months.

A. Conditions in the city continued to deteriorate.
1. As winter approached, there was insufficient firewood, so the soldiers began dismantling houses, stripping them of doors, windows, and roof beams to use for fuel.
2. The unburied dead rotted in the streets for some time, and eventually, many bodies were thrown in the Tiber, the source of much of the city's drinking water.
3. Disease and hunger began to spread among the army and those few citizens remaining in Rome.

B. After some months, Pope Clement managed to escape the city in disguise.
1. In negotiations with Charles V, Clement was forced to recognize the power of the emperor in Italy, including sanctioning all of his claims to Italian territory.
2. An imperial coronation was granted, and Charles was duly crowned in Bologna in 1529, the last imperial coronation in Italy.
3. Rome was desolated for almost a decade, with its population depleted and even those who returned

suffering from disease, made worse by serious flooding of the Tiber in the years immediately after the sack.

    4. The thriving papal culture in Rome ceased for many years, with artists having fled the city, taking their talents—and the new style—to other centers in the peninsula.

C. The Protestants exulted, saying that the sack was God's judgment on the Antichrist.

    1. Broadsheets and woodcuts of the sack and the humiliation of the pope spread across Europe.

    2. Charles V was sincerely regretful of the event and offered condolences to the pope, but never did he accept any responsibility for the sack.

D. After this event, Italians had difficulty in continuing to believe in the dignity of man and the ideals of Humanism.

Primary Source Texts:

Benvenuto Cellini, *The Autobiography of Benvenuto Cellini.*

Secondary Sources:

André Chastel, *The Sack of Rome, 1527.*

Supplementary Reading:

Judith Hook, *The Sack of Rome.*

Questions to Consider:

1. Why was the sack so unspeakably savage?
2. Can the sack of Rome be seen as the end of the Renaissance?

Lecture Twenty-Nine—Transcript
The Sack of Rome, 1527

We've seen how the situation in Italy was reduced largely to chaos. We've seen that first decade of the 16th century being a time when the rival claims of Aragon and France challenged the Italian peninsula. The entire peninsula was, in fact, the battleground of Europe for the hegemony of the continent. And the stability of Italy, therefore, was compromised to the point that it was difficult, if not impossible, for the Italian states to exercise much independent control.

Many of them saw themselves as merely brokering the great powers through a system of alliances and attempts to build some sort of collective security in the face of overwhelming power. This situation was made much worse by the Habsburg inheritance of the Spanish crown in the person of the Archduke Charles, who became, after his election as Holy Roman Emperor, the Emperor Charles V.

The House of Ferdinand of Aragon and Isabel of Castile had become extinct. It passed then to Charles, who then united the enormous power and wealth of Spain with the power of the Holy Roman Empire, his Low Countries' inheritance, and also, of course, much of the new world that had been claimed for Spain.

Italy, then, was a battleground not just between two regional powers, France and Italy, but, in fact, the two mega powers of the 16th century, France and the Empire, who wanted not just hegemony of the continent, but also to exercise authority over an expanding European world.

The succession of Francis I in 1515 renewed this struggle in a very personal way. The young Francis I—who was handsome, ambitious, and extraordinarily charming—also wanted to prove himself through military glory. He wanted to be the ideal and perfect chivalric knight, and the way to do this was through war. And he immediately, then, followed the example of his predecessors, Charles VIII and Louis XII, and crossed the Alps in search of glory and Italian conquest.

In 1515, the year that he became king, he claimed and attacked Milan, defeating the Swiss mercenaries who had been hired to defend it at the Battle of Marignano. Marignano was one of those events that, to some extent, changed the nature of Italian history because it proved that a small, highly professional band of soldiers, like the Swiss, could not withstand the great power of a feudal army arrayed as the French king had managed in his attempt to build an empire based upon military force. But a decade makes a big difference.

Early in 1525, Charles V—realizing that the French and the north of Italy, in fact, challenged his ability to control the rest of the peninsula—invaded Italy himself, and at the Battle of Pavia, just outside of Milan, Charles V defeated the French in such a total and complete way that Francis, King of France, was captured and brought as a prisoner to Spain.

This complete humiliation of the French, this lack of a central power in the country—France was ruled by the king's mother as regent—resulted in Italy being, once more, the extension almost of imperial authority. Charles V decided that the way to rule Milan was through a French traitor. The Constable of Bourbon was the cousin of King Francis, but one who had fallen out with Francis's mother. This fight resulted in the money for the French troops and, in fact, in particular, the payment of the Constable of Bourbon, himself, to be stopped. Bourbon, in anger and personal humiliation, went over to the other side as a traitor. And this French aristocrat, this cousin of the French king, was named by the French king's jailer and victor, Charles V, as the governor of Milan.

The problem was that Charles V had financial problems of his own. Charles wasn't able to provide sufficient funds to Bourbon or to the Spanish-German army that was in the city—the army, in fact, that had defeated Francis I, and was now waiting, not only for pay, but for, in effect, future orders.

By the late summer of 1526, all of the money was gone. Bourbon had nothing to pay his soldiers with. He even stooped to the selling of his own property. He even started to alienate his personal patrimony in France in order to pay his soldiers a little bit longer because he realized that once they were altogether without pay, he would lose whatever power he had over them. Unable to pay them, his fears were realized.

These brutal, battle-hardened soldiers fell largely into two categories: a large number of professional Spanish veterans who had been fighting constantly since the 15th century; and a group of German mercenaries who were largely Protestant, having listened to the message of Martin Luther had brought it into their military camps. This mixed army of Spaniards and Germans began taking their pay from the local countryside. They moved outside the city and began looting and living off the land of northern Italy. They savagely looted the small towns around Milan and the Milanese.

Not really having enough to loot, realizing that they had exhausted the possibilities of the Lombard Plain, the army decided—and there was not much Bourbon could do to stop them—to march south where there was greater looting to be had. The army began to march. It had abandoned all discipline. It felt that because it had not been paid, and because there was no one really able to impose order and discipline on them, that they could do anything they wanted. They had become, in fact, like that barbarian horde that had invaded Italy a millennium before—a new group of barbarians equally intent on plunder, and they marched down the center of Italy in search of more and more wealth.

They reached Florence, but the Florentines bought them off, paid them ransom so they would avoid the city. All this succeeded in doing was speeding their march towards Rome. There was some sense that they would be held up somewhere on the peninsula by one of the Italian powers. It didn't happen. By May of 1527, they had, in fact, reached the outskirts of the Eternal City.

The situation in Rome while this was happening was equally as confused. This was in part because of the conditions in Europe, which were chaotic, which in themselves had largely created this problem and that also reflected the kind of impossible situation the pope found himself to be in. The pope, moreover, was Clement VII, that cousin of Leo X de'Medici, that illegitimate son of the murdered Giuliano, that brother of Lorenzo the Magnificent murdered, as we've seen, in the Pazzi Conspiracy.

Clement VII was a truly remarkable man, but he had exactly the wrong character at this moment of crisis. It was precisely the wrong mix of elements at a time when desperate action had to be taken, when there needed to be decisive moments, where there needed to be someone who could galvanize fighting men. This wasn't Clement VII. Clement was extremely learned, very polished, civilized, shrewd. But he was, by nature, vacillating, indecisive, and really naïve—especially where politics were concerned.

Clement, in the terrible struggle between Habsburg and Valois over control of the continent and all of its wealth, tried to be neutral. Both France and the Empire and Spain, of course, part of the empire at that point—the empire of Charles V—they were Catholic. The pope believed that he was the head of a universal Church. He tried to steer a middle course between them. The result was he was despised by both sides.

Francis felt that the pope should be putting more emphasis on some kind of reasonable balance of power in order to reduce the enormous authority that Charles V had acquired. Charles V despised the pope because Charles saw himself as the sword of the Church and the defender of orthodoxy against the rising heresy of Martin Luther, the defender of Europe against the Turks, the protector of Catholic orthodoxy in this dangerous time. Charles didn't understand why Clement VII simply didn't see him as his secular counterpart. The result was that trying to be fair and equal to both sides, Clement found himself in the middle and respected by none.

Francis tried almost everything in this period of his humiliation. He tried making alliance with the Protestant powers. He even encouraged the Turks to attack Europe, and, in particular, attack the world of Charles V, that world of central-eastern Europe that was, to some extent, part of the Habsburg hegemony. And it was successful inasmuch as the terrible Battle of Mohács in 1526. The Turks destroyed the Hungarian and international armies then to stop them, and the Turks then could march to Vienna.

This was actually done at the urging of Francis's mother, Louise of Savoy, as an attempt to try and force the emperor to release her son. This is the situation in which the pope found himself. This was the chaotic situation in Europe, and everything then was focused on Italy and this moment in Rome when the Imperial army—largely leaderless, largely without pay, composed of very, very vicious individuals—found itself in front of the richest city in the peninsula, the center of Catholicism and the capital of that pope that no one seemed to greatly respect.

Clement tried to stop the Imperial army, and he did what he could. He engaged his cousin, Giovanni de'Medici, known as Giovanni delle Bande Nere, Giovanni of The Black Bands, who was a mercenary captain, whose Black Bands consisted of a professional army sent for hire. But this *condottieri* army proved it impossible to stop the Imperials. And, indeed, in a skirmish, Giovanni himself was killed.

He was killed in one of those ways that provides a measure of evidence why putting young men in charge of armies is perhaps not the best thing. Giovanni was actually only wounded. He was hit by a cannonball, and his leg was shattered. But he insisted as the surgeon amputated the leg that he hold the torch so he could watch the process, and he died of shock. With the death of Giovanni, the only army between the Imperials and the walls of the city evaporated, and there was nothing to stop Bourbon and his completely undisciplined followers from attack.

Clement called for all able-bodied men to rally. The call yielded 500 individuals—nothing, no one to stop the attack. The following day after the Imperial army's arrival at the Aralian walls of the city, the weather was impossible. It was so foggy that you could only see a foot or so in front of your hands. Nothing could be seen. The top of the walls couldn't be seen from the moats around the city.

As a consequence, the soldiers rushed the walls. They put their scaling ladders against the Aralian walls of the city, those walls that had protected Rome for 1,300 years, and they started to climb. It's not likely that Bourbon gave the order; it's more likely that Bourbon couldn't control his soldiers.

Bourbon, though, French knight that he was, found himself at their head. He was the first to reach the top of the wall and the first to die. Bourbon died almost immediately after the Imperial army had reached the top of the walls of the city. Things were bad with Bourbon unable to exercise much control, but with Bourbon gone and no general, no leadership whatsoever, the army simply turned itself from a fighting force into a group of violent, vicious murderers, rapists, and looters.

There was nothing to stop them from entering the city. No one had expected an attack so soon after the army arrived. Nothing had been done to prepare. The bridges over the Tiber hadn't been severed, so the entire city lay open to them. The army fanned out in small groups into the huge city, only part of which was occupied—but, nevertheless, full of great riches and the accumulated treasure of the Renaissance papacy.

The city was totally unprepared. The pope and a few hundred very fortunate individuals of his *Curia* managed to escape from the apostolic palace along that escape route that had been built between the palace and the Castel Sant'Angelo, that fortress that had been built in ancient times as the tomb of the Emperor Hadrian, but was fortified as an almost impregnable fortress in the center of the city. It was from this spot where they could see everything happening. Pope Clement, his cardinals and bishops and their servants, including Benvenuto Cellini, that great artist and great liar who said that it was his shot that actually killed the Constable of Bourbon, watched the city being destroyed.

The soldiers worked in small groups throughout the city, choosing their areas of plunder and their areas of destruction. They looted churches. They took wealthy citizens that they identified by their clothes or their place of residence and held them hostage. Many were redeemed at great price by their families; others were simply killed. All women, young and old, were repeatedly raped, and when they passed out or were no longer of interest to the soldiers, they were killed. Companies of German Protestant soldiers diced for whole convents of nuns so that they had the pleasure of raping these virgins first. And then after a week of the most terrible brutalization, they were simply slaughtered.

All nuns were really killed in the city. Most priests suffered abominably. Bishops and cardinals were not only held at ransom, they were tortured, largely again by the German Protestants who saw this as ideological, as well as simply pathological. Not even the dead escaped. The soldiers pried open the tombs of popes, cardinals, and bishops so they could be stripped of their vestments of their cloth of gold; stripped of their mitres and their rings. The dead bodies were then thrown into the street or onto the floors of churches.

Art was not spared. The wonderful paintings that Raphael had so recently completed in the *stanza*, and in particular the *Stanza della Signatura* in the apostolic palace, lay open to the soldiers as they broke into the pope's quarters. A group of German pipe men scratched "Martin Luther" in letters three or four feet high at the bottom of the disputation in the Holy Sacrament in the *Stanza della Signatura*, that room that contained not only the *Disputation*, but the *School of Athens*. And, indeed, this image of Martin Luther's name can still be seen if the light is absolutely right, as it reflects on the bottom of that wonderful fresco.

The Sistine Chapel fortunately was completely protected, not by any sense of the magnificence of Michelangelo's art on the ceiling or the great 15th-century artist frescoes on the walls, but the Sistine Chapel, the private chapel of the pope, had been chosen as a place to put the body of the Constable of Bourbon. As it lay in state, it was, in effect, protected from those savages that destroyed so much beauty and so much accumulated art.

There was no hope. There was no help. The great Roman nobles had been completely and totally alienated from the power of the papacy from the time of Julius II. That warrior pope, Julius II, at the beginning of the 16th century, had done what so many other popes had wanted but had not succeeded in doing, and that is humbling the power of the great Roman noble families of the Campagna. He had, in fact, not only humbled them, he, in fact, had broken their power—and in some instances, particularly that of the Orsini, had actually resulted in the death of a number of them, including an Orsini cardinal.

The consequence was the great nobles in the countryside offered no protection, and the Orsini in particular, which had a long tradition of Imperial association, actually fell in with the barbarians themselves. The Orsini, then, didn't protect the pope; the Orsini cooperated in the destruction of the city. In particular, the Orsini abbot of Farfa, in a monastery just outside the city, used his bands of thugs in order to rob those who were trying to flee the city with their possessions. And he wasn't alone. The peasants, seeing the success of this, set up roadblocks on the roads leading away from the city. They stopped those fleeing with their possessions, robbed them, and, in most instances, simply killed them on the spot.

The initial brutal period of the sack and the destruction of the city lasted just over one week. But Europe had not seen anything this barbarous, had not seen this scale of savagery, for a thousand years.

Nothing in the previous millennium had been equal to this barbarism. At least 40,000 people were killed. And if you count those who were slaughtered outside the city, probably far more.

The Orsini and the peasants killed large numbers of those who simply happened to be in the wrong place at the wrong time. Rome was reduced to no more than 15,000 inhabitants by the end of that summer of 1527. A city that, at the time of Constantine, had over a million inhabitants—that once more had become the center, not just of the Church, but of art, and culture, and that marvelous moment of the Renaissance papacy—was now, in fact, just a breeding ground of disease and poverty. The city was being destroyed.

Seeing all of this from the Castel Sant'Angelo was the pope, and he could do nothing. He was in such a state of depression and despair that he refused, in the classical model, to cut his beard, beginning that moment, again, when priests and clerics were permitted to grow hair on their faces. This sense of the bearded pope, who said that he would not shave until there had been some form of reconciliation, became a symbol of not just the humiliation of the Church and his own personal papacy, but also of a new form of savagery.

The frenzy of slaughter and destruction ended because there was no one else to kill, and there was very little else to loot. After stringing cardinals and bishops up, and after driving the wealthy from the city or killing them, the army simply put down roots and decided to stay. There was nothing much for them to do, though, and winter began to arrive.

With the coming of winter, there was insufficient firewood in the city, so they began dismantling it. The soldiers took the doorframes, the doors, the window frames, the roof beams that held the roofs of buildings and palaces, and used them for firewood. The unburied dead that had been rotting in the street for weeks were ultimately just thrown in the Tiber. But the Tiber still, despite the rebuilding of the aqueduct by Nicholas V, remained the source of drinking water for much of the city. The consequence was not just destruction and poverty, but also disease.

Disease began to claim those few who had survived the sack, and it began to deplete the numbers of the Imperial army. Something had to happen because the city was simply dying literally.

The pope, Clement VII, managed to escape. He managed to get a disguise and escape the city dressed as a monk—in fact, dressed as his own servant. He managed to reach the Emperor Charles V through correspondence, and they negotiated some kind of reasonable truce. The pope knew that he had to completely capitulate because he had no argument to make. He had nothing with which he could bargain. He, essentially, gave in to every demand that Charles made, and the demands were huge.

First was the recognition of all Imperial—that is, Spanish—and Habsburg claims on Italy. All of the Habsburg claims on Naples, on Milan, were all to be accepted and recognized. Also, there was to be an Imperial coronation. This actually took place in 1529, not in Rome, because Rome was still uninhabitable—it was impossible for it to happen—but in the city of Bologna. And there in the great cathedral of San Petronio, Charles V was crowned by Clement VII as Holy Roman Emperor, the last Imperial coronation that ever took place in Italy.

Rome was desolated for over a decade as a consequence of these events. The city was not only physically destroyed and seriously damaged, but there were no inhabitants. Those who hadn't been killed had fled the plague and the starvation. Those who managed to hide when the soldiers were living in the city for eight months came out of their cellars and their places of hiding to find the city almost completely derelict. The disease was claiming almost anyone who was left, and the only solution, really, was to flee.

Once more, it seemed as though nature was cooperating with these savages because the Tiber engaged in some of the worst flooding in decades immediately following the sack. The flooding of the Tiber made everything much worse because it brought silt and the bodies of drowned animals and men back into the city. It made reconstruction almost impossible, even if there had been people there to rebuild.

But as in all terrible, unspeakable disasters, there was, in fact, something that we can look at that perhaps was a positive result, if anything could in any way compensate for those terrible months. The destruction of the city, and the ending of papal rule in the city, and the end of papal patronage, drove those artists and craftsmen, who had all been drawn to Rome by the magnetic power of papal patronage, out of the city. Those workshops, the workshop that Raphael had put together in the city to paint the apostolic palace, the model of Michelangelo and those who had come to look at his work, and to follow, and to decorate, the goldsmiths, the tailors, the makers of furniture—all of these were driven from Rome, and they sought employment elsewhere.

What they did is spread the model of Renaissance culture into small cities, and to cities in which the depth of the penetration of Renaissance humanist culture wasn't very deep. Cities like Genoa benefited enormously, and other cities that previously had been not really part of that first wave of Renaissance art exploration began to benefit. So, it was in this diaspora of art, this diaspora of artists, and this diaspora of culture, that much of the high Renaissance models of Rome began to spread throughout the peninsula. Still, it meant that Rome was that much poorer.

Also, it was a great propaganda victory—not so much for Charles V, who actually was somewhat embarrassed by the events. Charles did send a note of personal condolence to the pope saying, "I'm sorry all of this happened, but it wasn't my fault." Charles blamed everyone else. He blamed the Constable of Bourbon; he blamed soldiers that hadn't been paid. The reality was he was the person who should have paid them and simply chose not to, spending the money elsewhere.

Charles V was, in many ways, responsible for this terrible sack, although he never accepted any responsibility whatsoever, and, indeed, he made the humiliation worse under subsequent popes when he demanded an Imperial entry into the city. The great victors in this psychological battle were the Lutherans. They, of course, saw the sack of Rome as God's judgment on the anti-Christ, being the pope. They saw this as a moment when God's judgment on an imperfect, impure Church was being reaped. They saw, then, the sack of Rome as something that made their cause that much stronger and more attractive. Woodcuts and pamphlets spread throughout Europe, exulting in the sack of Rome and the humiliation of the pope.

And, indeed, the Lutheran soldiers in Rome during the eight months of the sack itself put an enormous example of this right on the walls of Castel Sant'Angelo, which they didn't bother to storm. They left the pope there, in part because the Spanish Catholics weren't terribly anxious to see the pope slaughtered. But, at the same time, it was almost better to leave him and force him to watch the humiliation of his city. On the walls of Castel Sant'Angelo, there was a huge image of the horror of Babylon riding upon a donkey. And this, of course, was to symbolize the papacy and the Roman Church.

The victory of the Protestants, in their perspective, was, in fact, a religious and psychological victory. The destruction, though, of the city and the psychological damage were much greater than anyone could ever anticipate.

What we'll see in subsequent lectures is that sense of self-confidence that the Renaissance had been building, really, from the time of Petrarch, that belief in the dignity of man so eloquently described by Pico della Mirandola, that belief that man is the measure of all things, is now shattered. Who could possibly believe in human dignity after seeing and hearing, and seeing the woodcuts and broadsheets illustrating the terrible events of the spring and summer of 1527?

It was impossible to sustain ideas based upon humanist concepts of the ability of man to do anything in this world when it seemed as though it was too easy to reduce the human condition to that of savage beasts.

The Renaissance, it has been suggested by a number of historians in the past, ended in 1527 with the sack of Rome because it was impossible to sustain the ideas that had given birth to it. I don't agree. The Renaissance didn't end with this moment, but it was turned into a more melancholy and, to some extent, almost nostalgic moment. But what it also did, it made a series of circumstances possible. It made the Habsburg control of the peninsula inevitable—a control that would last until the second half of the 19th century in the Risorgimento. It also made the idea of monarchy and ruthless, brutal power simply something to be sought after, rather than to be rejected as incompatible with human dignity.

We'll see authors like Machiavelli and Guicciardini recognizing that power and ruthlessness were, in fact, the new skills that statesmen needed. The idea of broadly based government, republicanism, liberty, and human dignity was secondary. These things require peace and security. The sack of Rome illustrated so powerfully that there could never be peace and security again in Italy without the exercise of power.

Lecture Thirty
Niccolò Machiavelli

Scope:

Machiavelli (1469–1527) was one of Renaissance Italy's most interesting thinkers. Best known for his political writing, such as *The Prince*, and historical works, such as *The History of Florence*, he was also a fine dramatist, letter writer, and diplomat. Born into a patrician Florentine family the year Lorenzo the Magnificent assumed control of the city, he pursued his career through the turbulent years of Savonarola's ascendancy and the restoration of the republic. He served as second chancellor, responsible for diplomatic work and, eventually, the creation of a citizen militia. Unfortunately, the militia was a failure, and his skill at negotiation did not save Florence or Italy from the scourge of foreign incursions and the ambitions of the Borgias. Still, his observations on these events and the lessons he learned entered the Western political consciousness. *The Prince* is his most read work. Written after the return of the Medici in 1512 removed him from power and relegated him to his small family villa outside the city, this book reviews the situation of Italy, particularly Florence, in an uncertain age. *The Prince*, using the ruthless Cesare Borgia as model, counsels harsh medicine, based on the need for strong leadership to protect Italy from the northern "barbarians."

Outline

I. Niccolò Machiavelli was born in Florence in May of 1469, the year Lorenzo de'Medici assumed control of the city.

  A. Machiavelli's early life corresponded to the glorious years of Laurentian Florence.

   1. His family was of the most honored ranks of the patriciate but relatively poor.

   2. He received an excellent Humanist education and was extremely well read in ancient authors, especially the Roman historians.

  B. But when he was just 25, his world was shattered by the French invasions of 1494.

1. He was in the city and witnessed the expulsion of the Medici, the regime of Savonarola, and the friar's execution in 1498.
2. The restoration of the broadly based republic that followed Savonarola's death in 1498 saw the appointment of the 29-year-old Machiavelli as second chancellor of the republic, responsible for translating executive decisions into policy.

C. As all noted, Machiavelli was brilliant at his job: He was a natural administrator, a shrewd observer of current events, and a brilliant synthesizer whose reports and diplomatic dispatches still read as models of their genre.
1. He was sent on an embassy to Louis XII of France in 1500, an embassy that was to be a formative moment in his career.
2. He realized that the fate of Italy was being determined north of the Alps at the courts of the kings of France and Spain, rather than in Italy itself.
3. For Machiavelli, this was a painful lesson, given his Humanist education and his unshakable belief that Italy was the heir of Rome and the northern monarchies were still barbarians.

II. Soon after his return to Florence in 1501, Machiavelli was sent as ambassador to Cesare, son of Alexander VI Borgia, to represent Florentine interests.

A. Machiavelli learned much from Cesare on this first mission.
1. First, he saw an Italian who appeared to be taking events into his own hands and directing them using the ruthless, brutal methods of the barbarians.
2. Second, he heard Cesare's advice that Florence should take back the Medici, because republics lack constancy and states need a firm leader in dangerous times.
3. Although a committed republican, Machiavelli listened to this advice, and he saw it as prudent counsel during times of crisis, if not as a universal principle.

B. Florence came to agree with Cesare and the French, as witnessed by Piero Soderini's election as *gonfaloniere* for life in 1502.

1. Because Soderini was Machiavelli's mentor and close friend, Machiavelli's career seemed assured and his influence was recognized.
2. In 1503, Soderini sent Machiavelli back to Cesare Borgia for three months, again trying to negotiate Florence's protection from the Borgias' ambitions in central Italy.
3. However, Machiavelli became entranced with the energy, ruthlessness, and single-mindedness of the Borgia and began to see Florence with some detachment.
4. He recognized that Florence was a small player in a life-and-death game and that changes would have to be made if the republic and the city's liberty were to survive.

C. Machiavelli had listened carefully to the French and others about the dangers of relying on mercenary armies.
1. As a keen student of Roman history, he knew that the Romans had conquered the world using armies of volunteers, well trained and rewarded and dedicated to fighting for their native land.
2. He also thought that war would help encourage discipline and unity among the fractious, luxury-loving Florentines, just as it did during the Roman Republic.
3. Soderini gave Machiavelli permission to establish a citizen militia in 1507 by appointing him secretary to the recently established war office.

D. The citizen militia saw its first action when the Holy League, under the newly crowned Pope Julius II, directed itself against the French army in Italy in 1503.
1. Florence, as a close ally of France, was left desperately exposed as the league army, composed mostly of battle-hardened Spanish veterans, invaded Florentine territory.
2. At Prato, a town just outside Florence that boasted excellent walls and defenses, Machiavelli arrayed his citizen militia to halt the Spanish mercenary advance.
3. However, after the first breech of the walls by the league artillery, the members of the militia threw down their weapons and fled, leaving the road to Florence open and undefended.

4. Soderini recognized there was no hope and fled into exile, allowing the Medici, as we saw in Lecture Twenty-Eight, to resume their role as first family in the city.
5. Machiavelli first lost his job and later was implicated—falsely—in a plot against the Medici and was tortured and thrown into prison.
6. Poor, suspect, and even in danger of his life, he decided to leave his beloved Florence and retire to a small farm owned by his family at San Casciano, just outside the city, in 1513.

III. Machiavelli's forced retirement gave him enough leisure to concentrate on his historical and literary work.

A. *The Prince* arose from the correspondence that took place in the spring of 1513 between Machiavelli, in exile in San Casciano, and his friend Francesco Vettori.
1. Machiavelli began by rehearsing the dangers to Italy resulting from the ambitions of Louis XII and noting how the barbarians had disrupted the peace of Italy since 1494.
2. He focused on how Italians might drive out the barbarians and form a united front against them, using national rather than mercenary armies and learning the skills of brutality and ruthlessness from the barbarians, at least until they could be expelled and Italy given collective security.
3. From Machiavelli's side of this correspondence came *The Prince*.
4. And from this book, the passage from Machiavelli to Vettori describing his life in the country and the birth of *The Prince* is perhaps the most famous letter in the Italian language.

B. *The Prince* has been greatly misunderstood since its composition.
1. It is an occasion piece addressing a particular moment in Florentine history, rather than an abstract work of political theory.
2. It must be read as the work of a committed republican who is looking temporarily to tyranny as an instrument

to save Italy and expel the barbarians, largely by using their methods, which have evidently succeeded so well.

    3. It is also a wake-up call for Italians to rise to their collective defense: If they failed to avoid internal strife, the barbarians would always exploit their fractious self-interest.

  C. Machiavelli was also writing his *Discourses on the First Ten Books of Titus Livius* at the same time.

    1. This text purports to be a Humanist commentary on Livy but is, in reality, a reflection on the recent history of Florence and Italy.

    2. It is much more abstract and self-consciously republican than *The Prince*.

    3. But it is also an indictment of Machiavelli's fellow Florentines for allowing luxury, lack of military rigor, factional strife, and class interest to weaken the republic, just as the Romans' weakness led to the collapse of the republic and the establishment of a tyrannical empire.

IV. As a result of his constant importuning of the Medici (including his dedication of *The Prince* to Giuliano de'Medici), Machiavelli was commissioned by Cardinal Giulio de'Medici as official historian with the responsibility to write *The History of Florence and the Affairs of Italy*.

  A. Machiavelli found this a difficult task, however, because he would have to discuss the republic between 1494 and 1512 from a pro-Medici perspective.

    1. But by 1525, he had brought the already large work up to the year 1492, the year Lorenzo the Magnificent died.

    2. This was not a problem, given that Machiavelli had respect for Medici foreign policy after 1450; by concentrating on that, he could avoid any comment about the decline of liberty, especially after 1480.

    3. In 1525, Machiavelli went to Rome to present his history to Giulio, now Pope Clement VII.

    4. Machiavelli was granted an annual stipend and offered some minor official work.

  B. The Medici were pleased with the *History of Florence* and Machiavelli now enjoyed a pension that allowed him to live again in Florence and reenter official life, although far from the level he had enjoyed under Soderini.

1. The crisis in Italy and the sack of Rome in 1527 was, for Machiavelli, a human disaster and illustrative of all he had hoped to prevent.

2. The expulsion of the Medici in 1527 as a consequence of the sack gave Machiavelli hope that he would be restored to high office and could contribute to the salvation of Italy.

3. Ironically, his having been accepted and pensioned by the Medici now made him suspect to the ferociously republican regime, despite the fact that many of them had been his friends and colleagues before 1512.

4. Again shut out of office, partly shunned as a Medici fellow traveler, in despair over the unbelievable barbarism of the sack of Rome, Machiavelli died sad and somewhat embittered in that terrible year, 1527.

Primary Source Texts:

Niccolò Machiavelli, *The Prince*.

Secondary Sources:

Maurizio Viroli, *Niccolò's Smile: A Biography of Machiavelli*.

Questions to Consider:

1. Oscar Wilde suggested that cynicism is the last refuge of the idealist. How is this illustrated in Machiavelli's writings?

2. As with Machiavelli and, later, Guicciardini, politicians forced from office often write important histories of their own time. Why do out-of-work politicians so often turn to letters?

Lecture Thirty—Transcript

Niccolò Machiavelli

The conditions that gave rise to the sack of Rome also created Niccolò Machiavelli, at least the Machiavelli that we know from the single work of *The Prince*, which is the most-read of all of his rather voluminous writings. Machiavelli is greatly misunderstood because usually people only read the prints.

It's necessary, in fact, to understand why this fervent, brilliant republican could write a book about the need for tyranny. And to understand Machiavelli is, to some extent, to understand the world in which he lived, and that is the world that produced the sack of Rome and other terrible events, which we shall be discussing in the next few lectures.

Niccolò Machiavelli was born in Florence in May of 1469, the very year that Lorenzo de'Medici assumed control of the city. And Machiavelli's early life, then, corresponded to that great moment of promise, the glorious years of Lorenzo de'Medici's patronage. Laurentian Florence was, indeed, an almost ideal and wonderful place, especially for one of Machiavelli's birth and training.

His family was from amongst the most honored ranks of the patriciate, but a relatively poor branch to the point that his father actually worked for a living. He practiced law, although he himself enjoyed a very elegant humanist education. Young Niccolò himself was given a superb humanist education in the classics, which you know extraordinarily well, and he was allowed to follow his particular interest in the Roman historians.

But his life, in fact, followed the history of the republic. He was just 25 when his world was shattered by the French invasions of 1494. He was in the city, and he witnessed the expulsion of the Medici in that year. He watched the rise of Savonarola and watched that regime unfold. He was also present in the Piazza della Signoria for the friar's execution in 1498.

The restoration of the broadly based republic that followed Savonarola's death in 1498 saw the appointment of the 29-year-old Machiavelli as second chancellor of the republic. This was a job that gave him the responsibility for translating the executive decisions of the government into actual policy. And everyone noted that Machiavelli was brilliant, and brilliant at his job: he was a natural administrator; he was a shrewd observer of current events; and he was a brilliant synthesizer of reports and diplomatic dispatches—these, in fact, are read to this day as models of their genre. Not only his insight, but his elegant style and his remarkable clarity gave the impression that, not only did he understand the events going on around him, but that, in fact, he was able to use this evidence to counsel others.

Because of his skills, he was sent in 1500 as a representative to King Louis XII of France. This, for the young man, was a formative moment. It was one, in fact, that influenced the way that his mind would develop over the next few years. He realized there—and this was a terrible shock to him—that the fate of Italy was not being determined in the peninsula itself, but the fate of Italy was being decided north of the Alps, at the courts of the King of France and the court of Ferdinand and Isabella.

In Italy itself, there was nothing but division. There was no force strong enough to actually stand against these great dynastic monarchies. And what a painful lesson it was for Machiavelli, given his humanist education and his belief that Italy, really, was the heir of great Roman empires and republics: he saw Italy as the natural, intellectual, and cultural heir of the ancient world. He saw the northerners as "barbarians," a term that he used almost constantly to describe the barbarians. They were the ones who were the descendents, not of the great Romans, but of the tribes that had destroyed that empire. They were, in Machiavelli's eyes, truly the scions of barbarian chiefs, and he also realized, like those late Romans, he was witnessing a time when the fate of Italy was determined by them.

Soon after his return to Florence in 1501, Machiavelli was sent as an agent to Cesare Borgia, the son of Alexander VI Borgia, in order to try and further Florentine interest and to protect the Florentine Republic as far as possible. And here Machiavelli, who learned as much as he could from every situation in which he found himself, did acquire a great deal.

First, he saw Cesare Borgia in action. He saw an Italian who appeared to be taking events into his own hands and directing them using the same techniques as the barbarians—using those techniques of ruthlessness, of brutality, that had made the barbarians—that is, the northern Europeans—successful in their attacks on Italy. So, here was an Italian who may, in fact, have been able to learn the lessons and to do something to protect Italy against those savages.

Second, he heard Cesare's advice to Florence, which Cesare repeated to Machiavelli on a number of occasions. He said Florence lacked constancy, and policy, and resolution. Florence was not resolute because it was a republic. It had to reach consensus decisions. It had to compromise. "In times of crisis," he said, "cities need a single voice, a single ruler." His suggestion to Machiavelli was to convince the Florentines to take back the Medici—not very likely, but, nevertheless, more information that Machiavelli filed away.

Machiavelli was, after all, a committed ideological republican. He listened to this, and he didn't particularly like the advice. But at the same time, he saw that there was a kind of reasonable consistency to it. What he learned from the French and what he learned from Cesare were all put together as part of his memory bank to be spent later when the situation became truly critical.

Florence came to agree with Cesare and the French, though, as witnessed by Piero Soderini's election as *gonfaloniere* for life in 1502, as we discussed before. Giving Soderini the position almost of a kind of Venetian doge allowed for that singular policy and that continuity of policy that would allow, then, Florence to stand against the concentrated efforts and brutality of the northerners.

In 1503, Soderini was extremely close to Machiavelli; in fact, Soderini was Machiavelli's mentor. Those in Florence at the time used to refer to Machiavelli as *il mannerino di Soderini*—that is, Soderini's puppet. They were very close. Machiavelli was often seen as Soderini's spokesman, and Soderini felt his responsibility to further the career of this brilliant, young man who seemed to be able to see everything, and digest it, and turn it into good, clear advice.

Once more, Machiavelli was sent to Cesare Borgia. The year 1503 was a very dangerous year, and Florence [sic Machiavelli] realized the ambitions of the Borgia; he also realized that it was absolutely necessary to try and protect Florentine interests and the integrity of the territory of Florence against the expansion of the papal states through the arm of Borgia. However, Machiavelli became entranced once more with Cesare. He was entranced by his energy, by his ruthlessness, and by his single-mindedness. Cesare would not let anything—not pity, not religion, not oaths or promises—interfere with what he saw as necessary policy. Machiavelli didn't particularly like this, but he also realized that perhaps it was the only solution to the situation of Italy.

Machiavelli also, at this point, had been so long out of Florence that he was able, almost for the first time, to see Florence with some measure of detachment. He was separated from the humanist ideology and environment of republican liberty in which he had grown up, and to which he was so completely and absolutely committed. He saw that Florence was, in fact, a very minor player in a game of life and death. He realized that the very existence of Florence was in question—not just the ability of Florence to remain free, but whether Florence would survive at all.

He also came to the conclusion, very reluctantly, that there are times when concepts like freedom and liberty might have to be temporarily sacrificed for greater goods like existence, and safety, and security. Machiavelli, then, had met the Duke Valentino of the prince, that Cesare Borgia figure who had come to represent the man on horseback that Machiavelli saw as, perhaps, the savior of Italy.

Machiavelli, then, had listened carefully to the French and others about the circumstances in which Florence found itself—in particular, the French who despised the Florentines for not fighting their own wars. The chivalric tradition of the French knights saw the Florentines hiring others to fight for them as so low as to be beyond contempt made Machiavelli wonder, in fact, whether the French had something. He wasn't wondering about their chivalric traditions—he had no interest or use for those—but he, in fact, remembered his reading of the Roman historians.

He remembered Livy, and he remembered that the Romans had conquered the world using citizen armies of volunteers: disciplined, well rewarded and respected, and honored. These citizen armies could galvanize a people, could reinvigorate them and give them strength and a sense of purpose. So, Machiavelli began filing away this information as well. He saw it, perhaps, as the necessary antidote to the fractious, luxury-loving Florentines. It worked for the Roman Republic, why couldn't it work for his own people?

He pressed Soderini heavily on this, and, ultimately, in 1507, Soderini gave Machiavelli the chance to do something about it. Machiavelli was given the right to establish a citizen militia, a citizen army, when he was appointed the director of the Ten of War, in effect, the military commissariat of Soderini's republican government.

Machiavelli spent much of the republic's treasure and a good deal of his own time and energy on the training and equipment of this army. They had the latest equipment. They were superbly trained. Everything looked towards the future of Florence defending itself and not having to spend treasure on others—mercenaries taking the money away from Florence—rather spending it internally in order to reward citizen soldiers.

The citizen army had an opportunity to prove itself. The Holy League, under the direction of the pope, directed itself against the French army in Italy, to the rallying cry of Julius II, "Out with the barbarians. Drive them out of the peninsula." Florence, though, was a close ally of France, and was left desperately exposed as a result of the League against the French, organized by the Holy See.

The French army, moreover, was largely defeated, as we've seen. What was left was a very powerful army of Spanish veterans— battle-hardened and experienced—and it was against this army that Machiavelli was told he had to leave his militia. He gathered them at Prato—a town just outside of Florence that boasted excellent defenses and very stout, thick walls—and the militia outnumbered the Spanish veterans considerably. But it just took a small breach in those walls by Spanish artillery for the citizen army—so expensively trained, so well equipped—to throw down their arms and run away.

With the evaporation of Machiavelli's militia, there was nothing between this group of Spanish veterans under the control of the papacy and the walls of Florence. Soderini saw there was no hope for his regime, as we've seen in Lecture Twenty-Eight, and he simply resigned and fled into exile. The Spaniards, under the influence of Giovanni de'Medici, that second son of Lorenzo the Magnificent, entered Florence. Machiavelli, of course, was on the losing side.

With the return of the Medici in 1512, he lost his job, and he was later implicated falsely in a plot against the Medici. He was tortured and thrown into prison. All that was found on a member of the anti-Medician party was a list of names, and on that list was Machiavelli's name. It only took that for Machiavelli to not only lose his freedom for a period of time and be tortured, but also to be so completely and absolutely isolated from the new regime that he had no hope of employment. He was poor, suspect, indeed in danger of his life, so he wisely decided to leave Florence and retire to a tiny farm that his family owned at the village of San Casciano, just outside of Florence. And, indeed, on a clear day, he could see the tower of the Palazzo della Signoria and the top of Brunelleschi's dome from his small farmhouse. It was 1513, and Machiavelli seemed to have no prospects and no future.

But this forced retirement, as in the case of so many out-of-work politicians, allowed him to think and to write. It gave him the leisure to work on his literary and his historical works that have given him his reputation up to this day. The most famous book he wrote was a very, very small one in the context of his very, very large output. *The Prince*, in fact, arose from a correspondence, a series of letters between Machiavelli in exile in San Casciano and his very close friend and republican associate, Francesco Vettori; this began in the spring of 1513.

Machiavelli, with his experience at the court of Louis XII, began rehearsing the dangers to Italy that the French posed. Louis XII clearly was still a great danger, and if his successor, who would clearly at that point be Francis I as Duke D'Angouleme, would, in fact, follow his desire for glory, Italy would, once more, become a battleground. Machiavelli began by rehearsing the situation of Italy that had started with the French invasions of 1494; he began by rehearsing a set of events that took the control over the peninsula away from his fellow Italians.

He focused on how the Italians had the responsibility, the duty, to protect their culture, in fact, to protect civilization altogether by driving out the barbarians, by presenting a united front to them, by overcoming the division and the factionalism that characterized Italian life. It was necessary to learn the methods of the barbarians themselves, as he had seen with Cesare Borgia.

The Italians, then, had to become brutal and ruthless. They had to be like the barbarians if they were to survive. And once the barbarians were expelled, and once the Italians could live in peace, then those terrible days could be forgotten and abandoned, and Italian liberty restored.

It's from Machiavelli's side of this so-called peace correspondence with Vettori that his little book, *The Prince*, arose. In fact, the letter between Machiavelli and Vettori on the December 10, 1513, that announces the birth of the prince, so to speak, is perhaps the single most famous letter in the Italian language. And it's worth quoting at some length because it reflects the life of a great man in exile and his attitudes, and it also indicates his continued Humanism and his belief in the role of history, and learning, and republican freedom.

Machiavelli writes:

> I get up early in the morning and go into some woods I have, which are being cut down, and I spend a couple of hours inspecting the work that the workmen had accomplished during the previous day. I spend some time with them, and they always have some dispute. It's usually over nothing, but, nevertheless, it's between them or their neighbors. I leave the woods and from there I go to a little spring, and from there to an *uccellare*, [a bird snare], and there I am happy. I sit because I have a book under my arm. I read Dante, Petrarch, or one of the minor poets like Tibullus or Ovid. I read about their passion and their loves, and I remember my own, and this for a while makes me happy. Then, I make my way along the road to the inn, and I talk to those who come in, and I ask of news of where they're from and about various matters, and I simply observe mankind. And I look at the variety of their tastes, and experiences, and the huge diversity of their fancies. But at that point, I return home. I go to my small house and eat the poor food that my modest patrimony can provide. But when I finish dining, I go back to the inn, and there usually is the innkeeper, a butcher, a miller, a few brick makers, and with them I play the rustic for a while, playing cards, playing backgammon, and these games lead to shouting matches and could be heard all the way to San Casciano. They're only over a penny or

two, but, nevertheless, it is what gives us our day. Cooped up amongst this vermin, I thereby get the mould from my wits. I curse fortune, accepting to walk down the road that she has directed me. If only she shows some sign of contrition of how I have been treated by her. But when evening comes, I return home and enter my study. On the threshold, I take off my daily mud-stained clothes and put on instead the robes of court and palace. Dressed in this way, I step back into the venerable court of the ancients, where they so graciously received me, and I'm nourished on that food for which I was born and which is mine alone. I'm not ashamed to ask them questions, to ask the motives for their actions. And they in their great humanity reply to me. They answer me. And for four hours at a stretch, I feel no boredom. I forget all of my misfortunes. I no longer dread poverty. I no longer even fear death. I am totally absorbed in them. And because Dante reminds us that no one can understand or remember anything without writing, I have recorded my thoughts on this matter in a short treatise: *De Principatibus* [*On Principalities* in Latin]. And in this I look deeply into the topic of principalities and define the categories of principalities and how they are acquired, how they're sustained, and why it is that princes lose power. And if any of my fancies has interested you, this should not be of no importance. And it could be particularly useful to a prince, especially a new prince, hence I plan to dedicate it to His Excellency, the Medici.

The Prince, then, is a product of a particular moment. It's why it's so totally misunderstood. From the time of its composition, it's been seen as an abstract work of political theory that suggests that tyranny is the solution to all political problems, and that faithfulness and all of the other elements that come out of the tradition of the medieval *speculum principis*, that advice to princes that Machiavelli takes as a genre and then turns on its head, all of this is, in fact, wrong. It's not a work of abstract political theory; it's an occasion piece. It's the product of a particular moment in Florentine history, a desperate moment, a moment that drove Machiavelli into despair, and a moment that cost him his own job.

It has to be read, then, as the exercise of a committed republican who is looking temporarily to tyranny as the instrument to save Italy, to expel the barbarians and use their methods against them. Machiavelli, then, is not counselling this as a way for the future, but as a necessary example of how the barbarians will have to be beaten at their own game. The Italians, he implies, are actually too civilized to stop the barbarians. You have to behave like them to drive them out, so that civilization and liberty can reign.

He also saw it as a wakeup call for the Italians. He wanted to raise their collective defence, their collective sense of being Italian. He wanted them to avoid the internal factionalism in strife. The barbarians, he said, will always capitalize on the division of the Italians until they actually get their act together and behave as one people. It's for this reason that the final chapter, Chapter 26 of *The Prince*, is part of a poem, the *Italia mia* of Petrarch, in which he notes that in the Italian breast, the Roman heart is beating still. And this is Machiavelli's advice to his contemporaries.

Well, Machiavelli, at the same time he was writing *The Prince*, was writing a book of political theory, a book much more abstract, which purports to be a kind of humanist commentary on Livy, *Discourses on the First Ten Books of Titus Livius*, that is the decades of Livy, the early historian of Rome. And it isn't really about that at all. It's really about Florence and the condition of Italy in the first decades of the 16th century. It's self-consciously republican. The real Machiavelli shows himself. He, too, talks about the need of a man on horseback, a dictator, someone who will function as a kind of drill sergeant who will reenergize the Italian people. And so, what he does, then, is he says, "This is the necessary moment." But then, as with the example of Cincinnatus, "Once he has done his job, he should retire and allow freedom once more to reign."

It was, like much of Machiavelli's brilliant analysis, essentially naïve. How can one escape one's humanist learning? How can one escape the ideology of republicanism that formed him so completely? Well, he can't. *The Prince* is one side of this, the commentaries on Livy, the other. And without the two together, Machiavelli's complex vision can never be fully understood.

As a result of his continual importuning of the Medici, including his dedication of *The Prince* to Giuliano de'Medici, and this to Giuliano who was represented by Michelangelo in the new sacristy of San Lorenzo in Florence, Machiavelli was finally given a job. He was given a job by Cardinal Giulio de'Medici, that is the cousin of Leo X, as official historian, with a responsibility to write *The History of Florence and the Affairs of Italy.*

Machiavelli found this a rather difficult task. He was a brilliant historian, and he had written forms of history, really, through much of his life. But this was a problem because he would have to praise the Medici regime, and he would also have to denigrate the republican period between 1494 and 1512. He, in fact, would have to interpret this from a pro-Medici perspective—when he himself had been not only a supporter of the republic, but an active agent of Soderini.

Still, he did his work extremely well, and by 1525, he brought the very large work up to the year 1492—that is the year of the death of Lorenzo the Magnificent. And Machiavelli did it in his usual clever and brilliant way. He had the greatest respect for the foreign policy of the Medici, beginning with Cosimo and the Peace of Lodi. He saw these as the examples of what Italy needed now: the Italian states working in concert in order to achieve goals. He attributed much of the peace and stability of the peninsula and the lack of foreign intervention to the success of the foreign policy of Cosimo de'Medici and his successors. He was then able to sustain a pro-Medician perspective, and he could then limit what he truly felt about the loss of liberty, especially after 1480.

In 1525, happy with his work, he went to Rome to present it to Giulio, who now, in fact, was Pope Clement VII. Giulio was extremely pleased. The pope liked the work, and he also liked what Machiavelli had done. So he offered him an annual stipend and some very minor official work. It seemed as though Machiavelli had finally been reconciled with the new regime, and that he had entered the service of the Medici.

The Medici were so pleased, in fact, with the *History of Florence* that he was offered a pension, and, indeed, Machiavelli had enough money to return to Florence and live amongst his old friends in this intellectual and cultural environment that he so respected and loved. He had no high rank as he had under Soderini and the republic, but he now had a regular income; he had some measure of respect; and for Machiavelli, very importantly, he had work.

But the crisis in Italy that would culminate in the unspeakable barbarism of the sack of Rome in 1527, was, for Machiavelli, both the terrible cosmic disaster that he had worked so hard to try and prevent, and it was also a personal disaster because it led to his second fall. As a result of the sack of Rome and the loss of Medici authority, with Clement VII a prisoner, in effect, of Charles V, and Castel Sant'Angelo unable to do anything, the Medici were thrown out of Florence, and the republic reasserted itself.

Machiavelli believed, that fervent republican that he had been, and given that the new republic of 1527 was largely driven by some of his closest friends and associates, including Francesco Vettori, he thought there was no problem whatsoever about his reentering government at the level that he had enjoyed under Soderini. He would then be able to contribute, not just to the recovery of liberty, but to the salvation of Italy, so necessary now as the events of 1527 had proved.

Ironically, his having accepted a pension from the Medici now made him suspect amongst the ferociously republican regime. They had observed that he had reconciled himself to the old regime. They saw him, in short, as a Medici fellow traveler. Those who had been his friends and close colleagues now rejected him. He was refused high office, and, in fact, he was seen with suspicion.

Shut out of office once more, shunned as a supporter of the Medici—which, in fact, he never was—he was someone who just needed to have access to work and government; in melancholy—in fact, in many ways personally shattered by the events of the sack of Rome, which seemed to illustrate so well the dangers in which all of Italy and Italian Renaissance culture saw itself—Machiavelli died embittered in that same year of 1527.

The death of Machiavelli wasn't a direct result of the sack of Rome, but, in many ways, it was collateral damage. Machiavelli had dedicated his life to the idea of republican freedom, and the idea of the dignity of the individual, and the concept of Humanism being the instrument that would sustain these in the face of the most barbarous actions then imaginable. He couldn't imagine the sack of Rome. It went beyond even his rich knowledge and experience. He also saw his own humiliation, and he realized that he was not part of the solution. He couldn't offer what he thought he had, and that is experience and wisdom, that could help save Italy from the barbarians.

Lecture Thirty-One
Alessandro de'Medici

Scope:

In negotiations with the Holy Roman Emperor, Charles V, to end the sack of Rome, the Medici Pope Clement VII made the recovery of Florence part of the treaty. With the collapse of Machiavelli's citizen army and after a terrible siege of the city, Florence fell to imperial troops in 1530. The last Florentine Republic had exhausted the republican patricians. Their courageous sons had died on the ramparts and outside the walls in fruitless attempts to break the siege. Pope Clement VII made it clear through the use of Spanish arms that the Medici were back to stay. Not having a more appropriate member of the family to rule in his place, Clement sent the 19-year-old Alessandro de'Medici as non-hereditary duke of the city. Alessandro, who was universally believed to be Pope Clement's natural son by a Moorish slave, was clearly mentally unstable. As long as Clement was alive, Alessandro listened to his councilors and to the bodies representing the political classes in the city. However, with Clement's death in 1534, the duke ruled ever more tyrannically, obliterating the symbols of the republic and making arbitrary decisions. He was also showing signs of madness, especially in the company of his favorite, his bizarre, insane cousin Lorenzo (Lorenzaccio). These two together engaged increasingly in depraved behavior until Lorenzaccio, for no apparent reason, assassinated Alessandro in 1537.

Outline

I. The collapse of papal authority with the sack of Rome galvanized the republican Florentines to drive out the pope's representatives, family, and garrison.

    A. The republic was restored for what was to be the very last time before the age of Napoleon.

        1. The Great Council, designed by Savonarola, was reinstated.

        2. A new *gonfaloniere* was elected from the anti-Medici faction.

        3. Clement, a virtual prisoner in Rome, could do nothing.

B. In negotiating peace with the Holy Roman Emperor, Charles V, Clement acquiesced almost totally, with his sole absolute demand being the re-conquest of Florence through the use of the same brutal army that had sacked Rome.

    1. In Florence, wiser counsel suggested a compromise with the pope, leaving the republic intact but under Medici hegemony as before.

    2. However, zealots, hoping for another change of fortune and fearful of the young Medici bastards, carried the argument: Florence would fight.

C. The entire city mobilized, with Michelangelo put in charge of the defensive walls, soldiers hired and trained, and grain brought in to help last a siege.

    1. In early fall 1529, the enormous Spanish army of 40,000 reached Florence but decided to lay siege to the city rather than attack.

    2. The siege lasted 10 terrible months, with the youth of Florence sacrificing itself in pointless but heroic sallies and plague and famine reducing the population.

    3. In 1530, the city surrendered.

II. The Medici had returned to Florence once again, but this time, there was no attempt to accommodate the sensitivities of the republican patricians.

A. A pro-Medici emergency council was appointed, supported by a Spanish army.

    1. The republican *gonfaloniere* was executed, and a Medici supporter was chosen to replace him.

    2. The republican leaders were tortured to death in search of evidence against others.

    3. Hundreds of leading citizens were banished in perpetuity and their property was confiscated.

    4. The republican constitution that had governed Florence from the time of the Ordinances of Justice in 1293 was dead.

B. Now the Medici were to rule as princes.

1. The prince chosen was an unstable young man of curious appearance, the 19-year-old Alessandro de'Medici, universally acknowledged to be Pope Clement's VII's son by a Moorish slave girl.

2. Given his age and his reputation for strange behavior, he was not proclaimed duke until nine months after the city fell to the Spanish army.

3. Even then, he was not to be a hereditary ruler, only duke in his own person.

4. Also, he was to be carefully controlled.

5. The councils of the republic remained in place, and these the duke had to consult and heed.

III. As long as Pope Clement lived, Alessandro obeyed these restrictions; indeed, he even appeared to be trying to improve his reputation and cleanse his personal life.

A. But in September 1534, Clement VII died, and with him, any control that Alessandro recognized also vanished.

1. Alessandro ruled in an increasingly arbitrary manner, ignoring the councils and his advisors.

2. Soon, he signaled the character of his regime by ordering that the great bell in the Palazzo della Signoria be smashed; from the foundation of the republic, this bell had sounded the call for a *parlamento* whenever the adult heads of household needed to assemble to grant ultimate sovereignty.

3. In further insult to this symbol of republicanism, he ordered the bronze melted down to fashion medals of himself.

4. He tore down the public symbols of the republic, such as the lilies, and replaced them with his coat of arms.

5. He also had constructed the Fortezza da basso, the huge fortress within the city, which exists to this day.

6. For the first time in Florentine history, the guns of the state were turned inward, on its own citizens, rather than outward in defense.

7. The Spanish garrison was stationed in the fortress to defend the duke and ensure that Florence remained a loyal client state of the empire of Charles V.

B. These acts of tyranny angered the patricians and even other members of the Medici family, who saw Alessandro's arbitrary and increasingly erratic rule as a threat to their futures.

1. The duke's cousin Ippolito de'Medici, another illegitimate member of the family, tried to control Alessandro and convince him to honor the traditions of the city.

2. Ippolito conveniently died in August of 1535, almost certainly by poisoning ordered by his cousin.

3. Republican patricians in exile approached Charles V with charges of both tyranny and sexual impropriety against Alessandro on the occasion of Alessandro's request to marry Margaret of Austria, Charles's natural daughter.

4. The exiles' shocking charges were delivered by the respected scholar and historian Iacopo Nardi, but they were answered by the brilliant careerist lawyer Francesco Guicciardini with such force that the charges were denied.

5. Alessandro married Margaret, bringing both the Medici and Florence more deeply into the imperial orbit.

IV. The assassination of Alessandro reflects how accurate the charges of Nardi and the republicans had been and that the court had become a bizarre place of wicked depravity.

A. Another Medici cousin, Lorenzo de'Medici, had been sent to Florence for his own and others' protection.

1. He was called Lorenzaccio, a derogatory diminutive, because of his loathsome personality and ugly appearance.

2. In Rome, he had been subject to outbreaks of violent mental illness, attacking classical statues with weapons and endangering the property and lives of those around him.

3. It was felt that he could be more easily controlled in Florence by Duke Alessandro, a young man of similar age.

4. The two deviants shared much in common: drunkenness, sexual ambiguity, and a love of violence and cruelty.

5. Soon, the drunken, disturbed Lorenzaccio became Alessandro's favorite at court, where they often shared the same bed and lovers of both sexes, often very unwilling partners.

B. At some time in 1537 in this depraved environment, Lorenzaccio hatched the plan to murder his cousin Alessandro; the reason for this is not clear, but the young man was evidently mad.

1. His scheme reflected the disgusting depravity of the two men.

2. He lured Alessandro into a trap by promising to share with him the rape of their very young, pious, and chaste cousin, who had recently been married to a Florentine noble.

3. Suspecting nothing and acting according to the plan, Alessandro entered the young woman's bedroom naked, only to find Lorenzaccio and a hired assassin waiting for him under the bedclothes.

4. Alessandro fought savagely, biting the end off one of Lorenzaccio's fingers in the process, but he was ultimately stabbed to death, leaving Lorenzaccio to flee to Bologna.

V. The city fell into chaos with Alessandro's murder.

A. Had the republicans acted swiftly and decisively, they might have been able to take advantage of the chaos following the murder to restore the republic.

1. But it was the pro-Medici party, led by Guicciardini and Francesco Vettori, and the pope's ambassador, Cardinal Cibò, who acted first.

2. The Medici were to continue to rule, but which Medici?

3. Cibò demanded that the 4-year-old illegitimate son of Alessandro be named duke.

4. Guicciardini demanded instead the teenaged cousin of Alessandro, the son of the late *condottiere* Giovanni delle Bande Nere, a solitary, distrustful but shrewd young man, Cosimo de'Medici.

5. Republican patricians tried to break the impasse by suggesting a return to an oligarchic republic, hoping the city would respond to the traditional call for liberty.

B. The dangerous stalemate was broken when Guicciardini bribed the captain of the garrison to bring troops into the Piazza della Signoria and call for Cosimo's elevation.

1. This show of force destroyed the confidence of the other parties.

2. Young Cosimo was proclaimed duke, with Guicciardini confidently expecting to be the power behind the throne.

3. It was believed that the poorly educated and young Cosimo would need a powerful chief minister to help cement his rule in the dangerous environment of 1537 Italy.

4. This belief was wrong.

Secondary Sources:
Eric Cochrane, *Florence in the Forgotten Centuries, 1527–1800.*

Supplementary Reading:
Christopher Hibbert, *The House of Medici: Its Rise and Fall.*

Questions to Consider:

1. How could an educated, cultivated, and sensitive man like Pope Clement VII permit a ruler like Alessandro de'Medici to rule in his native Florence?

2. In the 19th century, in the play *Lorenzaccio* by Alfred de Musset, the murderer of Alessandro is portrayed as a freedom fighter and tyrannicide. Can this interpretation be sustained?

Lecture Thirty-One—Transcript
Alessandro de'Medici

The events of the Italian peninsula in the first decades of the 16th century also gave rise, not just to the physical destruction of much of Renaissance culture, but also a moral issue: how, in fact, individuals with very, very little sense of the traditions of, not only Humanism, but even that sense of human dignity that had been one of the foundations and platforms of Renaissance thought, could achieve levels of great power?

We've seen occasionally in the principalities how individuals could, in fact, be depraved and simply inherit power, and we've seen cities like Florence being largely immune from that because of the distribution of authority amongst many citizens who had to be chosen because of their personal qualities. However, with the events of the early 16th century, and the collapse of republicanism, those restraints evaporated in cities like Florence as well. And we see the beginning of regimes that did not have much moral suasion, moral power, or moral example. And the regime of Alessandro de'Medici perhaps represents that most effectively.

The collapse of papal authority with the sack of Rome galvanized the Florentine republics to drive out the pope's representatives, drive out the family and the garrisons that the pope had placed there in order to continue his family's rule of their native city, and replace them with the republic.

The republic was restored for what would prove to be the last time until the age of Napoleon. The Great Council, the one designed by Savonarola in his constitution of 1495, was reinstated. A new *gonfaloniere* was elected from the anti-Medician faction. And Clement, a virtual prisoner in Rome within Castel Sant'Angelo, could do nothing.

In negotiating the peace between the Holy Roman Emperor Charles V, Clement agreed to, as I suggested earlier, everything that the emperor demanded. Clement had only one non-negotiable item on his side, and that is to use that same vicious, brutal army that had so destroyed the city of Rome to restore the family of de'Medici to Florence.

In Florence, the situation was seen as truly grave once peace was established in 1529, and the arrangement between Clement and Charles allowed for the Spanish Imperial hegemony of the peninsula. The situation was grave to the point that there was divided counsel amongst the patricians as to what to do in this situation that was proving to be so grave. The wisest counsel was that Florence really had to make some form of accommodation with the Medici to re-establish the republic, but the republic to be managed by the Medici. Allow the Medici to return and allow them to stage-manage the republic as they had from the time of Cosimo il Vecchio in the 14th and the 15th centuries. There were zealots, though, powerful voices who wanted to fight.

Those who believed that there would be another change of fortune— that the situation in Italy was just so volatile that there was a good chance that Florence would be able to steer a course amongst the varying competing powers on the peninsula and sustain their freedom—they, then, were ideological republicans who refused to compromise with the Medici. They saw the republic restored, and they had no desire whatsoever to compromise it.

Also, there were those who were merely practical. They saw the members of the Medici family who would probably be used by Clement VII to rule the city—in particular, the Medici bastards who were recognized as not only incompetent, but also of very, very weak moral character. The sense was with them ruling, the idea of some form of republicanism and a power behind the republic seemed unlikely. What was to be expected was rather, in fact, a return of some form of principality, some form of Medici rule that was not in any way compatible with republican liberty.

The result was the republicans won the debate. The entire city mobilized in order to defend itself against the Spanish army sent by Charles V and Clement VII to claim the city for the Medici. Michelangelo was chosen the engineer to build the defences and to maintain the walls that would protect the city. Huge amounts of grain were brought in to withstand a long siege. Soldiers were hired and trained, and the republic waited for the armies to reach Tuscany.

In the early fall of 1529, the Spanish Imperial army arrived. It was enormous—40,000—one of the largest armies on the Italian peninsula. But rather than risk their soldiers, the simple decision was to simply starve the city into submission. And so they invested the city in siege, a siege that was to last for ten terrible, awful months. The youth of Florence sacrificed almost an entire generation in order to try and break through the lines. Heroic sallies out of the city and moments of almost suicidal heroism on the part of young patricians reduced their number greatly. But all was pointless. Soon after, the city began to run short of food, and the usual threats to any besieged city in the early modern period, famine and plague, began to take its toll. By 1530, there was really no hope, and the city submitted without condition.

The Medici, then, entered back into Florence, back into their ancestral city, but this time as conquerors. Moreover, there was no sense whatsoever, given the events of 1527 to 1530, to make any accommodation with the republicans. The republicans, by refusing to compromise with the Medici, had destroyed any hope that their sensitivities would be recognized, and even Clement VII's knowledge of the traditions of the city and his experience when he was governor in the name of his cousin Leo X, all of these things were now without value because of the war and because of the siege.

Also, because of the changed political situation in the peninsula, Florence now had been delivered not just to the pope, but as a loyal client state of the Emperor Charles V. Florence had to remain stable because Charles needed a stable state in central Italy. Clement, really, had no choice, and the republicans, really, had no hope.

A pro-Medici emergency council was appointed, supported by that Spanish army that remained as a garrison within the city. The republican *gonfaloniere* was executed and a Medici supporter chosen to replace him. The republican leaders were tortured and imprisoned. They were tortured continuously in order to try and exact information about who was supporting them, which members of the patriciate were unsound, which could be counted upon to allow the new Medici regime to prosper. Hundreds of leading citizens, as a result of this, were banished in perpetuity and all of their property confiscated.

And the republican constitution, based upon the 1293 Ordinances of Justice that had really governed Florence during that period of the efflorescence of the Renaissance, was really, in effect, dead. The Medici now had no intention of trying to allow the republican sensitivities to thrive; rather, the intent was that they would rule as princes.

The person chosen as prince was almost a necessity, given the lack of appropriate young men to fulfil this role. The one chosen was a mentally unstable young man of very curious appearance, the 19-year-old Alessandro de'Medici. He was, as we noted before, universally acknowledged as the illegitimate son of Pope Clement VII by a Moorish slave girl.

Given his age and his terrible reputation, his reputation for extremely bizarre behaviour, he was not proclaimed duke immediately, but had to wait for nine months under the protection of the Spanish army, just to see what was going to happen, and to make certain that there would be some measure of calm. Even then, when he was given the title Duke of Florence, it was not initially to be a hereditary title. Rather, he was duke only in his own person. It was clear then that he was representing the dual authority of Clement VII de'Medici—that is the pope—and Charles V, who required Florence to be an allied state.

Also, it was recognized, given their knowledge of his character, that he had to be controlled. The Councils of the republic were to remain in place, and these the duke not only had to consult, but he had to take their advice. The assumption was that the small element of the memory of republicanism, the small element of consensus, would bring the political classes closer to the Medici regime, as well as simultaneously doing something to restrain some of the stranger habits of Alessandro de'Medici.

Moreover, as long as the pope lived, as long as Clement VII was alive, Alessandro obeyed these restrictions. In fact, he appeared to be trying to improve his reputation, trying to cleanse his personal life, which was widely reputed to be less than salubrious. But in September 1534, Clement VII died, and with the death of Alessandro's almost certain father, with him ended any control that Alessandro recognized and that Alessandro would, in fact, obey.

He ruled in an increasingly arbitrary manner. He more and more ignored the Councils. He ignored his advisors. And he then signaled the character of his new regime by ordering smashed the great bell in the Palazzo della Signoria that had, from the foundation of the republic, stood in the tower—the bell that hung in the tower that Arnolfo di Cambio built at the time of the creation of the republic, the bell that called all of the heads of households together in a *Parlamento* in the piazza—that would represent the ultimate authority in the state.

This bell was not only to be smashed, but, as a final insult to the patrician republican sympathies of the city, he had the bronze melted down and made into medals of himself. He tore down all of the public symbols of the republic, such as the lilies, the *gigli*, and the *Marzocco*, that lion of Florence. These were all replaced with Alessandro's personal coat of arms. And he had constructed within the city the *Fortezza da Basso*, that enormous urban fortress that exists to this day and still plays havoc with the urban bus routes.

For the first time in Florentine history, the guns of the state were now turned inwards, against its own citizens, rather than outward in defence of them—a fundamental shift, and one that Alessandro was well aware would signal, together with the smashing of the bell, the end of the republic and his refusal to allow any sympathy for the old regime to exist.

The Spanish garrison was stationed in the *Fortezza* in order to defend the duke and also to ensure that Florence would remain a loyal client state of Charles V. Now that Charles had conquered all of Italy, he wanted to make sure that he would keep all of Italy, and he had no desire whatsoever for republican traditions to try and thwart that.

These acts of tyranny angered the patricians and even other members of the Medici family, who saw Alessandro's behavior as not only arbitrary, but, in fact, threatening continued Medici power. They wondered exactly what he was doing. Why was he behaving in such a tyrannical way when, in fact, a small amount of reconciliation would have allowed for the patricians to accept Medici rule much more easily? They began to see that his erratic behaviour was, in fact, not just the reflection of a policy, but, increasingly, the reflection of a deranged mind.

The duke's cousin in particular, Ippolito de'Medici, another illegitimate member of the family, counselled Alessandro constantly, tried to control him, to convince him to honour some of the republican traditions—to at least not insult the pride of the great families. Ippolito conveniently, but very mysteriously, died in August of 1535, almost certainly poisoned by orders of Alessandro. The point was not just to silence someone who criticized him, but also to ensure that there would be no rival around that an alienated faction of patricians could then gather. Ippolito's death reflected that Alessandro intended to be a tyrant and would let nothing stop his ambition.

The republican patricians—those in exile who, in fact, had been in exile since the siege of the city—approached the Emperor Charles V with charges of tyranny and extreme sexual impropriety against Alessandro. The reason for this is that Alessandro had petitioned the Emperor Charles V to marry his illegitimate daughter, Margaret of Austria. This was something that Charles saw as a good alliance because it would link Florence even more closely to the Imperial alliance, but it was something that the republicans thought might succeed in driving a wedge between the Spaniards on whom Alessandro relied to rule and the duke.

Led by the brilliant scholar and historian, Iacopo Nardi, the republicans argued that Alessandro was not a fit husband, giving examples of his depraved sexual activities. But, in this trial almost, representing Alessandro, was the brilliant lawyer and careerist, whom we will get to know very well in a subsequent lecture, Francesco Guicciardini. Guicciardini argued with such force and such cogency that, ultimately, Charles was convinced that the republicans were simply sore losers—that they simply saw this as an opportunity to manipulate the emperor and get rid of an unpopular Medici prince. Charles allowed the marriage to take place. Alessandro married Margaret of Austria.

The assassination of Alessandro reflects just how accurate the charges of Nardi and the republicans had been—and, in fact, how the court of Florence, after 1534, had declined into a bizarre place of the most wicked, almost unimaginable depravity. It's represented not just by Alessandro, but by his very curious cousin, Lorenzo de'Medici, usually called Lorenzino, the diminutive, to separate him from other members of the family with that name. However, Lorenzino was usually called Lorenzaccio, using the derogatory diminutive because not only of his extremely ugly demeanor, but also because of his patent madness.

Lorenzaccio was sent to Florence for his own protection and for the protection of others. He had outbreaks of madness while in the papal palace and while in the Medici properties in Rome that caused him to pick up swords and attack classical statutes and smash them, to threaten the lives of those around for no reason, to seem to lose control of himself under even the most normal of circumstances. No one's property or no one's life was ever really safe around Lorenzaccio.

It was thought that if Lorenzaccio should be sent to Florence, there his cousin Alessandro, who was about his age, might, in fact, be able to control him to a greater degree, and the two young men then might be able to reform one another and live in this smaller environment in perhaps a more civilized and humane way. However, it became clear as soon as they met that the two young deviants shared more than a name and a genetic code.

They were very, very similar individuals. They revelled in drunkenness and sexual ambiguity. They loved violence. They loved cruelty. They both had a streak of cruelty so deep that no one was really safe around them—and, in particular, the young men and young women they lusted after were seriously in a state of terror much of the time that they ruled the court.

Soon, the drunken, disturbed Lorenzaccio became Alessandro's favorite at court. He could do anything. The two of them were literally inseparable. They often shared the same bed. They often shared lovers of both sexes. And often, these lovers were extremely unwilling partners demanded by this tyrannical duke and his mad cousin, Lorenzaccio.

At some time in 1537 in this depraved environment, Lorenzaccio came up with a plan to murder his cousin, Alessandro. Why? We simply do not know. There is no reason for it. Here was somebody who had finally found a true soul mate, who had control of the city, who was above the law, who was engaging in the most depraved activity possible with the protection of the prince. Why would he destroy this? Why would he kill the only person who ever really liked him? All that can be said is that Lorenzaccio was mad; he was insane. And that probably is reason enough.

What I'd like to dismiss, of course, is the 19th-century romantic view that he was an instrument of republican freedom. The play of Alfred de Musset, *Lorenzaccio*, says more about 19th-century romantic European liberalism than it does about Florence in the 1530s. Lorenzaccio did not want to restore the freedom of the city. He had no idea what he would do with it, and it was something that he had no sympathy for whatsoever. He was a madman. He was insane, and the effects of insanity would, in fact, ultimately turn out very badly for the city of Florence.

His scheme was not just depraved in itself, but really reflected, almost by way of morality play, just how far the city of Florence had fallen; this city of Napoleonic ideals of Lorenzo de'Medici; the city of Pico and Ficino; the city of the republican liberty of Salutati and Bruni; the city of the great works of the 15th-century and 16th-century painters had now become a kind of horror show—a horror show of two depraved young men who could do anything because one happened to be the prince.

The scheme that he put in place really reflected the nature of their relationship, Alessandro and Lorenzaccio. Both of them shared a young, beautiful cousin, a very young girl who had just recently been married to a Florentine noble. She was extremely beautiful, but she also was very, very shy and had a reputation for piety and chastity. Lorenzaccio suggested to Alessandro that this is exactly the kind of girl that would be most fun to rape. Wouldn't it be charming for everyone to think that this pious, chaste young girl could then be ravaged by the two Medici princes? What fun that would be. Alessandro, of course, fell into it immediately, thinking that this was a wonderful Saturday night's entertainment.

Everything was put in place by Lorenzaccio. First, Alessandro was to send the young girl's husband out of the city on a mission to make sure that she would be alone in her palace. And then Lorenzaccio ordered Alessandro to take his bodyguards—Alessandro travelled everywhere with a group of very, very large thugs, known as *i giganti*, the giants, and they were to protect Alessandro against everything, and Lorenzaccio had to get rid of them, so this plan. In order to rape her, the guards would have to stay at the door of the palace, and regardless of what they heard inside, they were to let no one in and no one out. They were to protect that door with their lives.

Lorenzaccio told Alessandro this was to make sure that they could get away with their heinous crime without anyone coming to the rescue of the young girl—when, in fact, the purpose was to get Alessandro alone. Alessandro usually wore armour and was armed, and so that was the next problem. So Lorenzaccio said the whole scheme should be then that they would surprise her in her bed at night, and that Alessandro should remove not only his armor, but all of his clothes and then get into bed with the young woman completely naked. This, of course, was to be the surprise because in the bed was not the young woman, but Lorenzaccio and a professional murderer, both wearing armor, both heavily armed.

Alessandro, when he removed the covers and he saw Lorenzaccio and the murderer prepared to kill him, fought desperately. He fought so hard that he actually bit the end off one of Lorenzaccio's fingers. And the effect of this will be significant, as we will discover later. Nevertheless, there was nothing that the naked Alessandro could do against two heavily armed and armoured young men.

Alessandro was killed. Lorenzaccio stole out of the palace as he had planned and escaped to Bologna. This, of course, proves that he had no desire to restore the republic or even rule in Alessandro's place, because the whole plan was that he was to escape; he was to run away. It was something that he simply wanted to do.

With the death of Alessandro, Florence fell completely and totally into chaos. Had the republicans acted quickly, if they had acted decisively, if they had been able to put together a candidate or group of candidates who could then behave in a way that would provide calm and security, it's not impossible that the murder of Alessandro would allow for the restoration of some form of republican rule. But as usual with the republican faction, they were weakened, they were leaderless, and they vacillated.

It was a pro-Medici party, then, led by Francesco Guicciardini and Francesco Vettori—yes, the same Francesco Vettori who was the interlocutor with Machiavelli in the peace correspondence—and the pope's ambassador, Cardinal Cibò of Siena. They are the ones who acted first. They're the ones who took advantage of the chaos in order to impose their solution on who would rule Florence in the absence of the Medici.

The result was that there was a general agreement amongst those who exercised power that the Medici rule would continue. Then the debate became which Medici? Cibò demanded that the 4-year-old illegitimate son of Alessandro be named duke. This, of course, was an improbable solution—in part because not only was the child still very young, but also because he was illegitimate, and also he was associated with this court environment. Cibò, of course, hoped that he then would be able to manipulate the situation and act in the duke's name.

Guicciardini, though, had another candidate, a candidate of a collateral branch of the family. He nominated the teenaged cousin of Alessandro, the son of the now dead *condottiere*, Giovanni delle Bande Nere—the Giovanni who was killed in that skirmish trying to stop the movement of the Spanish and German army towards the sack of Rome in 1527. Giovanni had a son named Cosimo, a son who was protected by his mother, Maria Salviati, by simply moving him around constantly from one rural villa to another. Because of your cousin, Alessandro, and your other cousin, Lorenzaccio, you didn't necessarily want to share the fate of Ippolito de'Medici.

Francesco Guicciardini truly believed that he would be able to manipulate the young Cosimo. Cosimo was completely inexperienced. He was largely uneducated because he wasn't able to stay in one place long enough. He was raised to be extremely fearful and distrustful of others, but he was incredibly intelligent, and he was shrewd, and he was absolutely ruthless. Nevertheless, Francesco Guicciardini felt he was the perfect candidate, and that Guicciardini and his close associate, Francesco Vettori, would then be able to be the powers behind the throne, manipulate this inexperienced teenaged boy and rule Florence for their benefit.

The republican patricians then entered the debate. They demanded that the oligarchic republic be restored; that this was an opportunity that would allow families like the Guicciardini and the Vettori to achieve some measure of influence by restoring an oligarchy that would then be ruled by the great patricians. "The Medici—well we could talk about the Medici later. But right now, let's re-establish an oligarchic republic." They hoped that simply by putting the word out that the Florentine love of the memory of liberty would be such that there would be a groundswell of support. The events, however, of the

16th century had so smothered that memory of republican liberty that there was no support.

Guicciardini then broke the impasse in a way that indicates, again, his ruthlessness and his ability. He bribed the captain of the Spanish garrison in the *Fortezza da Basso* to send a group of heavily armed troops to ring the Piazza della Signoria. He demanded then that Cosimo de'Medici, the son of Giovanni delle Bande Nere, be brought as ruler of Florence. The soldiers clambered for the elevation of Cosimo. They rioted and demanded, with force of arms, that Cosimo be chosen.

Fearful of what would happen to them if they should not agree, all of the other parties largely acquiesced. Many of the republicans went into exile, but then the other parties simply said, "It is a compromise with which we can all live." Cosimo was proclaimed duke, and Guicciardini was, at that time, by his side.

It also ironically fulfils a prophecy. When Giovanni delle Bande Nere was riding off to the war from which he would not return, he stopped his horse outside the Palazzo Medici and he called to the window where his young wife, Maria Salviati, was holding his baby son, Cosimo. He demanded that the baby be dropped into his arms. The height from the second floor of the piano nobile window was very high. Maria Salviati first refused. Giovanni demanded it, and being the good Italian wife she was, she threw the baby. Cosimo, when he fell into his father's arms, didn't cry from fear, he laughed and smiled. And Giovanni said, "Here is a child worthy to be a prince of Florence." And he then rode off to his death.

Francesco Guicciardini thought that he could control this young man with this prophetic past. He thought he would be able to control the city in his name. He was, of course, absolutely wrong. Cosimo had no intention of listening to anyone. Cosimo was that young child thrown into the arms of Giovanni delle Bande Nere, and his experience was such that he would never be accountable to anyone, ever.

He had saved his life, and his mother had saved his life through being shrewd and being distant. He wasn't about to stop now that he was Duke of Florence.

Lecture Thirty-Two
The Monarchy of Cosimo I

Scope:

When 19-year-old Cosimo de'Medici (1519–1574) was installed as prince in 1537, many assumed that the architect of his victory, Guicciardini, would be the chief advisor to the inexperienced young prince. But as soon as he was installed, Cosimo decided to rule personally and dismissed the influential politician. A revolt led by patrician exiles followed but was brutally suppressed after the Battle of Montemurlo in 1537. Cementing his regime by allying with the Habsburg emperor Charles V, Cosimo married Eleonora of Toledo (d. 1562), daughter of the rich and influential Spanish viceroy of Naples. He enlarged the Florentine state through the conquest of Siena with Spanish help in 1557. And, in 1569, he was invested with the title of grand duke of Tuscany by the pope. Cosimo's intention was to build a centralized, despotic monarchy on the ruins of the republic. The patrician families were offered titles and attached to his court; he created orders of knighthood; and he initially turned the symbol of republican government, the Palazzo della Signoria, into his palace, before moving into the Palazzo Pitti to house his large family and increasingly elaborate court. He provided patronage to artists, including Giorgio Vasari (1511–1574), who designed the Uffizi; Bernardo Buontalenti (c. 1531–1608), and Bartolommeo Ammanati (1511–1592). The Florentines had lost their freedom but had achieved stability in return.

Outline

I. The elevation of Cosimo de'Medici as duke of Florence in 1537 established the hereditary Medici monarchy that would last until the death of the Grand Duke Gian Gastone in 1737, the last of the Medici male line.

   A. Cosimo de'Medici (d. 1574) had an unusual background.

       1. His strong-willed mother was herself a descendant of Lorenzo the Magnificent. Her husband's death when he was in his 20s during a skirmish with the imperial army that sacked Rome had left her exposed and fearful.

    2. She had moved Cosimo constantly about Tuscany during the reign of Alessandro. As a result, her son grew up very intelligent but poorly educated, extremely distrustful and secretive, cruel, ruthless, and poorly socialized.

B. True to his character, Cosimo, rather than honoring Guicciardini and Vettori for securing his succession, distrusted their motives.

    1. He declared immediately that he intended to rule as an autocrat rather than serve their ambition.

    2. Guicciardini was effectively exiled to retirement at his villa.

C. Having rid himself of those who believed he owed his throne to them, Cosimo then had to turn against the republicans, the last significant republican movement in Florence until the time of the French Revolution.

    1. Exiles, driven from the city in 1530, had been joined by republican patricians who hoped to restore the republic with Alessandro's death.

    2. These young men, representing the oldest and most distinguished families in Florence, gathered an army to depose Cosimo.

    3. Cosimo had at his disposal, courtesy of the Holy Roman Emperor Charles V, the Spanish army garrisoned in the city.

    4. The republicans and Cosimo's Spanish army met at Montemurlo, near Florence, late in 1537; the republicans were defeated and many prisoners were taken.

D. Cosimo seized victory with ruthless cruelty.

    1. He beheaded all the rebel leaders publicly over four consecutive days in the Piazza della Signoria; those executed were the sons of the leading families of the city, related by kin and marriage to almost all the great patrician clans.

    2. Cosimo's arbitrary decisiveness was calculated to forewarn the old families that the republic and republican sentiment were dead.

II. Cosimo, however, was anything but secure: He had defeated his enemies but he was ruler only *de facto*, not *de jure*, and he depended upon the Spanish garrison in the city for protection.

A. Wishing to strengthen his connection to Charles V, he petitioned the emperor to marry Alessandro's widow, Margaret of Austria.

   1. Charles refused, because he needed her more as the consort of the grandson of Pope Paul III Farnese, but in 1539, Cosimo received an attractive compromise proposal.

   2. He was given the hand of Eleonora of Toledo, the daughter of the immensely rich Spanish viceroy of Naples; what is remarkable is that this couple formed an almost bourgeois union of great mutual respect and loyalty.

   3. They produced many children, with Eleonora providing the cold and ruthless Cosimo with domestic happiness and comfort until her early death from malaria in 1562.

B. The Spanish marriage placed Florence and Cosimo deep into the Spanish-Imperial allegiance.

   1. Cosimo had relied on Spanish arms to secure his rule, but he knew that he would always be seen as a tyrant as long as his throne rested on foreign power.

   2. The large Spanish garrison stationed in the Fortezza da basso did not make the situation better, prowling the streets at night, robbing citizens, brawling, and molesting Florentine women.

   3. When Cosimo first petitioned Charles to remove the garrison, the emperor refused; he did not trust Cosimo sufficiently to risk a hostile power in central Italy.

   4. Ultimately, however, seeing that Florence was stable and convinced by Cosimo's reliance on his Spanish wife, Charles withdrew the garrison.

C. Internally, the only remaining opposition was a memory of the crisis of the 1490s.

   1. The Dominican monks of San Marco kept the memory of Savonarola and his theocratic message alive.

2. Duke Cosimo emptied San Marco, sending the remnants of the *Piagnoni* out of the city.

3. He was now a completely independent ruler. He had shattered all internal opposition, he no longer relied on the Spanish, and he owed no debts.

4. He could proceed to create an absolute monarchy and remake the shape of Florence.

III. The result was the destruction of the still potent symbols and remnants of the republican constitution that had governed Florence for almost 250 years.

    A. Duke Cosimo decreed the abolition of the *Signoria*, including the offices of prior and *gonfaloniere*.

        1. He himself became the head of the traditional councils, making them rubber-stamp appendages of his will.

        2. Any official or patrician who resisted was thrown into the horrible prisons of Volterra.

    B. Cosimo knew that the republic would only truly die when its memory was tainted with failure and patrician disdain.

        1. He worked on the traditional competition and jealousy among the great families by offering titles of nobility and sinecures at court to those who proved their loyalty.

        2. In this way, the proud republican traditions of Florence were replaced by a servile aristocracy.

        3. Cosimo restored feudal land tenure and encouraged the patricians—now his new court nobility—to abandon trade as unbecoming and live as landed aristocrats.

        4. He encouraged the Humanist scholarly interests to be channeled through ducal academies under official control, patronizing historians to describe the republican period as a failed experiment.

        5. He created crusading orders of knighthood and built a fleet of galleys to fight the Turks.

        6. He supported maritime trade by constructing the port of Livorno and used his war galleys to protect Florentine commerce.

    C. Florence was also expanding and winning wars that the republic had not managed to complete.

1. Cosimo was intent on the conquest of Siena, Florence's ancient rival city to the south.

2. With the help of a Spanish army and after a terrible siege, Siena collapsed and was finally added to Florentine territory in 1557.

3. Cosimo was no longer content to be duke of Florence.

4. After years of importuning the pope, Cosimo was finally granted the title of grand duke of Tuscany and the honorific of *Altezza*, or "Your Highness."

IV. After a half century of instability, danger, conquest, and suffering in Florence, Cosimo seemed to be bringing back a new Golden Age, reminiscent of the time of Lorenzo the Magnificent.

A. Cosimo had symbolized his destruction of the republic by moving from the Palazzo Medici into the Palazzo della Signoria, transformed by the duke's architect and painter, Giorgio Vasari, into a royal residence.

1. The old building was designed, however, as a town hall, not a palace.

2. It was very small, uncomfortable, and unsuitable for court ceremonies.

3. Also, Cosimo and Eleonora had eight children, a large family for the old town hall.

4. In 1549, Eleonora used her great wealth to purchase the unfinished early-15th-century Palazzo Pitti, designed by Brunelleschi for the banker Luca Pitti, but his bankruptcy left it incomplete for more than a century.

5. It required a year to refurbish and expand the enormous palace and lay out its gardens, but in the end, the Pitti became one of the great palaces of Italy.

6. Cosimo moved there with his family and court, leaving the Palazzo della Signoria forever with the denomination of Palazzo Vecchio—the "Old Palace."

B. Cosimo was not only ruthless but hardworking, insisting on knowing everything that happened within his state and everywhere else, as well.

1. He had Vasari build the Offices (*Uffizi* in 16th-century Tuscan) of his growing bureaucratic civil service, attached to the Palazzo Vecchio, so he could walk into any office at any time.

2. His routine of punishing work began to take its toll, and his health grew worse after the tragic death of Eleonora and several of his children just two years after moving into the Palazzo Pitti.

3. Always emotionally dependent on his wife, Cosimo grew ever more melancholy, irascible, secretive and solitary.

C. Cosimo effectively ceased to rule in any significant way after 1564, leaving the government of the state to his eldest son, Francesco.

1. The loss of Eleonora drove Cosimo into a number of unsuccessful liaisons, including a disastrous second marriage.

2. Soon after, Cosimo seems to have suffered a series of strokes that reduced him to an invalid, incapable of speech.

3. Cosimo, first grand duke of Tuscany, died in 1574.

4. He left a united, enlarged, peaceful, and very well if harshly governed principality.

5. There were few, if any, who wanted a return to the republic: Freedom came, they believed after their experience between 1494 and 1537, at far too high a price.

Secondary Sources:

Christopher Hibbert, *The House of Medici: Its Rise and Fall.*

Michael Levey, *Painting at Court.*

Supplementary Reading:

Eric Cochrane, *Florence in the Forgotten Centuries, 1527–1800.*

Questions to Consider:

1. Consider why Florentine patricians turned their backs so completely on the republic after 1537 and rushed to become the courtiers of the new duke.

2. Despite the fact that he owed his position to the death of Alessandro, Cosimo pursued Lorenzaccio assiduously for 10 years (by questioning physicians about a young man with a severed finger) until he was discovered and assassinated in Venice with a poisoned dagger. Why would Cosimo have done this?

Lecture Thirty-Two—Transcript
The Monarchy of Cosimo I

The elevation of Cosimo de'Medici as Duke of Florence in 1537 established the hereditary Medici monarchy that would last until the extinction of the male line with the death of the Grand Duke Gian Gastone in 1737, and the line that Cosimo established would, in fact, prove to be an autocratic line of rulers that would give character to Florence quite different from the traditions of the republic of the 15th century.

And much of this came from Cosimo's own personality. He had an extremely unusual background, as we've seen. His strong-willed mother was herself a descendant from Lorenzo de'Medici, Lorenzo the Magnificent, and to whose family the Salviati had married. The death of her husband, when only in his twenties, during that skirmish with the Imperial army that sacked Rome, left her exposed and fearful in an extremely unstable and dangerous time in not only Italian, but also Medicean, history.

She moved, together with her young son, Cosimo, constantly about Tuscany, from one rural villa to another, from one fortified castle to another, fearing Alessandro. Seeing the fate of the other members of the Medici family, she was very concerned that this young man, descended as he was from two branches of the family, might, in fact, be in particular danger.

As a result, her son grew up to be an extremely secretive, private young man. He was distrustful of all around him. He was cruel by nature. He was ruthless, extremely poorly socialized, and had difficulty dealing with others. And true to his character, Cosimo, rather than honoring Guicciardini and Vettori for securing his rule, for arranging for him to be chosen as the candidate to become the prince of the city, distrusted their motives. He had no intention whatsoever of being anyone's creature, despite his young age. He was only 18 years old. He was, in fact, very, very concerned that ultimately what would happen is that he would be but the extension of the ambitions of Guicciardini, in particular.

Consequently, he instantly announced that he would be an autocrat; he would take advice from only those whom he chose to consult, and, while he was at it, it would be better if Guicciardini left

Florence, and, in effect, he exiled him to his villa on the outside of the city. We'll see that this, in fact, benefited not only Guicciardini in some ways, but also the study of history a great deal, because in his leisure Guicciardini was then able to complete his great literary works.

Cosimo, then, had rid himself of those to whom he believed he owed his throne. He now had to make sure that there was no opposition whatsoever, either within the city or without—no one who could challenge his desire to be an autocrat, to be a true prince. And he decided that he had to, in fact, destroy what was left of not just republican sentiment, but also the republican movement, and he did just that. He, in fact, crushed the last republican movement that Florence would experience until a time of the French Revolution.

The republican movement in Florence had not only long roots, but, in fact, had also had a very powerful impetus caused by the events between 1527 and 1530. The exiles who had been driven from the city in 1530, those who had been able to escape after the siege of Florence, had been joined by republican patricians who had been exiled earlier, and they were all committed to the idea of the restoration of the republic.

There were others who came to their aid with the assassination of Alessandro. When their position was ultimately overruled by the Medici, in particular, by the machinations of Guicciardini and Vettori, they saw that their hope was not within the city, but without. Most of these were young men representing the oldest and most distinguished families in Florence, and they gathered an army in order to oppose Cosimo, thinking that perhaps they would be able to defeat him in battle and then restore the republic and rekindle, once more, the republican fever for which Florence was known.

Cosimo, though, had at his disposal, courtesy of the Holy Roman Emperor Charles V, the Spanish army that was garrisoned in the city in the *Fortezza da Basso* that had been built by Alessandro. The republicans and Cosimo's Spanish army met at the town of Montemurlo, near Florence, late in 1537, and the republicans were crushed by the hardened professional soldiers under Spanish command. The republicans were not only defeated, but most of their leaders were captured.

For Cosimo, this was a perfect moment to illustrate the character of his new rule. He responded with his characteristic ruthless cruelty. Without trial, and through summary justice, he beheaded all of the rebel leaders publicly in the Piazza della Signoria over four consecutive days before the assembled people. Those whom he executed were the sons of the leading families. They were related by kin and marriage to almost every great patrician clan in the city. At least one member of almost all the great families suffered. The point that Cosimo wanted to make could not be escaped—that is, not only were these young men and their ideals gone and dead, but the ideals themselves were gone. That any sympathy with, or action in favor of, republicanism would lead to the block in the Piazza della Signoria. Not only was the republic dead, but the republicans were too.

He also, then, felt he had to respond to the murder of Alessandro. He himself owed his rule to the murder of Alessandro, but he had no sympathy with Lorenzaccio. First of all, he knew him to be mad; and secondly, he felt that if anyone could escape regicide, then the principle could perhaps be recovered.

He sent professional murderers throughout Italy, tracing Lorenzaccio wherever he went. The means of following him really were quite interesting. The murderers went to every physician and asked whether a young man who had lost part of a finger, because it was known to have become infected, had come for treatment. And by asking at the physicians, they eventually traced Lorenzaccio to Venice, where he was murdered with a poison dagger in the streets by the murderers hired by Cosimo in order to ensure this last act of Medici vengeance would be exemplary. With Lorenzaccio's death, there is no question but that Cosimo paid all of his debts and ensured that he would be challenged by no one.

Cosimo, though, was anything but secure still, and he knew it. He knew there were other elements in the city that were the product of the rich and complex history, especially of the past half-century. He knew that first of all he needed immediate protection from the Spanish garrison, and he needed to be seen as actively part of the Spanish Imperial alliance that was formed around Charles V. It was clear to everyone that the Habsburgs had the control of the peninsula, and to be associated with them was to have a measure of protection that no one else could enjoy.

Consequently, he petitioned Charles V to marry Alessandro's widow, Margaret of Austria. He argued that it was an appropriate thing—that it would keep her in the city, that it would maintain the alliance. But Charles, who was actually quite fond of his natural daughter, Margaret, had other plans for her. He needed her more as the wife of the grandson of Pope Paul III Farnese, who was then the ruler of Parma. To make sure that the papacy would remain loyal and to make sure that that city in north Italy would also remain a good source of Imperial support, he decided that Margaret was better spent in the Farnese, rather than in the Medici.

However, in 1539, Cosimo was offered a kind of consolation prize. It was suggested by the Imperials that he might be interested in the hand of Eleonora of Toledo, the daughter of the immensely rich and powerful Spanish viceroy of Naples, and Cosimo agreed. Not only would she bring a huge dowry, but she would also bring Cosimo more closely into the Spanish Imperial alliance, link him more closely with Naples, and also indicate clearly to Charles V that he was a dutiful subject and quite willing to sustain his connection with the Habsburg cause.

They married, and what is truly remarkable, especially given the personality of Cosimo, they formed an almost instant, rather bourgeois union of great mutual respect and loyalty. Cosimo had almost no social skills, as one might expect. Eleonora was extremely refined and somewhat distant. She was, in fact, a remarkable woman. We can see her here, in fact, together with her young son in this portrait by Bronzino. This is Eleonora of Toledo, painted as a court portrait. And this is much the way she looked when the marriage took place.

They produced eight children. They produced a large family. She provided comfort and support to Cosimo in very, very difficult times, and, indeed, he began his own decline with her early death from malaria in 1562. The Spanish marriage, then, not only succeeded in giving Cosimo something like a normal domestic life—something he had not enjoyed for the early part of his existence—but also made Florence deeply engrained as a fundamental part of the Imperial-Spanish control of the peninsula.

Cosimo, then, relied on Spanish arms in order to secure his rule. But he also knew that eventually he would have to compromise, because as long as he was protected by a Spanish, a foreign, garrison in the *Fortezza da Basso*, the Florentines would always look upon him as a tyrant, supported by foreign arms. He knew that he had to become a domestic tyrant. He was quite happy to rule tyrannically; that wasn't the problem. But he wanted to associate his rule with the future of Florence, and to do that he needed to rid himself of the Spanish army that was always at his back.

This became increasingly necessary, as the soldiers in the *Fortezza da Basso* were behaving more and more without discipline. They would brawl through the streets at night when all Florentines were supposed to be at home safe in their houses. They robbed citizens, and, in particular, they would molest and embarrass Florentine women as they went about their daily activities.

Also, it was becoming clear that Charles was gaining the sense that Florence was really a reliable ally. Cosimo felt secure enough to ask Charles to remove the garrison. Charles refused. Charles realized that in the period of the 1540s, it was still too dangerous; the situation in Italy was still too volatile to risk having a potential enemy, or not a completely dependent vassal state in central Italy in Tuscany. So, he refused.

But, as the years passed, it became clearer to him that, largely as a result of Cosimo's marriage to Eleonora of Toledo, that there was a powerful Spanish influence at court, that Cosimo had no interest whatsoever in supporting any other power, particularly the French, and that eventually those troops were more useful elsewhere. So, ultimately, the soldiers were withdrawn. Charles trusted Cosimo as a loyal retainer and as a client state, without feeling he had to enforce that allegiance.

There was another element of Florence's past that Cosimo had to address. There was a world that still existed below the surface in Florence that Cosimo knew he had to root out because of the possible danger to his rule. This resulted from that period of experimentation and that period of millenarian theocracy that surrounded Savonarola in the 1490s.

The monastery of San Marco still remained a hotbed of Savonarola and chiliastic, theocratic dreams. They still believed that the second coming was at hand. They still believed the prophecies of

Savonarola. That moment under the prior had been, in fact, their great historic moment; they weren't about to yield it easily. So, as long as the monks of San Marco maintained the memory of Savonarola, Cosimo knew that *Piagnoni* sentiment was there, and *Piagnoni* sentiment was republican sentiment, and it was based upon the idea of freedom, closely linked to religious enthusiasm. These were dangerous, dangerous concepts for a tyrant like Cosimo.

He then, in a very theatrical gesture, got on his horse, surrounded by his court and servants, and rode to the gates of San Marco. He pounded on the door and demanded to see the abbot and monks, who dutifully came down. Cosimo looked at them and said, "Who established this monastery and set you up?" The Abbot replied, "Cosimo il Vecchio"—that is the Cosimo de'Medici of the 1440s. Cosimo then replied, "But now Cosimo il Duca is closing you down. Get out of town." And so he drove the Dominican monks from San Marco, and he repopulated it with another Dominican congregation that was much more suitable to this monarchic rule.

With the expulsion, then, of the *Piagnoni* memories, with the expulsion of the Dominicans, it was clear that Cosimo was willing to not only impose his order on the state, but also on the Church. Cosimo saw himself as omnicompetent. There was nothing in the state that was to be beyond him or above him. There was no power greater than the power he enjoyed within his own principality.

Now that the Spaniards were gone, and now that all of the republicans were shattered, and now that Lorenzaccio was dead and vengeance was his, and now that Charles rested quite comfortably knowing very well that Cosimo was part of his alliance, Cosimo could then focus on what he really needed to do, which was to establish a monarchy on the ruins of the republic, and on those terrible moments of experimentation with principality with the Medici bastards after 1530.

Cosimo proved he had no debts. Cosimo was now his own man. He could shake Florence into whatever design he chose, and he chose well. Cosimo was, in fact, completely ruthless and badly socialized. He was a man of enormous cruelty. But he was also more than intelligent. He was, in some ways, an administrative genius. He also was capable of hard work, to which he ultimately sacrificed his life.

The first thing you had to do was destroy the remaining symbols and the ideas of republicanism itself. Alessandro had begun this process by smashing the great bell in the tower of the Palazzo della Signoria, and the taking down of the symbols of the republic; but the ideas were still there. And Cosimo was sufficiently sophisticated to know that the Florentines loved abstractions and loved ideas, and he knew that if you were to be truly a ruler and autocrat without restraint, those ideas had to go.

So, then, he began to dismantle the constitution and the structures of the republic that had existed for almost 250 years, since the 1293 Ordinances of Justice. He first of all decreed the abolition of the Signoria—that is, that collectivity of central office government that the Florentines had established in order to rule the republic in the interest of the mercantile patricians. He then abolished the office particularly of the prior and of the *gonfaloniere*. So the collective executive that distributed power broadly was now gone.

He allowed Councils to remain in place, but he became their head. They became nothing but rubber stamps of his own personal will. Any official or any patrician who even challenged his action was then arrested and thrown into the unspeakable dungeons at Volterra, from which very few ever emerged. It was clear that questioning Cosimo was dangerous; challenging him was fatal.

Cosimo also knew the republic would die only when its memory was tainted with failure and with patrician disdain. The pride of the republican families, the pride of the great clans of Florence, had always been in the number of magistracies they had held over the generations—the number of times they had been elected prior or *gonfaloniere*. They kept their *ricordanze*; they kept their merchant memoirs and their family histories in order to record such things. Cosimo knew that this memory had to be rooted out and not just destroyed—but actually turned into something that was embarrassing.

He first of all worked upon the sense of jealousy and competition that had always existed among the Florentine patrician clans. He made a statement; he said, "I am now the Duke of Florence. I need a court. I need those around me who will serve me loyally, and I will recognize them. I will not only give them court appointments, but I will give them grand titles. I will call them *conte*, or count, or *marchese*, or marquis. They will be able to then hold these ranks, and wear coronets and wear robes around me. I will give them positions in my bedchamber and positions in my chancellery. They will, in fact, have a new hierarchy, not based on the number of republican magistracies that they've held, but upon how close they can get to the sacred person of the duke." And, of course, it worked brilliantly.

The Florentine patricians who, just a few years before, had sacrificed almost an entire generation of young men on the battlements of the city during the siege of 1529 to 1530; similarly, those terrible, terrible times when the republicans had tried to overthrow Cosimo, resulting in Montemurlo and the executions in the Palazzo della Signoria; these same families—the fathers of these young men, their brothers—then went to the family muniments room, searched through every documentation to show that they deserved the title of count, or the title of marquis, and they then should be admitted into the service of the duke.

And the service was very often court service, positions that were dependent upon the person and the ceremony of this new aristocratic environment. There was nothing, then, clearer to anyone than that the republic was dead. From being a group of proud and jealous republican magistrates, struggling amongst themselves to achieve some measure of leadership and honor, they then became the servants of the duke, quite happy to be called by almost absurd names.

A servile aristocracy, then, replaced the great mercantile patriciate. And it happened so quickly that it was clear to everyone that the republic was truly dead—that its memory, in fact, had passed—that its foundations had been so weakened that it collapsed without any noise.

Cosimo, then, continued, and he began the reorganization of the economy, as well as the social structure of his new state. He did something that is still discussed as an experiment —a move backwards so profound that it's hard to imagine a contemporary example. He reintroduced feudalism to his state—the same feudalism that had been abolished in the 1280s to destroy the power of the old magnate clans. He introduced feudalism because he wanted to turn this new servile aristocracy into landholders, a land of nobility gentry that would take their money out of trade and put it into land;

he wanted to make them aristocrats in the northern model, like those Spanish and Imperial nobles that he had surrounded himself with during the period of the Spanish garrison in the city. And, again, it worked extraordinarily well.

There was a huge flight of capital from trade into landed rents, and with it, the Florentine economy—which was already in freefall because of the changes to the European economy caused by the voyages of discovery and the period of dislocation during the Habsburg-Valois wars—simply collapsed.

Florence became an agricultural state, in essence. Cosimo tried to address this in other ways dependent on the duke. But, ultimately, Florence began that decline that would turn it into one of the poorer states of Europe—into an economic and social backwater, a memory of what it had been, a kind of stage set or almost a theme park of Renaissance architecture. Cosimo then realized that this flight from trade and this movement into landed wealth would create a new form of nobility—that whatever memories of the old regime that the patricians might have would no longer have the wherewithal, the wealth, and the independence to sustain it. Now they were happier, really, with their titles and their offices at court.

He also realized that Humanism had to be turned to his own interest. Cosimo was shrewd and realized that the whole tradition of Humanism in Florence was based upon the concept of republican liberty. He, after all, was familiar with Leonardo Bruni. He knew the traditions of Machiavelli. So his solution then was, as with everything else, not to destroy it by saying you couldn't do it, but co-opt it and make it, in fact, the solution to his problems.

He then founded and became patron of the great Medicean ducal academies. He created academies and filled them full of the most learned and scholarly of the patricians and their followers. He gave them funny titles. He allowed them to wear costumes. He allowed them to debate in front of him. But they were dependent on the duke. He gave them their topics for discussion. He told them the answers that he wanted them to achieve, and so they did.

The historians then looked at the past and saw it as a failed experiment, as something not to be repeated. The scientists in the Crusca actually began to extend knowledge far beyond the 15th-

century knowledge of the humanists and the politicians. Well, there were no more politicians; there were servants of the duke.

He also created orders so he could give orders of knighthood. He created a Crusading order, the Knights of Santo Stefano. And he did this not just so he could gain the support of the pope, which he so desperately wanted, but also so that he could contribute to the great endeavor that all of Christian Europe was working towards—and that is the war galleys that would fight at the Battle of Leponto and defeat the Turks in 1571.

Florence became, in fact, a Mediterranean power as a consequence of the Knights of Santo Stefano and his Crusading orders. Cosimo's desire was, again, to give them funny titles and costumes so that they, in fact, could be proud of themselves to walk around, and swagger, and say that they are better than others simply because the duke had recognized them. It also weakened, of course, that sense that they were better than others because they had achieved something in their own right. Now they were dependent upon Cosimo, and he made it clear.

He also built the port of Livorno, oddly in English, "Leghorn." Livorno was a port that would compensate for the silting up of the harbour of Pisa, and then also be something that's particularly Cosimo's gift to the economy of his city. He saw Florence not as part of the European economy, but much more in terms of long-distance trade, and in order to do that, he began building war galleys and mercantile galleys that did integrate Florence much more into the European economy. But it didn't dominate it. In fact, it was a dependent state. It became increasingly agricultural, and less and less the bankers and the carriers of Europe.

Florence was also expanding and winning wars that added to Cosimo's lustre. Cosimo was intent, as were the Imperials who wanted to destroy this point of French influence in Tuscany, with a conquest of the ancient Republic of Siena, Florence's old rival, just to the south. Provided by Charles V, an army led by Cosimo ultimately captured Siena in 1557, extinguishing the long republican history of that great state. And after 1557, Cosimo then was no longer content to be merely the Duke of Florence. He petitioned the pope, who, ultimately—largely because of his support of the Crusades—made him the Grand Duke of Tuscany, with the honorific of Your Highness, or *Altezza*. The Grand Duchy of Tuscany was created.

After half a century of instability, danger, and suffering in Florence, Cosimo seemed to be bringing back a new kind of Golden Age. It was a new age and completely different, but one that at least the Florentines could feel proud of. He symbolized new rule by moving out of the Palazzo Medici and taking over the Palazzo della Signoria—turning it, through the exercise of Giorgio Vasari's skills as an architect and painter—into a palace. Cosimo wanted to symbolize his victory over the republic by turning the republican town hall into his private residence.

But, symbolic as it was, it was also extremely uncomfortable. It was too small. It wasn't appropriate for court ceremonies, and Cosimo and Eleonora had eight children. So in 1549, Eleonora used her enormous wealth to purchase the unfinished building that Brunelleschi had designed for the banker, Luca Pitti, in the 15th century, and the family moved in a year later to the much enlarged and beautifully decorated Palazzo Pitti. This became the Grand Ducal residence, and with the addition of the Boboli Gardens behind, became one of the great royal residences of Italy, as it is to this day, where it functions as the Palatine Museum of Florence.

With the Palazzo Pitti, Florence, then, not only had an appropriate court and palace and a ruling family, but everything that really put Florence into the category of a monarchy. Now the Palazzo della Signoria became the *Palazzo Vecchio*—the "Old Palace," and the memories of the republic were truly dead.

Cosimo also wanted to make sure that he could watch everything that was going on, so he had Vasari build a series of Offices, or in 16th-century Tuscan, *Uffizi*. These *Uffizi*, these Offices, were to be built contiguous with the Palazzo della Signoria, the Palazzo Vecchio, so that Cosimo could walk from his own study through and look over the shoulders of those who were working on his behalf. He could, in fact, check everybody's work, and he did. He read everything. Having read the documents from the time of Cosimo, and seeing his own hands scribbling questions and commentary in the margin, you realize what a hard-working individual this was.

He worked so hard that he began, in fact, to decline physically. The death of Eleonora, as a result of malaria because of a visit to Livorno during malaria season, shattered him. It also made him more secretive. It made him more distant. He began turning the rule of the state, in fact, over to his son, Francesco, even before he suffered the series of strokes that ultimately would leave him speechless and incapable of ruling.

A series of unfortunate liaisons and a disastrous second marriage alienated him even more from his own court and his own community. And weakened as he was, but not terribly old, but worn out by work, he died in 1574. The first Grand Duke of Tuscany was dead, leaving the crown to his son, Francesco, whom no one questioned would rule.

He also left a united, enlarged, and peaceful, if harshly governed, tyrannical republic, leaving a tyrannical state. He, in fact, left Tuscany a stronger place, one more suited to the world of the late 16th and 17th centuries. And there were none who really bemoaned the republic. So many Florentines simply believed that liberty had been purchased at too high a price, and they no longer believed that it was a price worth paying.

Lecture Thirty-Three
Guicciardini and *The History of Italy*

Scope:

Guicciardini was a remarkable, if flawed genius. Born into the highest ranks of the Florentine patriciate, he studied law in order to further his ambitions. A brilliant man, he attracted the attention of the republic and served, despite his youth, as an ambassador to Spain in 1511. The fall of the republic affected him not at all, as he was appointed by the Medici Pope Clement VII as governor of Modena in 1516, followed by ever greater responsibility until he became one of the pope's chief advisors. Unfortunately, it was, in part, his advice that resulted in the sack of Rome in 1527, after which he retired to Florence, where the restored republic had little use for him. The return of the Medici rehabilitated Guicciardini, and he assisted in the irresponsible despotism of Alessandro, on whose murder he hoped to advance. Cosimo de'Medici, however, intended to rule personally, and Guicciardini sought refuge in scholarship. During his diplomatic and political career, he had written some history and a collection of maxims that reflected his belief in experience over abstraction and his cynical belief in human fallibility. He himself had little loyalty and did whatever those in power required. However, his monumental work, *The History of Italy*, completed just before his death, became the model for new Humanist historiography, using documentary evidence and making balanced judgments on men and events. This book has been called the most important work of history between Tacitus and Gibbon.

Outline

I. Guicciardini was a flawed genius who illustrated brilliantly the unprincipled servant to great powers, able to deliver whatever was required without question, and the astute, cynical observer of his own time.

    A. Guicciardini was born to public responsibility and high office.

        1. He was born in 1483 into one of Florence's greatest families; in every generation, his family had provided the leaders of the republic.

2. His grandfather had been one of the leaders of the Medici faction and had facilitated the return of Cosimo de'Medici from exile in 1434.

3. The family was richly rewarded, not only by Cosimo but by Piero and Lorenzo, as well.

4. Guicciardini's father broke from this tradition under the influence of Florentine Neoplatonism.

5. Not attracted by politics, he devoted his life to scholarship and philosophy, as was appropriate for a godson of Marsilio Ficino.

6. He and his family consequently escaped becoming suspect after the 1494 expulsion of the Medici and the return of the pristine republic under Savonarola's influence.

B. Francesco Guicciardini reflected his father's deep commitment to philosophy and learning.

1. His early training in classical literature was superb, but he was not attracted to pure scholarship; instead, he wished to study the law and was far more given to empirical knowledge and Aristotle than to the abstractions of Plato.

2. He attended the universities of both Ferrara and Padua to study civil law, and his time there already described his character.

3. Always looking for better opportunities, he showed no loyalty, moving from professor to professor and from one university to the other when he thought he had gained as much as possible.

C. In 1504, Guicciardini's cynical ambition was again made evident when he came very close to entering the Church at the age of 21.

1. His uncle, the bishop of Cortona, had just died but made provision for his nephew to assume his see, if his nephew so wished.

2. Guicciardini saw this as an opportunity, as his rank, legal training, astounding intelligence, and raw ambition would certainly, he thought, quickly lead to Rome, the Sacred College, and perhaps, the papacy.

      3. His father, however, strongly discouraged him, saying he lacked the spiritual qualities necessary.

II. Francesco listened and continued his studies until he was named, at the remarkable age of 23, the professor of law at the University of Florence.

    A. He also married at this time, but again, his choice of a bride indicates his personality.

        1. His wife was a member of the powerful Salviati family, related to the Medici by marriage and leaders of the aristocratic opposition to the republic of Soderini.

        2. As Guicciardini was to write about his marriage: "The Salviati, in addition to their wealth, surpassed other families in influence and power, and I had a great liking for these things."

    B. A man of Guicciardini's qualities could not be held long by a university professorship.

        1. In 1511, he was named Florentine ambassador to King Ferdinand of Aragon and Naples, the youngest ambassador to a major monarch in Florence's history.

        2. Guicciardini made much of this opportunity in Spain, beginning to write those pithy political aphorisms known as his *Ricordi*.

        3. He also continued to write a history of Florence that he had begun just before 1511, a history that was to cover the years between 1378 and 1509.

        4. It was to be superseded by the author's own later work, but for that time, it was the most sophisticated work of history of the Italian Renaissance.

III. The fall of Soderini in 1512 and the return of the Medici occurred while Guicciardini was conveniently in Spain.

    A. He returned to Florence in 1515 and was immediately named, as a supporter of and relation by marriage to the Medici, to the new *Signoria*.

1. Guicciardini's skill as an administrator caught the eye of Pope Leo X, who in 1516, asked him to serve as papal governor of Modena, a territory that was traditionally part of the Este duchy of Ferrara, with its nobles and people little inclined to obey the papacy.

2. Before Guicciardini arrived, there had been four failed administrations in six years: Leo had given him a great challenge.

3. This opportunity made Guicciardini's career: He imposed order ruthlessly, used his exceptional intelligence to reorganize the territory, and reduced the powers of the great feudal families and city patricians.

4. Most remarkable, he was incorruptible, completely honest, a trait quite absent from most Renaissance governors.

B. This success motivated Pope Leo to give Guicciardini additional responsibilities that led to a string of spectacular diplomatic achievements.

1. In 1517, Guicciardini subdued Reggio with the same brilliance with which he had governed Modena.

2. In 1521, he accomplished the extraordinary feat of holding Parma against the French, using his gifts for flattery, reward, and brutal ruthlessness to strengthen the city and its resolve.

3. In 1524, he was appointed governor of the Romagna, where government and commerce had virtually ceased because of the

   instability and unrest caused by feuding great families, papal officials, and independent towns. Guicciardini imposed once more a ruthless order, and calm and security returned to the province.

C. By 1525, the international situation required Guicciardini in Rome, as chief advisor of Pope Clement VII.

1. Guicciardini counseled Pope Clement to keep his options open and not to abandon the French in favor of Charles V.

2. Guicciardini was made lieutenant general of the papal army and sent north, but he was unable to stem the advance on Rome.

3. In May 1527, Rome was sacked, with terrible consequences, which can be seen, in part, as Guicciardini's fault because of his advice that the pope not altogether desert the French.

D. Still, Clement gave Guicciardini another major task: acting as papal representative in Florence after the restoration of the Medici under Alessandro in 1530.

1. Despite his own probity and honesty, Guicciardini advised the depraved duke.

2. On the duke's murder in 1537, Guicciardini tried to take control of the situation for his own benefit.

3. He intimidated the republican leaders and manipulated the papal representative by staging a military show of force in favor of his candidate, Cosimo de'Medici.

4. As we have learned, Cosimo surprised Guicciardini by deciding immediately to rule as an autocrat and, in effect, exiled Guicciardini to his villa outside the city.

5. Guicciardini's political career was over.

IV. However, during the imposed retirement of the last three years of his life, Guicciardini ensured his fame by revolutionizing the writing of history and producing one of the great books of the Italian Renaissance, the *Storia d'Italia* (*The History of Italy*), a book largely regarded as the greatest work of history between Tacitus in the 2nd century and Edward Gibbon in the 18th.

A. Guicciardini was 55 years old when he began writing this great book in early 1538.

1. It is a personal history, discussing events during his lifetime.

2. He lets events speak for themselves: He has no agenda whatsoever.

3. God is not a factor, but neither is the ideal of republican freedom so central to other writers, such as Bruni and Machiavelli.

4. If Guicciardini has any transcendent or overarching values, they are completely hidden.

5. Indeed, Guicciardini argues that in governing or politics, principles are worse than useless because they get in the way of opportunity and necessity: All that matters is experience and information.

B. *The History of Italy* becomes, as a consequence of Guicciardini's singular vision, a very coherent study, almost a tragedy in the classical sense of the fall of princes.

1. Guicciardini traces how the French invasions of 1494 set off a chain of events that the leaders of Italy could not control.

2. First rulers suffer, then their states, then the whole peninsula: Poor decisions, bad information, or insufficient force account for much of this tragedy.

3. His conclusion is that self-interest ultimately undoes all ambitious men because they lose sight of the larger picture.

4. In other words, history will always turn out badly because those who shape it are motivated only by what serves them best, even at the expense of the greater good.

C. In many ways, there is another intention in Guicciardini's *History of Italy*: the story of why one man of exceptional ability, honesty, hard work, cynicism, and ruthlessness lost his job, and this he presents as an exemplum for others.

Primary Source Texts:

Kenneth R. Bartlett, "Francesco Guicciardini," pp. 381–391, in *The Civilization of the Italian Renaissance*.

Francesco Guicciardini, *The History of Italy*.

Secondary Sources:

Mark Phillips, *Francesco Guicciardini: The Historian's Craft*.

Supplementary Reading:

Felix Gilbert, *Machiavelli and Guicciardini: Politics and History in Sixteenth-Century Florence*.

Questions to Consider:

1. Guicciardini strongly believed that all men, regardless of what they claim, act only in their own interest. Do you agree?

2. History to Guicciardini is the complex web of events in which individuals are caught. Do you share this view?

Lecture Thirty-Three—Transcript
Guicciardini and *The History of Italy*

We have met Francesco Guicciardini on a couple of occasions already. It's necessary, I think, to pause and to look at the career of this most remarkable man, this seriously flawed genius who represents, so brilliantly, the concept of the unprincipled civil servant, those who were willing to serve great powers in order to achieve what they thought was the necessary conclusion, those who were able and willing to deliver whatever was required of them without question. The astute, cynical observer of his own time, and perhaps the most brilliant historian of early modern Europe, Guicciardini had a mixed reputation. His close friend and somewhat older contemporary, Machiavelli, survived the period of Italian unification well as a kind of hero because of this call for the unity of the peninsula. At the time of the unification, Machiavelli was seen as not just a hero, but as an object almost of cult veneration, where conferences were held and processions were arranged to associate his memories and his ideas with the creation of a united Italy; whereas, Guicciardini was seen as part of the problem, not part of the solution.

Indeed, Francesco De Sanctis, one of the great critics of Italian literature and thought at the time of the unification of the peninsula, wrote a famous essay called *The Guicciardinian Man*, and he identified Guicciardini as the kind of individual who actually allowed and supported Italian subjection. He saw Guicciardini as the kind of person who was willing to make accommodation with those whom the Italians should have not only resented, but struggled against.

It's necessary, then, to pause and to look at this remarkable, remarkable man; to see what he accomplished and to see why his reputation—in fact, only recently, in the past decades, to some extent rehabilitated—to see what he wrote and why, and to see why his very success in many ways was seen as part of the problem of the late Italian Renaissance.

Guicciardini was destined for high responsibility and public office from the moment of his birth. He was born in 1483 into one of Florence's greatest families, who, then as now, fulfilled the highest obligations to the state; who held the highest social status; and who always had provided the leaders of their respective generations. His grandfather had been one of the leaders of the Medici faction who had facilitated the return of Cosimo de'Medici after his exile in 1434.

The family was richly rewarded—not just by Cosimo, but by Piero and Lorenzo as well. There were Guicciardini close to the Medici during the entire period of the 15th century, until Guicciardini's father. Guicciardini's father broke with this tradition under the influence of Florentine Neoplatonism. He was not attracted at all to politics, and he devoted his life, instead, to scholarship—and, in particular, to Neoplatonic philosophy, as was appropriate for the godson of Marsilio Ficino.

The world of Laurentian Florence, then—that world of abstraction and the flight from the civic Humanism of the engaged citizen magistrate involved in the republic—was not really his choice. Guicciardini's father was happier in his study, looking to perfect himself through pure knowledge. He, then, was an exemplar of how the Humanism of Laurentian Florence differed from that of the period of Salutati and Bruni.

It was this, consequently, as a result of this flight from politics and the self-identification as someone more interested in thought than in action, that helped the Guicciardini escape all of the problems that attended those who were close to the Medici after the expulsion of the family in 1494. Under Savonarola's influence, the republic was restored, as we've seen, and the Guicciardini did not suffer because Francesco's father had not really been part of the Medici faction.

Francesco shared his father's deep commitment to philosophy and learning. He was a brilliant student, but very different in personality and in interest. His training was certainly in classical scholarship, as one might expect, but he was not attracted to pure scholarship or abstraction, as was his father. He was much more interested in applied learning. He was interested in the law. He was not interested in Plato and Platonic ideas; he was interested in Aristotle and empirical observation.

Guicciardini, with all of his learning, was always a very practical man. He was always an empiricist, and, to some extent, that's what made him such a great historian. He was able to build his own observations and insights into a narrative history of his time that really helps explicate one of the most confused and difficult periods of Italian history.

He, to study law, went to two universities, Ferrara and Padua; but even there, his character was being formed. He had no sense of loyalty. He left one professor for another; one group for another; one university for another. When he thought that he had gained as much as he reasonably could from one, he abandoned it without any remorse. He simply moved on in order to see what new fields there were for him to till.

In 1504, Guicciardini's cynical ambition was perhaps made most evident when he became very, very interested in entering the Church. At the age of 21, his uncle, the bishop of Cortona, died. His uncle, seeing the intelligence and amazing precocity of his nephew, arranged for young Francesco to take his place as bishop of Cortona, if he so wished. Guicciardini saw this as a great opportunity. He was very keen to, in fact, become the bishop because with his legal training, with his social rank and influence and associations, with his astounding intelligence and raw ambition, he imagined that he would very, very soon be admitted to the Sacred College and become a cardinal—and then, ultimately, a pope.

His father, though, strongly discouraged him. His father took him aside and said, "Francesco, you are brilliant. You are astute. But you lack any spiritual quality whatsoever. The Church is not the place for you. Follow the law. Follow politics, because that really is where you belong." Francesco wisely listened to his father and decided to choose a secular life, the consequence of which we shall see at some length.

His personality is also reflected in his marriage. At the remarkable age of 23, he found himself appointed as professor of law at the University of Florence. This is, in itself, amazing that a 23-year-old could hold this high office, but his intelligence was such that there was no question but that he really deserved this chair. And now that he had this solid position in society, he had the wealth of his family and his influence, he thought it appropriate to take a bride. And he began looking about for an appropriate young woman to marry. His wife was a member of the powerful Salviati family, related to the Medici by marriage, and the leaders of the aristocratic opposition to the republic of Soderini, the factional debate into which Guicciardini was really just beginning to admit himself.

Guicciardini, though, wrote about his marriage, something that reflects his personality, again, even at a young age. He wrote, "The Salviati, in addition to their wealth, surpassed other families in influence and power. And I had a great liking for these things." There is nothing about the young woman, and, in fact, he clearly disliked his wife intensely. He spent as much time as possible away from her, and he just did the requisite duty to ensure that there would be a continuation of a line. It was the Salviati that he had married—their influence, and their wealth, and their political connections. The young woman was completely immaterial.

A man of Guicciardini's qualities, though, couldn't be held long by university professorship. It's hard to even imagine Francesco Guicciardini grading papers. In 1511, he was named Florentine ambassador to King Ferdinand of Aragon and Naples. He was the youngest ambassador to a major monarch in all of Florence's history. Again, his fast-track career was recognized by those who saw his great ability, and as a very young man he began establishing a career that ultimately would lead him to the highest reaches of international diplomacy in government.

While in Spain, Guicciardini made a good deal of his opportunities. Not only did he prove himself to be an extremely shrewd and skilled ambassador for Florence, but also he began his writing. He began writing a collection of pithy political aphorisms, which he would continue to record and expand throughout his entire life, called his *Ricordi*. These *Ricordi*, or little memories, were observations on the state of humanity, the state of government and politics, the state of learning and reading. They, like Montaigne's essays, provide an insight into a mind that reflects the tenor of his age.

Guicciardini's *Ricordi* are still read and still studied, and what emerges is that remarkably astute, remarkably intelligent, but oh-so-cynical individual who saw the world driven only by self-interest. He, also, at this time began to write his first history. He was interested in studying why Florence was where it was, and how it really got there. So he started writing a history of Florence that covered the years between the period of the Ciompi revolt of 1378 until 1509. This was, then, a history that was to bring the history of his city up to his own time, because the first record of his starting to write it is 1511.

It was, in fact, to be the most sophisticated piece of historical writing of its age, only to be superseded by Guicciardini's own greater last work, the *Storia d'Italia*. But he was already seeing the writing of history and the insight into human motivation and circumstance, that web of events in which we are all caught, as the essence of the condition of Italy; a set of circumstances that are so complex that no one individual could ever master them all. And he was simply providing advice as to which ones you should choose, and how you should take your knowledge and your ambitions and use them towards ends that you can see as beneficial to yourself, because that's the only thing of which you can ever be sure.

The fall of Soderini in 1512 and the return of the Medici occurred while Guicciardini was conveniently in Spain. He returned to Florence in 1515 and was immediately named, as supporter of and relation by marriage to the Medici, to the new Signoria. There was no question but that he would enter this community—that he would be part of the Signoria merely because it was part of the role that he was to play in society, a role into which he was born, and one that he embraced with enthusiasm as well as a sense of dynamic dignity. Moreover, he was so skilled as an administrator, he was so intelligent and insightful, that it was only a matter of time before he caught the eye of the powerful.

Pope Leo X de'Medici, a distant relation by marriage, asked him in 1516 whether he would be willing to serve as papal governor of the city of Modena. Modena is a territory that traditionally formed part of the Este lands dependent on Ferrara. The pope, then, was interfering in a state that, for centuries, had enjoyed virtual independence of the Holy See, despite the fact that it was a papal fief. Its nobles and people were little inclined to obey the pope, and it was a difficult, difficult assignment.

Guicciardini knew just how serious the problem was because he instantly saw that there had been four failed administrations in the previous six years. But Guicciardini embraced it, realizing that it was only in hard cases like this that his mettle could be truly shown. And, indeed, this opportunity made his career: he imposed order ruthlessly; he used his exceptional intelligence to reorganize the territory completely and make it dependent upon the Holy See; and he reduced the powers of the great feudal families and the city patricians. He made himself the center of power, and he acted in the name of the pope.

Most remarkable, he was incorruptible. He was completely and totally honest—a trait that made him so different from almost every other Renaissance governor. Almost every other Renaissance administrator saw it as part of the perks of the job to be able to take bribes and do whatever they could in order to advance their own wealth. Not Guicciardini. Guicciardini saw himself as a servant of the pope. He had the mentality of the senior civil servant who was willing very, very much to sacrifice the immediate gain in terms of long-term recognition. In no way was he self-sacrificing, but in every way he was honest.

This success motivated Pope Leo to give Guicciardini additional responsibilities that led to a string of spectacular successes in his career. In 1517, Guicciardini subdued Reggio, very close to Modena, and again, part of that territory in Emilia Romagna that had been, by tradition, ruled by the Este. And he did so with the same brilliance and insight that he used to govern Modena. And in 1521, he accomplished the extraordinary feat of holding Parma against the French—using his gifts of flattery, reward, and brutal ruthlessness to strengthen the city and its resolve to maintain its alliance with the papacy.

In 1524, he was appointed governor of the Romagna—that unstable, ungovernable territory of the papal states across central Italy, where government and commerce had virtually ceased because of the political factional disputes and the unrest caused by the great families feuding amongst themselves, and the papal officials and the independent towns all seeking their own interest at the expense of the pope.

Guicciardini once more succeeded. He imposed a ruthless order. He imposed calm. He imposed security to a province that had been, by tradition, ungovernable. Guicciardini seemed to have a kind of skill that no one else did. He seemed to be able to take an impossible situation, see its opportunities, and turn it into a coherent, effective policy that not only gave him great glory, but then redounded to the glory of his superiors—in particular, in this case, the pope.

The result is, by 1525, the international situation meant that the pope, now Clement VII, required Guicciardini to leave these provincial appointments and come to Rome in order to be the chief advisor of the Holy See. He had been so successful in the provinces that now he had to apply that genius, and ability, and ruthlessness to a situation that Clement VII, with his vacillating mind, couldn't quite see how to escape.

Clement VII felt that Guicciardini was the perfect person to give him advice. Guicciardini was everything he was not. He was decisive; he was ruthless; he was extremely intelligent, but able to cut through all of the competing arguments in order to get to the one simple truth that would allow success to be ensured.

Guicciardini, then, was asked by Clement VII what he should do in the struggle between the Habsburg and Valois. And here comes the great mistake of his career. Guicciardini said, "We can't be certain what is going to happen. The Church is universal. I recommend, Pope Clement, that you steer a course between the two. Come out neither for the French, nor for the Habsburgs, to try and represent a Church that's above faction." And, of course, this was the advice that ultimately resulted in the humiliation not just of the Holy See, but of Italy.

Guicciardini, nevertheless, was still seen as exactly the right kind of person, and Clement followed his advice, as we know. He was made Lieutenant General of the papal army. He was sent north. But he wasn't really a soldier, and he knew that it was impossible to stop the march on Rome that would ultimately result in a sack. It also meant, though, that he was out of Rome during that terrible period that began in May of 1527.

Rome was sacked with such violence and viciousness, as we've seen, that the papacy was humiliated, and the pope himself found his policy of trying to maintain some form of equal representation amongst the Habsburg and Valois in tatters. The consequences of Guicciardini's advice now became clear to everyone. Nevertheless, Pope Clement still realized that Guicciardini was still the best servant that he had, and it was impossible for him to give up completely on his advice.

Still, Clement gave Guicciardini another chance so that something could be done to try and salvage the situation. And it was clear that someone of Guicciardini's personality and experience, as well as his social rank in Florence, was necessary to try and bring papal rule back to the city and to provide some kind of control for Alessandro, whose personality caused everyone a good deal of concern.

So it was Guicciardini who was sent by Clement VII in order to control the young Alessandro. He was sent there as papal representative, and it was his job not just to try and reconcile the Florentines to papal rule, but also to make absolutely sure that Alessandro would obey the pope, and to try and restrain and curtail his tendencies towards antisocial behavior and depravity.

It's hard to imagine two more unlikely colleagues. Alessandro—the depraved, partly mad tyrant, and Guicciardini—the shrewd, cynical, intelligent lawyer who was completely incorruptible and completely honest. Nevertheless, Guicciardini saw his responsibility as serving the duke, and whatever he thought of him personally, he served him well.

We've seen that it was Guicciardini who argued against Iacopo Nardi in front of Charles V to allow Alessandro to marry the emperor's natural daughter. Guicciardini, with his great skill at argument, his extraordinary reason, his knowledge of the law, was able to thwart the attempt of the republicans to try and drive a wedge between Alessandro and the emperor. And, of course, the consequences of this we know.

On the duke's murder in 1537, we've also seen how Guicciardini tried to take control of the situation for his own benefit. He intimidated the republican leaders, and he manipulated the papal representatives by staging that military show of force in favor of his candidate to rule Florence, the young Cosimo de'Medici, the son of Giovanni, Giovanni delle Bande Nere.

As we've learned, Cosimo surprised—in fact shocked—Guicciardini by deciding immediately to rule as an autocrat, and, in effect, he exiled Guicciardini to his villa outside the city. Guicciardini had made an error in judgment. He had completely misjudged this secretive, strange, young teenaged man who was so determined to not be dependent on anyone, and Guicciardini couldn't imagine any reasonable person in his position not needing someone like him.

However, it's during that period of imposed retirement, that period of the last three years of his life, where Guicciardini ensured his fame by revolutionizing the writing of history and producing one of the great books of the Italian Renaissance, one of the great books of the European tradition in the terms of the writing of history—that is, the *Storia d'Italia*, or *The History of Italy*, a book largely regarded as the greatest work of historical writing between Tacitus in the 2nd century and Edward Gibbon in the 18th century.

Guicciardini was 55 years old when he began writing his great book in early 1538. It's a personal history. He says at the beginning he will only discuss the events of his own lifetime—events that he knew about in detail, many of which he was involved with, and many of which he actually saw. He also lets events speak for themselves: he has no agenda. There is no intent, as in Bruni's history of Florence, to indicate how history produced the republican liberty that made Florence the chosen people and the beacon of freedom for the peninsula.

It's not the same as Machiavelli justifying Medici rule in terms of the traditions of Florentine politics. It's quite different. It's a book in which history takes its own course. It becomes, in fact, the driving force of events. History, then, becomes just as he always described, the circumstances of his own advice to popes and princes. History is a web of events, a series of circumstances—the more of which you know, the better you will be as a ruler, the stronger and the more able to confront the forces that are arrayed against you.

If Guicciardini has any transcendent or overarching values, they are completely hidden. It's clear that Guicciardini, in fact, rejects the concept of principle. Guicciardini argues—in fact in the *Ricordi* he says this again and again—that principles are worse than useless because principles get in the way of opportunity and necessity: all that matters is experience and information. He says about principle that if you follow what you think is right, you will always lose because you will then not have the broad perspective of options that you have foreclosed. You must act out of necessity, regardless of how brutal, how ruthless, how terrible, how criminal, that act might be—such as his defending of Alessandro—you must do it. It's your responsibility.

He begins, in so many ways, that long line of senior civil servants who do what they're asked or commanded to do without question, without asking whether it's right or proper, simply that he has the responsibility to do it and do it well, and he will perform as required. This he sees as a necessity of history, and he, like Machiavelli, has been created by the circumstances of his own time.

He sees Italy as being under the thrall of the barbarians. He sees his papacy as being humiliated by the Imperial army. He sees Florence under the control of a despotic and half-mad duke. He sees his own protégé turn against him. His conclusion, then, is that, ultimately, there is only one certainty, and that is your own self-interest; and whatever happens, you cannot sacrifice that, because if there is a principle, it's looking after your own concerns.

The History of Italy, then, becomes, as a consequence, Guicciardini's singular vision and a very coherent study. In fact, to read this great narrative is almost to read a tragedy in the classical sense of the fall of princes, because that's what it's really about: how Italy was a tragic situation because princes made the wrong decisions because they acted out of principle, or, more usually, because they acted as he did, out of self-interest.

Guicciardini completely agrees with his close friend, Machiavelli that the French invasions of 1494 began as calamity because they initiated a series of events that the leaders of Italy could not control. And by losing control, they really lost the game. Whoever controls the board, controls the movement of all the players, and Italy simply did not control the board.

He argues that first rulers themselves suffer, then their states, and then, ultimately, a whole people—the entire Italian peninsula. Poor decisions, bad information, or, like Machiavelli, insufficient force account for much of this tragedy.

His conclusion is that, ultimately, the only thing we can be certain of is our own self-interest. But he also says, in a kind of oxymoronic way, that self-interest undoes us as well because ambitious men acting in their own self-interest lose sight of the big picture. Their self-interest becomes ever more carefully defined as events progress, and they lose the ability to look in a more broad way at greater action.

His idea of self-interest, which he defines in Italian as the *particulate*, is something that he says will undo us all, but it's something that we all necessarily follow. The particulate, that sense of what is most important to us at that moment, is the only thing of which we can be certain. He says that he writes history, and that history itself is valuable to any ruler and any people because it provides information. That web of events that constitutes history, then, is something that will allow you to escape your narrow particulate and look at a wider sense of how your interest can be furthered by taking into account a huge number of events and conditions that only the broadest perspective can ever provide.

For him, then, the particulate is not just that momentary self-interest that he can identify so easily, but, in fact, it's the broad self-interest that comes from knowledge of how you are part of this process—the contribution that you make to the ability of history to unfold in a particular way.

In one of his *Ricordi*, he debates silently his friend Machiavelli by saying that quoting and speaking of the ancients at all times is worse than useless because their times were theirs. It's the past; the situation is different. There is no advantage or exemplum in history; there is only information.

Guicciardini, then, sees history not as a great series of ideas and principles to animate a people the way Bruni did, the way Machiavelli did. Guicciardini sees history, rather, as the kind of report that any careful civil servant should have on his desk in order to make a call about every moment of the day. In order to understand what things mean, you need a broader context. And Guicciardini wrote in the *Storia d'Italia* one of the great contexts of all time.

In many ways, there's another intention, then, to Guicciardini's *History of Italy*: the story of why one man of such exceptional ability, such honesty, such hard work, such cynicism and ruthlessness lost his job; and this he presents as an exemplum for others. It is a tragedy, indeed, and not just to the fall of princes, but the fall of Francesco Guicciardini.

And for me, there's a particular moment: As I was a student in Florence, my teacher of Italian palaeography and archival research also was the archivist of the Guicciardini counts, who still live in that same palace on the Via Guicciardini by the Palazzo Pitti. I was in the study, and my teacher gave me a book and asked me to comment on it, as was his want.

The book, I identified as being a 16th-century text written in a beautiful humanist hand, and my teacher kept saying, "Marco, Che cos'è? Che cos'è? —what is it, what is it? And then I looked at what it was I was holding. I was holding the autographed manuscript of Francesco Guicciardini's *Storia d'Italia*, a book that had shaped the practice of history and the concept of the individual in the Renaissance as an actor in events.

I was moved, and so Guicciardini has always meant something in particular to me. But also, as an historian, I realize he was one of the great practitioners of my art.

Lecture Thirty-Four
The Counter-Reformation

Scope:

It was not just the foreign invasions of Italy or the loss of economic power that affected the later Italian Renaissance. The revolt in the Church led by Martin Luther (1483–1546) from 1517 had a devastating impact. The Roman Church had seen itself as universal and confident and able to permit relative freedom of debate and belief. Only when the authority of the Church was attacked was there a strong response, as in the case of Savonarola. Luther's revolt changed that, especially as Protestantism spread so quickly and effectively through the printed word. The Church lost millions of adherents and much revenue as a consequence, and the unity of Christian Europe was shattered forever. To combat this danger, the Church responded by tightening controls. The Roman Inquisition was established in 1542 to determine centrally what and who were orthodox or heretical. In 1545, Paul III called a great council of the Church to meet at Trent whose purpose was to define doctrine and build discipline among Catholics; the council was to sit, with some interruptions, until 1563. As a consequence of Trent, the Index of Prohibited Books was created in 1559 to control what books were printed, read, and circulated, and the penalties for possession were severe. The claims of the reformers were also rejected and the authority of the Church and the papacy reinforced. The ultimate effect of these measures was to suppress open debate and original thinking. The principles that had stimulated the Renaissance initially were being overwhelmed by forces that demanded uniformity and obedience.

Outline

I. During the period of the Renaissance, the Church was latitudinarian in matters of academic or artistic debate, provided that the fundamental tenets of Catholic Christianity were accepted.

    A. As was illustrated by the works of many writers, Renaissance models had deep roots within the Church: There was no necessary wall between the two intellectual disciplines of Humanism and theology.

        1. Petrarch had been in minor religious orders and saw his journey to self-knowledge as fully compatible with Catholic teaching.

        2. Even those Humanists who had flirted with syncretic religion or paganism under the influence of classical letters or Neoplatonism ultimately returned to orthodox thought.

        3. For example, Marsilio Ficino, who prayed to "St. Socrates" and pretended to adhere to purely Platonic ideals, eventually came to the conclusion that there was no necessary exclusion between Christianity and Platonism and, ultimately, became a priest.

        4. Pico della Mirandola, who had argued for the Platonic Unity of Truth, in which all religions and philosophies participated in ultimate truth, ended his life as a devout follower of Savonarola.

        5. Lorenzo de'Medici, the Magnificent, as well as being a patron of Neoplatonism and Humanism, was a very devout Catholic.

    B. Primary ideals of Humanism, such as the dignity of man, free will, and the deep connection among the soul, reason, and speech all resonated with practical Catholicism; for this reason, the Church offered little opposition to the movement.

II. On the other hand, Humanism was not universally accepted, despite the attempts by so many Humanist writers to reconcile Christianity and pagan thought.

    A. The Spiritual Franciscan movement followed the letter of St. Francis's rule and example.

1. For these believers, wealth, secular learning, and public office interfered with the struggle for salvation and, hence, were to be avoided.

2. The Spiritual Franciscans were often seen as heretical in Italy, preaching social discord by prophesying God's retribution on the proud and rich and exaltation of the poor and meek.

3. In Florence, these mystical Franciscans were regularly outlawed and driven from the city; on occasion, they were publicly burned.

B. The example of Savonarola has already been presented: This mystical Dominican attacked "pagan" Humanism, classical literature, and secular art and practices.

1. His dominion over Florence after 1494 constituted a repudiation of Humanist values.

2. The burning of the vanities illustrated dramatically his hatred of the things of this world.

3. His ideas sparked a flame among devout Italians, who rejected classical studies, Humanism, and civic responsibility in favor of personal, mystical piety.

C. The institutional Church rejected much of Savonarola's message.

1. Pope Alexander VI Borgia's offer of a cardinal's hat to Savonarola had been simultaneously an attempt to co-opt his popularity and to bring him under control.

2. His attack on the papacy and institution of the Church in many ways reinforced in official circles the danger of mystical spiritual values and the advantages of practical secular wisdom and knowledge.

III. The initial stages of Martin Luther's revolt, the revolt that ultimately led to the establishment of the Protestant church, had little influence in Italy.

A. The pope was annoyed at Luther's attack on his authority, but Luther's theology caused less consternation than one might have supposed.

1. Pope Leo X thought that Luther, an Augustinian canon, was only engaging in traditional monastic rivalry in his attacks on the Dominicans' sale of indulgences.

2. It was only in 1520 that the pope finally felt forced to excommunicate Luther.

B. Powerful churchmen, educated in Humanism and theology and possessed of a deep spirituality, felt much sympathy with some of Luther's claims.

1. These included influential Church officials, such as Venetian noble Cardinal Gasparo Contarini (1483–1542); Reginald Pole (1500–1558), cousin of Henry VIII of England and soon to be named a cardinal; and Gian Matteo Giberti, bishop of Verona (1495–1543) and papal datary.

2. Together, they attempted to seek reform within the Church and even hoped for reconciliation with the Lutherans.

3. The death of Leo X and the surprise election in 1522 of an ascetic Dutchman, Adrian VI, who had never been to Rome and who also wished to reform the Church focused reformist ideas in Italy.

4. Consequently, Italian reformers, often termed *Spirituali*, attracted many followers, including powerful clerics, princes, and artists, such as Michelangelo.

C. Events in the 1520s made liberal accommodation with reform ideas more difficult.

1. Adrian VI died in just one year, having in that short time alienated many powerful ecclesiastics with heavy-handed attempts at reform.

2. The sack of Rome was a disaster for reform; Lutheran soldiers in Rome committed unspeakable atrocities and claimed they were wreaking judgment on a corrupt Church ruled by the Antichrist.

D. In 1536, Pope Paul III Farnese established a commission to reform the Church.

1. In 1538, the commission submitted a report, *On the Reform of the Church* (*Consilium de ecclesia emendanda*).

2. It was a radical document that reflected much of the Protestants' position.

3. Consequently, it failed to change anything at that time, although it signaled a need for reform.

IV. By 1542, it was clear that there could be no reconciliation with the Lutherans, and the Church responded in decisive ways, under the energetic Pope Paul III.

A. The Roman Inquisition was established in 1542.

1. There had been local or diocesan inquisitions to determine heresy for many years, but the Roman Inquisition was central: to decide from Rome who or what was orthodox, who or what was heretical.

2. A number of high-profile Catholic thinkers and clerics fled Italy to join the reformed confessions in that year, depriving Italy of many influential leaders.

3. Those left in Rome became increasingly conservative.

B. Paul III wanted to control the reform movement and direct what was now spiritual war against the Protestants from the center of the Church.

1. He called a council of the Church to meet in the northern Italian city of Trent.

2. In 1545, the sessions began that would last until 1563, with some breaks.

3. The council's mandate was to confront the Protestant threat by reaffirming Catholic doctrine, reforming the Church where necessary, and rejecting heretical ideas.

C. Trent revitalized the Roman Church.

1. The authority of the pope was confirmed.

2. Protestant notions of salvation by faith alone were rejected in favor of the Catholic emphasis on works.

3. All seven sacraments were confirmed.

4. The authority of Scripture was not sufficient; the teachings and traditions of the Church played a role in the faith.

5. The clergy were to be better educated and trained and subject to clear doctrinal control.

D. To stop the spread of heretical ideas and control a new technology that the Protestants had used greatly to their advantage, the Index of Prohibited Books was established in 1559.

    1. It determined from Rome what Catholics could and could not read.

    2. Penalties for possessing or reading proscribed books were harsh.

    3. All ideas now had to be approved before they could be spread.

V. The Church created new instruments and new religious orders to combat heresy.

  A. The Jesuit order, or the Society of Jesus, was recognized by Paul III in 1540.

    1. It was founded by a Basque noble named Ignatius Loyola.

    2. Wounded in battle, Loyola decided to be a soldier for Christ and the Church rather than in secular wars.

    3. He wrote *The Spiritual Exercises*, a book of discipline, helping the faithful yield their will to God and the Church.

    4. The order was to become the vanguard of the Catholic Counter-Reformation.

  B. Ignatius built his order around three elements: preaching, teaching, and missionary work.

    1. Jesuits were not cloistered but out in the world, wearing inconspicuous clothes to help win converts.

    2. They were to spread Catholicism and try to convert heretics.

    3. The order established the most progressive and effective schools in Europe, schools in which a Humanist education in the classics and in rhetoric were used not to open minds to new ideas but to confirm approved articles of faith.

Primary Source Texts:

Ignatius Loyola, *The Spiritual Exercises of Saint Ignatius.*

Secondary Sources:

Gigliola Fragnito, *Church, Censorship and Culture in Early Modern Italy*.

J. W. O'Malley, *The First Jesuits*.

Supplementary Reading:

Eric Cochrane, ed., *The Late Italian Renaissance, 1525–1630*.

Questions to Consider:

1. How compatible were the principles of Humanism with religion?

2. Do you agree that the Renaissance could only have flourished in Italy in an environment of lax Church control over men and ideas?

Lecture Thirty-Four—Transcript
The Counter-Reformation

In the course of this series, we haven't discussed specifically the role of religion. There have been many references to the institution of the Roman Church and the papacy; there have been discussions of religious moments, such as the regime of Savonarola.

But there is this sense that somehow religion was subsumed by the classical nature of Humanism, and that the personal confessional beliefs of the men and women during the Renaissance were continued in a way not terribly different from their medieval predecessors. This is generally true, and, in fact, far truer than that is the 19th-century concept that the Renaissance was pagan, that the recovery of classical antiquity drove Renaissance thinkers towards the rejection of Christianity.

The truth really is something quite different. The truth is that most Renaissance men and women still followed the traditional teaching of Roman Catholicism without much question. It determined the patterns of their lives; it determined those moments that punctuated human existence—of baptism, of confirmation, of marriage, of death. Also, it was the entire cultural reference of their time. If you look at the art of the Renaissance, it is very much religious art. If you look at the institutions of the Renaissance, they are often formed by Christian ideas.

So, the Renaissance was, in fact, a Christian idea. But this idea of Christianity as a single model began to break down under the same sorts of circumstances that we've seen affecting Italy in the first part of the 16th century. A set of circumstances occurred that drove Italians to reconsider their relationship with God and the Church. It also drove the Church to address some of the systemic problems that had been identified by the reformers, problems that we've seen manifested in the Borgia papacy and those elements of ecclesiastical impropriety that very often became the elements of Protestant sermons.

But during the Renaissance, the most important point to make is that the Church was wonderfully latitudinarian. In matters of academic or artistic debate, there really was no problem in having a relatively open mind, provided the basic tenets of Church teaching and acceptance of the structure of the Church were perfectly visible. So, it didn't really matter whether you engaged in an academic debate, as did the great Aristotelian philosophers at the University of Padua over the immortality of the soul; it was an academic debate. It wasn't anything that challenged faith.

Also, we can see in the work of so many of the Renaissance thinkers and those Renaissance leaders who actually define the period that they had deep roots within the church: To them, there was no necessary wall between the intellectual disciplines of philosophy and Humanism, and the belief that constituted religion and the structure of theology.

We've seen with Petrarch—Petrarch himself in minor religious orders, someone who worked for and with the Church. He saw no disjunction whatsoever between Catholic teaching and his desire to know himself and his world. Collucio Salutati, one of those founders of civic Humanism in Florence, was an extremely devout man, writing books of devotion at the same time he was writing those letters as secretary to the Florentine Republic, in which he served as chancellor.

Even those humanists who flirted with syncretic religion or who flirted with paganism as a consequence of recovering antique texts, they saw that there was no real difficulty in ultimately embracing Christianity. They saw that there was no disjunction between, for example, classical letters or Neoplatonism and basic orthodox thought. And all of them, ultimately, came back to complete communion with the Church.

The great example is Marsilio Ficino, who in his youth prayed to "St. Socrates," who celebrated Plato's punitive birthday on November 7 as a Holy Day of Obligation, who adhered completely to Platonic ideals. Well, he came to believe the more he studied Plato and the more he studied Christianity, that there was no necessary exclusion between the two. And, indeed, he ultimately became a priest.

Pico della Mirandola, who argued for the Platonic Unity of Truth—in which all religions and all philosophies participated in ultimate truth, who not only understood a new Christianity, but also Judaism, Islam, and Zoroastrianism, believed strongly that all religions partook of some form of truth, but ultimately came to believe that the Christian religion had perhaps the surest route to it. And late in life, he became a devoted follower of Savonarola and died just before he took his final vows as a Dominican monk. In fact, he was buried in the cowl of a Dominican.

Lorenzo the Magnificent, the ideal almost of Renaissance secular thought and Renaissance secular government and patronage, was an extremely devout Catholic. Besides his obscene carnival songs, he wrote some of the most moving religious poetry of the 15th century, some of which is still quoted, like those wonderful lines about "Oh God, oh ultimate truth, why is it that you force me to seek you always, yet never let me find you?"

These primary ideals of Humanism, then, and the practice of individual Catholics during the period of the Renaissance, even during those moments when classical antiquity was energizing them the most, there was no sense that you had to reject the traditional teachings of Roman Catholicism to be a good scholar, to be a good humanist, to be an active citizen in the world.

But, of course, there were others who didn't agree and who never agreed. There were those who saw Humanism as a movement away from what they saw as the secure traditional route to salvation; those who often had a somewhat contrarian view, even in the context of the traditional established Church. There were tensions. There were those who felt that they were excluded from the world of Humanism because of their religious thought.

The Spiritual Franciscans are probably the best example of this. They were the followers of St. Francis to the letter. The Franciscan order had divided at the time of Pope John XXII, soon after Francis's death, because Francis had become such a holy man and attracted so many followers, and it attracted so many gifts of wealth and land that those who wanted to be exactly like their founder felt that they were being compromised simply by having to organize others, by having to control property. They wanted to live as mendicants with no property.

There were others, though, who were quite content to accept the property, to live together in communities. So, the Franciscans divided between the conventuals, who lived in large monasteries who controlled vast tracts of land; and there was the ruse simply that this land did not belong to them, it belonged to the pope, and the pope simply let them use it. And then there were the Spiritual Franciscans, those who refused to compromise, who lived by begging, who worked among the poor, often in small groups or as individuals. These were seen often, especially in large cities, as dangerous.

They were seen as dangerous not because of the model of St. Francis and his poverty, but because they worked amongst the poor and sowed what those in power and those with property saw as social discord. They were the ones who preached against the rich and said that they would ultimately be punished by a vengeful God; they were the ones who preached that the meek would inherit the earth, and it was only a matter of time.

Cities like Florence regularly expelled and outlawed the Spiritual Franciscans, thinking that they were dangerous to society. Occasionally, when they came back, they were burned. The point to be made, then, is that the Church and the state worked very closely together in order to establish a regime that was open to everyone who accepted the basic rules. If you started to challenge those rules, you were often in some measure of difficulty.

We've seen how the Dominicans responded under the regime of Savonarola; how this millenarian preacher rejected completely the classical Humanism, the secular art, the practice of 15th-century classical learning. He called it "pagan." He said that it got in the way of salvation—that property, desire for things of this world, would simply impede your movement to the next.

His dominion over Florence after 1494, as we've seen, constituted a repudiation of almost everything that the classical humanists believed. The Burning of the Vanities, then, illustrated dramatically his hatred of the things of this world. It was a very clear signal of what he thought of the acquisition of wealth and treasure. He thought that these things were not just unnecessary; he saw them as evil intrinsically.

His ideas, as we've seen in Florence, sparked a flame. There was obvious resentment, especially by those who had been marginalized, who previously had been under the influence of the Spiritual

Franciscans. These people, especially the poor, women, those who were left out of the humanist explosion of culture and largely left out of the economic and political structure of the city, saw that their hope was in the Church and salvation. But it was not the Church that they saw around them headed by the pope and presided over by elegant bishops. Their Church was much more a kind of Church of the spirit, a Church that was often in opposition to the very structure that they saw in the Church in power. For them, then, they were concerned that there was a growing distancing, an alienation, between what should be the basic simple Christian message and the elaborate, powerful institution of the Church militant.

Well, we also saw how the Church responded. Savonarola was called by Alexander VI to Rome, and the pope tried the way the pope had succeeded with St. Francis to co-opt him; make him part of the solution; bring Savonarola so that he could take his spiritualism and actually use it to effect some form of reform, perhaps in the Church or, more likely, get him close to Rome, where he could be either silenced or even burned as a heretic.

But what was seen as a consequence of the pope's attempt to silence Savonarola was again a recognition of this tension—a tension between those who saw religion as a largely spiritual function, and those who saw religion as a set of sacramental and confessional responsibilities, presided over by a wealthy and sophisticated institution, which very often was quite separate from the actual beliefs that they held internally.

Well, this background, this set of assumptions, the two kinds of Christianity in Italy during the period of the Renaissance, became focused, in part, by the revolt of Martin Luther. When Martin Luther, on October 31, 1517, nailed his 95 Theses on the castle Church door at Wittenberg, he began a revolution, the likes of which Europe had not seen for a very long time. He began to challenge that institutional Church and its structure; he began to challenge the authority of the pope and the right of the Church to do certain things that Martin Luther said belonged, really, only to God. And he had a different model of faith that was, really, quite at odds with what the institutional Church, certainly in Italy, taught.

The pope and the institutional Church responded badly to Luther. Initially, the pope, who was Leo X de'Medici—that extremely civilized, polished young man who really thought this was just another quarrel amongst religious orders—thought that Luther, the Augustinian canon, was simply attacking the Dominicans the way religious orders had always squabbled. He failed to recognize what Luther was really about. And it was only in 1520 that he was forced to excommunicate Luther, when Luther had gone even too far for an irenic peace-loving pope like Leo, in calling for the German Church to be separated from the Roman confession.

But the institutional Church may have rejected Luther, but there were individual Churchmen and large numbers of individuals in Italy who listened to this message with a good deal of sympathy. Luther seemed to be saying, perhaps with more invective than they would like, but Luther seemed to be saying something that they, too, believed—that is that there was need of a deeper spirituality, a deeper sense of the personal acceptance of religion, rather than simply the following of the sacramental responsibilities of Catholicism.

This, I think, is connected with so many of the Renaissance ideas of individuality and the idea of the autonomous spirit. Many of these individuals were very, very highly educated humanists. They were those who saw that there was a connection between the ability to function in this world in a secular manner, and the responsibility of the individual to take some measure of action for his or her spiritual and personal lives. Consequently, these deeply spiritual, somewhat concerned individuals managed to put together not exactly a faction or a party, but certainly a movement of influential individuals. And influential they were.

This group consisted of powerful, wealthy nobles in the Church, such as Cardinal Gasparo Contarini, the great Venetian who was not only a Venetian patrician, but a prince of the Church; and Reginald Pole, the cousin of Henry VIII of England, who would ultimately be Queen Mary's Archbishop of Canterbury, who, too, had this desire for spiritual fulfilment and a desire to reform the Church in both a spiritual and structural way. There was Gian Matteo Giberti, the Bishop of Verona, who had been papal datary, one of the great offices of the *Curia*, with access to great wealth, great influence, and great power, but who chose to resign the office, and go to his see of

Verona, refusing all further offers of advancement in the Church so he could live as a model bishop.

These individuals, and those who were in sympathy with them, formed groups to talk about Church reform; they often galvanized the ideas that they saw coming from Germany and Luther. They wanted to reform the Church, then, in a way that would allow the Schism to be healed, so that the Roman Church could move closer to the Lutheran model and the Lutheran model could then accept some of the structural elements of the Roman Church.

The death of Leo X and the election—surprise election; no one anticipated it—of an ascetic Dutchman, Adrian VI—who had never even been to Rome, but who wanted to reform the Church in a profound way—gave them some measure of hope. He had reformist ideas. He thought that the Church should be altered in order to reflect a much more purely spiritual sense of calling, rather than the administrative needs of this large multinational corporation known as the Roman Church.

The Italian reformers—who broadly were called *Spirituali*, the spiritual ones—attracted followers that moved beyond the ecclesiastical institutions and eventually included princes, and artists, and poets. The most significant and interesting of these was Michelangelo, who was an active *Spirituali* and who wrote some of the most wonderful Neoplatonic religious poetry of his age. But the 1520s made any hope of reconciliation between the reformers in the Roman Church in Italy and the Lutherans impossible.

The events were such that it was really difficult to even sustain dialogue. Adrian VI was a total failure as a reformer. He himself lived in an extremely restricted ascetic life, and he tried to impose that on others. The cardinals and bishops of the Church didn't much like it; they didn't much like his high-handed methods, his lack of sympathy with Italian and Roman tradition, and his lack of sympathy for the city of Rome. When he died, he was not mourned, and in his place was elected another Medici pope.

Four years later, the sack of Rome happened. The terrible events of the sack of Rome weakened a good deal of sympathy for Luther's position, especially among common people. So many of the Lutheran soldiers who committed those terrible atrocities said they did so, not so they could just rape, and pillage, and destroy, but they said that they were punishing the anti-Christ. They said they were acting as God's instruments. Well, of course, they weren't, and the Spanish Catholic soldiers, who did exactly the same thing, didn't use that sort of vocabulary, but it was clear that their real interest had nothing to do with religion and a good deal to do with violence and personal gain.

Nevertheless, the idea of Lutherans, and the sack of Rome, and especially the propaganda campaign that followed the sack of Rome, in which the Lutherans argued that this was, in fact, God's judgment, did alienate those who thought that there could be reconciliation.

In 1536, the new pope, Paul III Farnese, realized, though, that there had to be an attempt to reform the Church, or the Roman Church would continue to lose large numbers of adherents, and whole provinces, and much revenue to the new religions. So, he decided that there had to be a commission, a kind of group of extremely well-educated individuals who had sympathy with reform, who could advise him. And he established a committee—a committee that consisted of men like Contarini; those who could engage in dialogue with the Lutherans because they were known to have sympathy with many of the things that Luther taught.

And in 1538, they submitted their report, one of the great documents of 16th-century Church history. It was called *On the Reform of the Church*, or in Latin, *Consilium de ecclesia emendanda*. It was a radical document that reflected not only the need for fundamental structural reform in the Church, but also some clear recognition that much of what Luther was saying could be compatible with Catholic theology and Catholic teaching.

It failed. It failed because in many ways it was too radical, and also events in Europe were overtaking any possibility that there could be reconciliation between the old and the new religions. There were meetings to try and attempt to bridge the chasm between the two groups, but they all failed. They failed either over an element of theology or, more usually, because the questions were simply too complex to really deal with such a volatile, changing political, and theological, and religious environment.

By 1542, then, it was obvious that something had to be done that wasn't simply an attempt to forge links with the new religion. And Paul III did what was necessary, and it was an act of great courage. Realizing that reconciliation was largely impossible, he established the Roman Inquisition in 1542.

The Inquisition was something that had long roots in Catholicism. We all know the Spanish Inquisition of the 15th century that was established just before the period of the re-conquest in order to link the Iberian peninsula through the only institution that really did provide some glue for all Spaniards, and that was the Church—and also an instrument that would be directed towards the heterodox groups on the Iberian peninsula, the Moors and the Jews.

We also know that each diocese had its own Inquisition. It was important for the bishop to make a decision about what someone was saying—if it was true in orthodox, or if it was false in heterodox. So the idea of Inquisition was always there, but it was always local. It depended on local circumstances. The degree of its severity depended on the personality of the bishop, or on the character of the circumstance of the politics, and economics, and social structure of the region.

The year 1542 was different. The year 1542 established an Inquisition from Rome: a central body—a central office—that would command what was true and what was false; a central office that would determine, through the office of the papacy, what was going to be accepted and what was going to be denounced.

As a result of the Roman Inquisition of 1542 and the centralization of belief and theology, there was a flight of a number of reform-minded Catholics from the Church in order to seek some kind of union with the Protestant forces to the north. A number of Catholic thinkers—some of them extremely influential, like Bernardino Ochino, the general of the Dominicans, the most popular and greatest preacher in all of Italy, who fled to the Protestants, ending his life ultimately in London, where he not only was the most popular preacher at the Italian Church, but also a powerful influence on the future Queen Elizabeth.

These individuals, with their active flight, reinforced in the Church the belief that there could be no reconciliation, rather that there had to be a firm line drawn, and the Inquisition was the instrument in order to do it. The Inquisition would make sure that that wall between Catholics and Protestants would be high and insurmountable. You either believed, or you didn't. You were one of us, or you were one of them.

Those left in Rome, then, became much more conservative. And Paul III realized that he had a responsibility to direct this and to try and control the circumstance—which, in a theological sense, was somehow getting out of control. He then called the Great Council of Trent to meet in a northern Italian city. It was brilliant to not have the meeting in Rome, but just across the frontier from the German-speaking territories; it was seen as an act of reconciliation. But the reality was that this long Council that was to meet between 1545 and 1563—with some interruptions, but almost 20 years of theological debate—would ultimately determine the nature of the Roman Church in contradistinction to the other sects of the Protestants.

Its mandate was to confront Protestant theology and to reaffirm Catholic doctrine by defining it clearly, and by enforcing and reinforcing the faith. It was to crush heretical ideas and clarify what was to be done and how. And the Great Council of Trent did revitalize the Church. The authority of the pope was confirmed, and the apostolic succession from St. Peter was recognized. The Protestant notion of salvation by faith alone was rejected in favor of the Catholic doctrine of works as being necessary to achieve heaven.

All seven sacraments were confirmed, again rejecting the Protestant reduction to three. And the authority of Scripture was not sufficient, but the teachings of the Church over the previous 1,500 years had to be taken into account, believing that the Church militant did, in fact, reflect the Church triumphant, and that there was a need for the inspiration of God to be acting among the faithful, even after the period of the Incarnation.

The clergy, though, were to be better-educated and better trained, sparking the explosion of seminaries across Europe. And the abuses in the Church that the Protestants could point to so effectively, represented by so many Renaissance popes and bishops—simony, and pluralism, and nepotism—these were to be abolished and not practiced anymore.

To stop the spread of heretical ideas and to ensure that those who were faithful would remain faithful, in 1559, there was established the *Index of Prohibited Books*. It was now established from Rome, from another central office, what Catholics could and could not read. If you owned a book on this *Index*, or if you were known to have knowledge of this content, the punishment was severe, because then you obviously had sympathy with heresy, and you, perhaps, could, in fact, be a point of heretical leadership yourself. All ideas now had to be approved before they could be spread.

We, of course, get our modern terms of *imprimatur*, let it be printed, and *nihil obstat*, let no obstruction be seen in the printing of this book, as the reaction to the *Index*. These are things that enter our vocabulary because the *Index* entered our collective unconscious as a sense of directing the faithful along carefully recognized lines.

Moreover, the Church created new institutions in order to confront the Protestant threat. The most powerful of this was the Jesuit Order. The Jesuits, or the Society of Jesus, was recognized by Paul III in 1540. It was established by a Basque nobleman named Ignatius Loyola who, wounded in battle, saw during his period of convalescence a book that he was to write. He had a vision that lasted eight days, the consequence of which was not just the shape of the Order he would found, but *The Spiritual Exercises*, his great book.

The book is not a book of theology; it's a book of discipline; it's a book to discipline the individual spirit to be always respectful of— and obedient to—the Church and its leader. The Jesuit Order was to be almost military in its structure because Loyola thought like a soldier. And these were, in fact, the vanguard, the shock troops, of the new Catholic Counter-Reformation. They were to build their Order around three basic functions: preaching, teaching, and missionary activity.

The preaching was not just to reinforce the faith of Catholics, but to try and win back those souls lost to Protestants. This was missionary activity, because Europe had now contacted the rest of the world and came into contact with people who had not known Christianity, and the Jesuits were concerned that when they were converted, that they be converted to its Roman model rather than to any other sect. And, it was also teaching activity; the Jesuit schools were amongst the best schools in all of Europe, and they remain so, to some extent, to this very day. And one of the ironies was that a classical education based on humanist models provided the foundation for the curriculum, but it was not to open minds for debate, but rather it was to provide ammunition to prove that those who were heterodox were wrong. It was to create a common culture so that the educated elite across the continent could still discuss, regardless of their confessional allegiance; but, those trained in the Jesuit schools would have the ability through logic and rhetorical skill to argue down those who believed the wrong things.

The structure of the Jesuits, the effect of the Council of Trent, the revitalization of the Roman Church as a consequence of that Council, and the intention of the papacy and its office to make sure that Catholicism would not only survive, but begin to win back some souls, meant that Italy became a different place. As we'll see, ideas that previously could be discussed freely, a world where ideas could flow easily in print and from the lips of learned men, a world in which what one believes in one's confessional life was largely between the individual and his confessor, had passed.

The circumstances of the first decades of the 16th century, then, were not only upheavals in politics and economics; they were upheavals in religion and in the very mental structure and cultural model of Italy. Italy was a very different place as a result of the Reformation, the Council of Trent, the *Index of Prohibited Books*, and so many of those other things that required a single belief that all adhered to. This was an anathema in many ways to Humanism, and it created a very different kind of world.

Lecture Thirty-Five
The End of the Renaissance in Italy

Scope:

It is very difficult to establish when a period such as the Renaissance ended. What is clear, however, is that the Italian world was a very different place in 1550 from what it had been in 1450. There are particular events that can illustrate why that dramatic change occurred: the French invasions of 1494; the failure of the Italian states to work together consistently to protect the peninsula; the sack of Rome in 1527; and the closure of free thought, debate, and experimentation by the Church and its secular supporters after mid-century. Moreover, the victory of despotic monarchical regimes in such states as Florence ended the competitive, energetic world of the republic, replacing it with a singular, official ideology and power that everyone, regardless of rank or genius, had to obey. Art and literature, then, reflected increasingly the patronage and needs of princes and their servants, and these were not universally talented. Furthermore, the voyages of discovery in the later 15th century had moved the economic center of Europe from the Mediterranean to the Atlantic seaboard. It was now cheaper to buy spices and luxury goods in Lisbon or Seville than in Venice or Florence, because the route around Africa was faster and incurred fewer charges and dangers. The incessant wars of the period drained money that could have been spent on patronage, and religious debate consumed everyone. The consequence was a loss of the forces that had initially given rise to the Renaissance mentality: confidence and will. The disasters that befell Italy ended the belief that "man is the measure of all things" and that "man can do anything if he but wills."

Outline

I. The Renaissance in Italy can be seen to have declined with the conditions that encouraged its development two centuries earlier.

    A. Italy lost control of its political destiny.

        1. The sack gave the Holy Roman Emperor, Charles V, control over the papacy and most of Italy, as was recognized in Charles's papal coronation as emperor in Bologna in 1529.

2. With Habsburg power dominant, every state had to craft policy that the imperials would find acceptable.

3. Milan and Naples were ruled directly by Habsburg governors.

4. Florence was a client state of the empire.

5. The only truly independent Italian state, Venice, was fighting a life-and-death struggle with the Turks in the Mediterranean; thus, it, too, wanted security in Europe and was unwilling to take chances.

B. Therefore, the competition among the states of the peninsula that had given rise to different experiments in constitutional structure, statecraft, and social organization ceased.

1. A singular model of monarchical government was adopted in every major state but Venice.

2. The new importance of princely courts, and the examples of the Spanish nobles helping to administer the peninsula, destroyed whatever memories remained of ideas of republican participatory government.

3. Even social mores, customs, and behavior became courtly.

4. Trade was shunned as "bourgeois" in favor of landed wealth.

5. Participation in society was accomplished through service at court, in the Church, in learned academies, or in the military.

6. Government was left to the prince.

II. The enormous concentrations of wealth that had resulted from the Italian monopoly over long-distance luxury trade collapsed by the turn of the 16th century.

A. The center of the European economy shifted from the Mediterranean to the Atlantic coast.

1. The fall of Constantinople in 1453 and Turkish aggression in the Mediterranean and in southeastern Europe signaled an end to Italian control of the Mediterranean.

2. The end of The Hundred Years' War in that same year permitted the economic recovery of the Low Countries, England, and France, now able to complete with Italy for markets.

3. The Portuguese voyages of discovery led to direct sea routes to Asia, making the Italian middlemen superfluous.

4. The Spanish voyages, especially those of Columbus, gave Spain access to the vast wealth of the New World.

B. The Italians did not participate in these expansions, except as the captains and cartographers who actually sailed for Spain, France, or England.

1. The problems of Italy meant that Italians could not imagine new, daring enterprises: They were focused on self-preservation.

2. The challenges to Italy drove the most dynamic Italians into a conservative, defensive posture and found them working to keep the known markets they knew in the Mediterranean rather than searching for new opportunities.

3. This can be best illustrated in ship design: The Portuguese had demonstrated the dramatic flexibility of new forms of ship architecture, but the Italians continued to build huge galleys that were useless outside the Mediterranean.

C. As early as the 1520s, the Italians knew that their economic dominance was over, but they did nothing about it.

1. They had lost their will as a result of decades of war, humiliating defeat, and foreign intervention.

2. They sought security in safe ground rents, secure but low-yielding investments, and conspicuous consumption.

3. Trade was just too uncertain and personally dangerous.

III. The Reformation and Counter-Reformation made ideas dangerous rather than exciting, inhibiting challenges to the status quo.

    A. Princes in Europe were encouraged to use force to convert their subjects and war to defeat Protestants.

        1. Charles V and his son, Philip of Spain, warred constantly in the name of Catholicism against the Dutch, the English, and the German Protestants.

        2. The French Wars of Religion were among the most terrible on the continent.

        3. All these events spilled into Italy directly as a result of Habsburg control of large parts of the peninsula and a desire on the part of the ecclesiastical establishment to keep Protestants and Protestant ideas out of Italy.

    B. By the mid-16th century, the free exchange of ideas that had given such an impetus to the Renaissance was suppressed through such instruments as the Roman Inquisition and the Index of Prohibited Books.

        1. Scholars, teachers, and educated individuals were afraid to speak if there was any chance their words could be construed as heretical.

        2. Secular rulers, wanting to keep peace with the Church and with the Habsburg power in Italy, supported this suppression of thought and speech, often enforcing the Index and arresting heretics.

        3. Religious oaths were required from those who wished to graduate from universities.

        4. Society became much more conservative, with people looking for safe, solid, and secure places, without the taint of controversy.

    C. Basic ideas central to the Renaissance mentality were questioned or rejected.

        1. Such concepts as the dignity of man were hard to sustain after the sack of Rome, the St. Bartholomew's Day Massacre (1572) in France, and the burning and persecution of heretics.

2. The suppression of new ideas shattered the belief that man is the measure of all things: Rather, the measure of all things was man as approved by God through the Church.

3. Man could no longer do anything if he but willed it: There were a great many things, carefully noted and circulated, that man could not do without incurring torture, imprisonment, and death.

IV. Although it is tempting to assign the end of the Renaissance to a specific date or event, such as the establishment of the Roman Inquisition in 1542, this is too sharp a break and too specific a moment.

A. On the other hand, there can be no doubt but that Italy in 1550 was a dramatically different place from Italy in 1450, as is most clearly illustrated through the example of Florence.

1. In 1450, Florence was a vibrant republic, managed with consent by the Medici family.

2. Civic Humanism was the dominant ideology among the political classes, with Neoplatonism offering an acceptable alternative for those more interested in scholarship than politics or trade.

3. The economy flourished, with the republican government providing support for the mercantile ambitions of its citizens.

4. Foreign policy was coalescing into a new alliance with Milan that would result in 40 years of stability and relative peace.

5. In every field, competition and genius were the means to success.

B. In contrast, Florence in 1550 was an absolute monarchy in which Cosimo, a creature of the Habsburgs in foreign affairs, supported the orthodoxy of the Church, which solemnized his rule.

1. The government functioned to preserve and increase the power of the duke, not his citizens.

2. Trade was increasingly seen as dangerous and inappropriate for those patricians wanting court appointments and noble titles.

3. Art and architecture were creatures of the singular patronage of the prince and served to flatter and aggrandize him.

4. Feudalism had been reintroduced into the countryside.

5. The route to success had shifted from ability to clientage, connections, and flattery.

V. In conclusion, then, what we see is a failure of the conditions that had permitted the Renaissance to develop and thrive.

A. But this is true not only in economic, military, and political spheres.

B. The end of the Renaissance represented a failure of will.

1. The self-reinforcing energizing myth that drove men to do great things, simply because they believed they could, evaporated into a tendentious acceptance of tyranny and, all too often, of mediocrity, because at least it was safe.

2. Freedom and struggle were just not worth the effort.

Primary Source Texts:

Giovanni Della Casa, *Il Galateo*.

Secondary Sources:

Chris F. Black, *Church, Religion and Society in Early Modern Italy*.

William Bouwsma, *The Waning of the Renaissance, 1550–1640*.

Supplementary Reading:

Gregory Hanlon, *Early Modern Italy, 1550–1800*.

Questions to Consider:

1. Can ideas die?

2. Are there other examples of a vital society giving up on freedom because it proved just too demanding to sustain?

Lecture Thirty-Five—Transcript
The End of the Renaissance in Italy

It's very difficult to determine why and when an historic period ends. In some instances, it's quite easy. The French Revolution clearly ended the ancient regime and began a new set of principles and values in which European society could be built. The First World War was sufficiently cataclysmic and altered so much of the European state system that it can be seen as ending the 19th century and that tradition of state building in the continent.

But the Renaissance is something different. I'm going to argue that the Renaissance declined and came to an end, in Italy at least, as a result of the cessation of those very principles and values that gave rise to it. The Renaissance ended because its energizing myth was no longer believed.

If you remember my introductory lecture—the idea of an energizing myth, the idea of people believing in a set of principles that then galvanized their action to behave in a particular way, to open their mind to certain sets of ideas and to change the way they looked at their world, and their relationship to their world, and to one another—all of this came to an end as a consequence of the circumstances that we've been discussing in the past few lectures.

It's necessary to look specifically and to see exactly how these things manifested themselves to prove my argument that, in 1550, Italy was a very different place from Italy in 1450. First of all, Italy lost control of its own political destiny. The sack of Rome gave the Holy Roman Emperor Charles V control over not just the papacy for a period of time, but, as a result of the arrangement with Pope Clement VII, control over the peninsula. The coronation of Charles in Bologna in 1529 wasn't just the last imperial coronation in Italy, it was recognition that Charles was, in many ways, Emperor of Italy.

With the Habsburgs dominant throughout the entire peninsula, then, almost every state had to craft its policy so that that policy would be, in many ways, compatible with imperial desire and imperial design. The idea of states acting independently—not just in foreign policy, but also in domestic policy—would be impossible, given the overwhelming authority that the emperor had throughout the continent, and in Italy in particular.

Milan and Naples were ruled directly by Habsburg governors. Florence was a client state of the empire. And the only truly independent Italian state, Venice, was fighting a life and death struggle against the Turks in the Mediterranean. And after the terrible events of Agnadello in 1509 and the War of the League of Cambray, with the almost complete destruction of a *terra firma* empire of the Venetian Republic, the Venetians were very circumspect. They had no desire to get involved in the struggles of the continent or of Italy. They wanted to husband their resources, and fight the Turks, and try and sustain some measure of their maritime empire. The Venetians decided to stay out of this debate, and in so doing, the only major independent Italian state did not take part in what was to become the complete and total reorganization of the Italian political world.

Therefore, the competition among states that I argued earlier as one of the fundamental driving forces of Renaissance experimentation and constitutional structure, and in statecraft and social organization, all stopped. That mosaic of states, that fragmentation of authority that constituted Italy during the period of the Renaissance, resulted in constant and almost obsessive competition. They wanted to not just perfect the internal operation of each individual place, but they wanted to outdo their neighbors. They wanted to succeed in all ways—not just economically and militarily, but also culturally and intellectually.

That experimentation, then, allowed for a thousand flowers not just to bloom, but, in fact, to be carefully cultivated. With a single model imposed, with a single Habsburg hegemony over the continent and over the Italian peninsula, there was nothing that was left of this experimentation. It simply no longer worked, nor could it work. All that mattered was that you met the needs of the emperor.

A single model, then, of monarchical government, with the exception of Venice, descended upon all of Italy. Almost every state, including those with very long republican traditions, became principalities, became monarchies. It was the requirement. It was a necessity. And in many instances, it was something that most of the citizens gleefully accepted because there was a belief that at least a prince, as

Machiavelli had argued, could provide some measure of consistent policy and some sense of security. This was not a time for experimentation. It was too dangerous. It was a time for safety, for security, for stability, and princes at least seemed to offer that.

With the spread of princely courts, the model of aristocratic behavior, the examples of the Spanish nobles who came with the Habsburgs in order to administer their territories and to attend them, the Spanish officers who were in the armies of the Habsburgs, these provided a different model of behavior from the republican magistrates in a city like Florence. These were aristocrats. Their traditions were feudal; their traditions were based upon landholding nobility; their traditions were fighting on horseback and chivalric romance.

They weren't interested in debates and the application of classical rhetoric to republican government, because they were irrelevant. And, in many ways, as they would find them somewhat loathsome because government was the purview of the prince, they served the prince; they did not serve one another.

The result is that the ideas of republican participatory democracy that we've seen as one of the engines of Renaissance culture—modeled on Florence, but also able to find residence elsewhere—simply stopped functioning. The new example, the new primary role of the articulate citizen, was to guide the prince and provide good counsel. It was no longer to argue the truth in the counsel of his fellows.

Even in social terms and social morass—aristocratic behavior, and dress, and means of interpersonal relations became standard. We see the growing number of books and manners of how to dress and act like a Spaniard, how to use the language in such a way as to provide the greatest amount of almost euphuistic praise. Gone then was that plain, effective, rhetorical speech modeled on Cicero and his republican virtue. These things no longer obtained.

The model of Cicero's republican virtue, in fact, was seen as a failure. It failed Cicero—he was murdered by Mark Anthony's thugs; it failed the republic because it died with him. So why address it now? Why keep it alive? Why argue for a system that not only didn't work, but, in fact, had failed once and seemed to have failed again? Let's go with the winner. Let's accept this monarchy, this stability, this order, this fixed world, and let's adopt the terms of address, and let's adopt those elements of interpersonal discourse that are based upon recognition of rank and honor. It's easier. It's more appropriate, and it also makes for good poetry.

Trade was increasingly shunned as "bourgeois." It was inappropriate for someone of noble rank, for a gentleman, to engage in trade. The Italians had not reached the stage of the French, for example, where to engage in trade was to result in your being *derogé*, losing your aristocratic rank automatically, but it was considered inappropriate. It was considered unsuitable, as the Italians would say *non sta bene*. It wasn't appropriate for a young man of some measure of hope, of good family, of good connections, to become a merchant. It was much more appropriate to serve the community in other ways: to serve at court; to become the servant of a prince; to be a gentleman of the prince's bedchamber; to be a page. It was better to serve in the Church, to help the spiritual nature of humanity—everything was fixed. There was a clear *cursus honorum*; the Church was a good, safe, and reasonable place for an intelligent and articulate young man.

Enter an academy if you want to marry, and have a family, and stay secular. The academies are safe and fine. They have the patronage of the prince, or the patronage of the Church. They allow you to engage in debate. They can permit you to use your flights of rhetoric and your classical knowledge, but not in a way that would disturb anyone. It's safe and secure. It's controlled. You know your limits. You know the purpose. And you know the conclusions that you have to reach.

Or serve in the army. The army is the easiest. Obey orders. Do what you're told. Be heroic. Be a hero. Be recognized. Be decorated. And you'll be able, then, to walk beside your prince as an honored companion. This, then, was safe and secure as well. Everything was made clear.

What was gone was the world of the elected magistrate—the idea of the individual recognized as having ability through the exercise of language and reason, and that person then being seen as someone with responsibility automatically because of his personal qualities to lead others. No longer were personal qualities required because government was no longer required of magistrates. Government was the independent, singular monopoly of the prince. The prince owned government and rule; others did what the prince told them. It was a government of obedience. It was a government of accepting authority.

The magistrate, then, was, in fact, not only no longer respected, but someone who, if insisting upon independent action, was dangerous. Added to that instability, that insecurity, do what the prince says, follow the rules, do what you're told and things will turn out much better.

If the political decline of Italy was tragic, the economic decline was even more so. The total collapse of the Italian economy by the 17th century was presaged clearly in the 16th century. It was not just that single greatest revolution, almost an economic history in the west, the movement of the center of the economic world of Europe away from that *media terra*, that center of the earth of the Mediterranean towards the Atlantic seaboard; it was also all the things that fell from that shift.

Why the shift happened, of course, we've already discussed. The conquest of Constantinople by the Turks in 1453, the expansion of the Turkish Empire, the challenging of the Italian trade routes to the east, the loss of the monopoly on those luxury goods—all of these things, then, drove the Italian economy into very, very much a subsidiary position.

But then other events—the end of The Hundred Years War and the rise of indigenous industries challenging the Italians, such as the woolen industry in the Low Countries—similarly, the rise of great territorial monarchies and nation states in the north allowed for them to develop their own money markets. Italians were no longer the only bankers available with large concentrations of capital.

By the 16th century, the great German firms of Fugger and Wesler had far more in capital than the Medici ever dreamed of, because they were able to finance an empire, the empire of Charles V, and they were able to launder—through their huge accounts and enormous numbers of branches throughout the Habsburg world—the vast sums coming in from the new world.

But it was the Portuguese voyages of discovery that really ended the Italian hegemony. Once the Portuguese proved that you could sail around the coast of Africa and sail directly from a seaport in Portugal to Asia, then that monopoly that had been celebrated from the time of Marco Polo that the Italians had enjoyed, that had give them such wealth and such influence on the continent, simply ended.

As early as 1510, spices from Asia cost 20% what the Venetians were charging. So, where would you buy? The decline of the Italian economy was catastrophic, and it was very, very quick. It was quick because it was part of a larger set of events that we've already seen developing and unfolding. These things coincided with the French invasions of 1494 and the French invasions of 1500, using Italy as the battlefield of Europe, and the struggle between Habsburg and Valois, the sack of Rome—so many of the things that we've touched upon. The Lutheran revolt and the loss of so much revenue for the Church that otherwise would have flowed to Rome and helped rebuild not just the institution of the Church, but the great buildings that represented that institution—all of these things came together. And the final moment was the vast wealth that the voyages of discovery brought into the Spanish and Portuguese crowns.

In particular, Spain seemed to have an inexhaustible amount of gold and silver as a result of their mines in South America and Central America. There were no ways that the Italians could possibly respond to this. The concentration of capital from trade was nothing like the looting of an entire continent and the destruction of another civilization. The Italians simply recognized it and wept.

One of the ironies, and something that's often pointed out, is that the great voyages of discovery often were directed by Italians; not just Cristoforo Colombo, but also John Cabot, Giovanni Caboto, Verrazano, and Amerigo Vespucci—who gave his name to our continent. But these were Italians who didn't sail for Genoa or Venice; they sailed for Spain, for England, for France. They set out for the new world, and they drew the maps, and they made sure that the ships got to where they were going. But they benefited others. They enriched the states of the north, rather than Italy.

The Italians didn't participate in these voyages of discovery, except as a servant of others. And this, of course, was a tragedy. And it illustrated so well why it was that the Italian economy and the Italian civilization of the Renaissance fell into such rapid decline. The challenges to Italy were such that the Italians themselves felt that they just didn't have the resources; they didn't have the energy; they didn't have the self-confidence to engage in this sort of thing themselves. They looked desperately to try and save what they knew. The Venetians struggled for over a century and a half against the Turks, trying to keep some of their empire in the Mediterranean and the eastern world alive, when they should have realized there was essentially no hope.

They struggled, then, to maintain their old world when a new world was being born, which they helped create, but they refused to recognize and participate in. A single example perhaps illustrates this best. The Portuguese were constantly experimenting with ship design and ship architecture, trying to find those flexible models that would ultimately create the Caravelle and other ships that would sail so brilliantly across the Atlantic Ocean and, ultimately, around the known world.

The Venetians and the Italians continued to build huge, wide-beamed, shallow-draft galleys. Galleys were perfect for the Mediterranean. But if they sailed out beyond the Straits of Gibraltar, they'd be smashed like matchsticks in the first great storm. The Italians didn't experiment with ship design. They didn't experiment with anything. They simply held on to what they knew. In times of crisis the natural response is a conservative knee-jerk to try and keep what you've got. And here was a failure. The Italians failed to confront the new reality, even though they were aware of it, perhaps better than anyone, because those who were creating and defining that new reality—the sailors, the captains, the cartographers—were, in fact, Italians. But the Italians got nothing from it.

As early as the 1520s, the Italians were well aware that their economic dominance was over; but, their response was to just try and salvage little bits and pieces, so they at least, in their generation, could lead comfortable lives. They had lost their will—the result of decades of war, of humiliating defeat, of foreign intervention. Why risk your life for fighting the Turks? Why risk your life for long-distance trade when at least you can live comfortably and raise your children relatively well? Or, if you have great wealth, why risk it on this terrible adventure? Why not just engage in conspicuous consumption and show everyone that you've got it? Why not just enjoy what you have because tomorrow is so uncertain?

The sense of terrible uncertainty, the sense of foreboding in doom, characterized—in so many ways—the Italian mentality. They had, in fact, been brutalized. They had been invaded. They had been subjugated. They had been economically, and militarily, and politically defeated. It's no wonder, then, that they didn't stand and try and resurrect their culture and their economic and political position. They essentially gave in. Stability and security, then, were bought at a very high price, but Italians were willing to pay it because they had come to believe, tragically, that they had no other choice.

The same is true in the realm of ideas. In the early lectures, I suggested the Renaissance wasn't really a time from one set of years to another, but rather it was a set of ideas that drove thinking men and women to adopt certain perspectives; to create different models and instruments; to try and define life and the world according to a set of terms and values they held dear. But the world of ideas they knew simply evaporated, crushed by circumstance once more.

The Reformation and, in particular, the Counter-Reformation in Italy made ideas themselves dangerous. Ideas were no longer exciting. They no longer galvanized individuals to try and find truth or the solution to complex problems through rhetorical exercise, and debate, and dialogue. Now, ideas were seen as suspect. They could be seen as being challenging to the status quo. It's best to simply do what you're told, to believe what you're taught, and leave ideas to others whose job it is to deal with them under close control: the academies, or the Church, or those around the prince. To engage in too much thought, too much speculative thought on your own, could lead to the wrong conclusions, and everybody knows what the punishment is for a wrong answer.

Charles V and Philip of Spain warred constantly in the name of Catholicism against the Dutch, the English, and the German Protestants. And the French Wars of Religion indicated what happened when there was a division in the nation between Protestants and Catholics, when those who decided to fight for their principles and ideas actually picked up arms to do so. Those terrible confessional wars that divided people, that resulted in internecine warfare in which brother fought brother, is not something the Italians particularly wanted. They had seen that already as a result of the French invasions and the fragmentation of the peninsula.

They were looking for something else. They were looking for a set of ideas that would at least keep them together, that would give them a basic element of security. So, thought, discussion, debate—enter into the religious debate of the time, even though it was the single, most powerful set of ideas on the continent—not at all; it was too dangerous, unwise.

By the mid-16th century, then, the free exchange of ideas that had given so much of an impetus and so much energy to the Renaissance mind, to the creation of Renaissance culture and the Renaissance ideal, was simply forgotten—more than forgotten, it was actively suppressed. The Roman Inquisition suppressed it. The *Index of Prohibited Books* suppressed it. Scholars, teachers, educated individuals, were afraid to speak because there was a chance that their words could be misinterpreted, misconstrued. It's possible they would reach the wrong conclusion, and there were spies everywhere. And those spies could easily turn you in. You could be tortured. You could be burned. You could lose your property. You could be separated from your family. So, is it worth it? No, it's not. Stick to what you're told. Read what you're told to read. Do what you're told to do.

Secular rulers even followed this. They wanted to keep peace with the Church. The Church was a powerful institution, and one that gave divine and numinous power to their rule. It gave them authority. It gave them significance. It gave them ceremony. So why challenge it? And what's more, the Church is useful. The Church controlled dangerous ideas because those who were suspect in religion could easily be suspect in politics. Let's use the Office of the Inquisition. Let's use those spies that the Church had in order to see whether, in fact, there were challenges, movements of revolution, or discontent against the prince.

So it was in the best interest of the prince to support—to actively support—the hunting of heretics, the enforcing of the *Index*, the enforcing of the Inquisition. Religious oaths were required of graduates of universities and schools. Society became, then, far more conservative because it was just too dangerous to speak your mind.

Anything with the taint of controversy can be interpreted badly, so let's be safe. Let's be mediocre. Let's talk about things we already know, because to move beyond that is to challenge the forces that are so powerful they could crush us in a moment.

Basic ideas central to the Renaissance mentality, then, were questioned or rejected; concepts like the Dignity of Man. Who can believe in the Dignity of Man after the sack or Rome, after the St. Bartholomew's Day Massacre in France, in 1572? Who could possibly believe this with the burning of heretics and with the events of the wars in the peninsula? No dignity to man. This is an absurd idea. If there is dignity, it's the dignity of the soul the Church tells us we have.

The suppression of these ideas also made us all question whether man really is the measure of all things. Well, rather, man is the measure of all things approved by God, and the Church, and the prince. These things were fine. But all things? No, that's overreaching; it's dangerous.

Man could no longer do anything if he but willed it. There are a great many things carefully determined, described, and printed that you could not do—things that you could not do without being imprisoned, without being tortured, without being punished, or without being killed. There were, then, limits to human imagination, human ability, and human power. And you knew exactly what these limits were because they were made clear to you constantly through the *Index of Prohibited Books*, through the preaching of the Church, through the power of the prince, and through the Inquisition.

Although it's tempting to assign the end of the Renaissance to a particular moment, such as the sack of Rome or the establishment of the Roman Inquisition in 1542, it doesn't really work. An historic period doesn't really hinge on a particular event. But there's no doubt that Italy in 1550 was different from Italy in 1450. Let's just look at Florence as an example.

In 1450, Florence was a vibrant republic, managed with consent by the Medici family. Civic Humanism was the dominant ideology among the political classes; Neoplatonism offered a reasonable alternative for those who preferred study to the magistracy. The economy flourished, and the republican government provided support for the mercantile ambitions of its citizens. Foreign policy was coalescing into that new alliance with Milan that would bring stability and security to the Italian peninsula for 50 years. In every field, competition and genius were the means to success. That was the Florence of 1450.

Let's look at Florence, in contrast, in 1550. It was an absolute monarchy. It was a tyranny in which Cosimo, a creature of the Habsburgs in foreign affairs, supported the orthodoxy of the Church, which solemnized his rule, and, of course, it was the pope who gave him the title of Grand Duke of Tuscany. He was, then, a ruler, *papae gratia*, in many ways, and he supported and respected the Church as a result.

The government functioned to preserve and increase the power of the duke, not his citizens. Trade was increasingly seen as dangerous and inappropriate for those patricians who wanted to serve at court and bear aristocratic titles. Art and architecture were the extensions of princely patronage. They had to flatter the prince. They had to serve his needs. They weren't the result of genius acting freely so the best could rise. Art became propaganda, and architecture came to glorify the prince. Feudalism was reintroduced in the countryside. The route to success moved from ability and competition to clientage, birth, connection, and more often than not, flattery.

In conclusion, then, what I'm suggesting is that the Renaissance ended because the sets of attitudes and beliefs in self-confidence, that energizing myth that Cabot identified as the motive power of the Renaissance mind, simply ceased to function. The Renaissance could not continue in the form that it had. It couldn't be sustained, because, ultimately, the failure wasn't military, or political, or economic—although all of these provided the context for the truly great failure, which was psychological: the failure of will; the failure to confront the crises that the Italians knew that they were in; the decision, the hard decision, the decision that is so natural in human nature—to accept what is known, and safe, and stable.

The self-reinforcing energizing myth, then, that drove Italians to do such great things, to extend human experience so far in such a short period of time, to recover an entire literature and culture and apply it to their own needs, this evaporated. It evaporated into a tendentious acceptance of tyranny, or princely rule, on the part of second-rate princes who simply either were at the right place at the right time, or they were able to take the advice of Machiavelli in *The Prince* and simply exert power when needed.

Often, what they supported and what the Italians accepted as a reasonable compromise was mediocrity. The thing about mediocrity—whether it's in government, or politics, or economics, or art—is that it's safe. If something is mediocre, it doesn't challenge the weak and the unable; it doesn't set a standard that others feel they can never reach; it doesn't set a set of principles that make those who are in positions of power and authority feel insecure. Mediocrity is always safe. And to some extent, the Italians embraced mediocrity with a good deal of energy and excitement.

What they had learned over the previous century, the effect of the terrible events of the last decade of the 15th century and the first decades of the 16th century, is that freedom and genius were just too expensively bought. Ultimately, freedom just wasn't worth the effort. The genius is fine as long as it's contained and controlled. Genius uncontrolled and unconfined can lead you in areas that you cannot control or even foresee. These are uncharted waters. This puts you outside the realm of the new definition of the citizen in the community—that is, an obedient group who accepts what they're told, and believes it, and practices it, and celebrates it. In many ways, the late Italian Renaissance is a celebration of mediocrity, and therein lies its failure.

Lecture Thirty-Six
Echoes of the Renaissance

Scope:

This course has introduced, developed, and discussed the Italian Renaissance as a cultural and intellectual phenomenon in the political and social context of the Italian city-states. The remarkable efflorescence of culture that Italy witnessed from the mid-14th to the mid-16th century stands as a monument to the human imagination. That Italy failed politically and economically by the end of that period in many ways puts this achievement into clearer perspective. Castiglione suggests in *The Book of the Courtier* that individual cultivation can be successfully achieved by any man or woman who seeks knowledge, truth, love, and beauty, regardless of the circumstances, although hard times make the process more difficult. In some ways, the Italian Renaissance continued strongly into the last century, as ideals of beauty based on Naturalism, proportion, and the ability to reproduce what the eye sees remained the foundation of academic art. The role of antiquity continued in the architectural vocabulary of public buildings, and the central place of the Greek and Roman classics was sustained in the education of elite groups in every Western nation. It can be argued, then, that the echoes of the Renaissance died only in the 20th century, with the triumph of objective science over purely human values.

Outline

I. It has been suggested that the Renaissance is, in many ways, still a part of our daily lives.

    A. The ideals of 15th -century Italian art and architecture remained the foundation of the Western traditions until the early decades of the 20th century.

        1. Naturalism in art, with correct anatomy and linear perspective, lasted in academic painting and sculpture until very recently.

        2. Reproducing what the eye sees is still an important Western ideal, whether in painting or in photography.

3. The use of a classical vocabulary in architecture remained fundamental in building until the end of the Beaux-Arts period in the 1920s.

B. Certain principles that we have traced from Petrarch until the 16th century remain important elements of our collective characters in the West.

1. The primacy of individual experience is central, as is the belief that we have the capacity to create ourselves according to a set of principles that we choose to follow.

2. Each individual also has some degree of responsibility to the community and the community to him or her: These ideas are found clearly in the Florentine republic of the 15th century.

3. Participatory government is one of the foundations of our contemporary society.

4. Quality is best assured through competition, whether in the arts or in ideas.

5. Speech—the art of communication—is a good index of the appropriateness of an individual for public office.

6. And to achieve its goal, speech must be free.

C. It was a set of Renaissance Humanist principles that dominated elite education in the West well past the late-19th-century rise of science.

1. Education was viewed as a preparation for citizenship.

2. Learning was not just instrumental but designed to build character and values.

3. Education was expected to equip a young person for useful leisure.

4. Physical training to effect a sound mind in a sound body was a necessity.

5. Knowledge of ancient texts and the Greek and Latin languages in which they were written would equip a citizen to fulfill any role.

6. The texts used to study the ancient world were those recovered by Humanist scholars and published according to their disciplines of philology and editing.

II. The Renaissance invention of the individual has remained a powerful force in our self-definition.

A. Petrarch's concepts of romantic love have infused our own.

    1. We all trace the progress or trajectory of our love for another in terms not very different from Petrarch's record of his feelings for Laura.

    2. Platonic ideals of love find resonance, as well, in the principles of the uplifting power of love and the links among beauty, goodness, and truth.

    3. All forms of human experience are valid in teaching us and others about our common humanity.

B. The forms of literature developed or recovered by the Renaissance remain important.

    1. The psychological autobiography, resurrected by Petrarch after a thousand years of neglect, is one of the most common forms of personal contemporary memoir.

    2. The sonnet sequence invented by Petrarch defined poetic literature through Shakespeare, Sidney, and Spenser to Elizabeth Barrett Browning in the late 19th century.

    3. The primary genre of the Renaissance, the dialogue, remains an important instrument for reflecting on the complexity of ideas and the multiple perspectives of human discourse.

    4. Renaissance theater is still produced and still meaningful, as we see our common humanity rehearsed across centuries.

C. Such ideals as free will, with human agency the cause of the events in the world, are found in Renaissance historians from Bruni to Guicciardini and drive us to accept responsibility for our actions and our lives even today.

    1. Belief in the improvement of the individual person through education, example, and social support all reached maturity during the Renaissance.

    2. Concepts so closely associated with this belief, such as the dignity of man, survive as well, although with a more tenuous hold on our imaginations after the terrible events of the past century.

3. Is man still the measure of all things? Can he still do whatever he will?

4. That depends on who is responding and the context. Still, such principles remain with us as powerful motives for improving our own and our society's condition.

III. The Renaissance, as we noted at the beginning of this series, has been described by historians of science as retrograde from the Middle Ages.

A. There is no doubt but that the Aristotelian model of empirical observation contributed profoundly to an understanding of nature before the Renaissance.

1. But these principles were not suppressed, as the continued interest in Aristotle as a primary source for antiquity indicated.

2. Also, the Galenic medicine practiced during the Renaissance accorded with medieval education and medical knowledge.

3. Classical sources did tend to be seen as the final arbiter of knowledge, but the recovery of certain scientific texts, especially the geographers and mathematicians, did assist the movement of science: Not everything was based on Pliny's *Historia naturalis*.

B. Other elements of the Renaissance mind, in fact, made modern science possible.

1. The artistic obsession with perspective and reproducing what the eye sees made the replication of observation possible and reproducible.

2. If a plant or animal is observed and described in one place, an image of that animal or plant can be reproduced and disseminated widely for others to comment on.

3. Also, with the privileging of individual experience, the very process of experimentation in science was validated, because experimental science presupposes the ability of the individual to see, interpret, and describe a phenomenon correctly and clearly.

4. Equally, the voyages of discovery could not have happened without the self-confidence of the Renaissance mind to imagine a world beyond what was described in Scripture or ancient texts.

5. Then, using the principles of linear perspective, these newly found places can be measured and drawn in space, with relative distances clearly indicated for others to follow.

C. The evidence of this developing scientific interest can be seen in the remarkable moments of the 1540s, when so many of these ideas reached maturity.

1. In 1542, Nicholas Copernicus printed his text disproving the Greek Ptolemy's theory of the universe as geocentric.

2. Working mostly in Italy, Copernicus, a Polish priest, used mathematical tables to follow the paths of the celestial bodies that were visible to him.

3. Believing his data and despite the teachings of the ancients and the Church, he printed *De Revolutionibus* (*On the Orbits of the Heavenly Bodies*), confident in his individual observations and judgment.

4. The next year, in 1543, Andrea Vesalius, a Fleming working in Italy, had printed *De humani corporis fabrica*, a richly illustrated—and anatomically correct—description of the human body. Modern medicine was born.

5. At almost exactly the same time, the university in Italy where Vesalius taught, Padua, instituted its botanical gardens, the first in Europe, for the production of medicinal plants.

6. This was based both on ancient texts and Renaissance interest, but the modern connection between the pharmacopoeia and medical practice was institutionalized.

IV. Your choice to listen to these lectures is ample evidence that the Renaissance still resonates for us in the modern world.

A. As you have followed this series of lectures with me, I hope you have found yourself identifying with some of the elements of the Renaissance mentality.

    1. We must always remember that the Renaissance was a state of mind in so many ways: The concrete effects followed from those fundamental attitudes.

    2. There was a clear end to these elements of Renaissance self-definition, caused by internal failures of confidence and will and by external forces that sapped their strength.

    3. It must be a lesson for every society to be watchful for the threats that can serve to undermine the essence of the civilization built on these shared values.

B. Equally, however, the Renaissance can show us, as did Castiglione in his *Book of the Courtier*, that ideas and culture have a powerful resistance to violence, brutality, and ignorance.

    1. There are things we must keep safe to protect us against our ruin.

    2. I leave you with a Renaissance Humanist principle as an assignment to take away. Humanists constantly asked the question: "How might I lead a more humane life [*Quam sit humaniter vivendum*]?"

    3. This is a question still worth asking.

    4. And, if you share the principles we have discussed in this course, you might respond as would most of our Renaissance Humanist friends: It is incumbent upon us all to turn our lives into works of art, that is, carefully crafted, elegant models of individual behavior, closely working with others in free association to achieve the mutual goals of our shared humanity. These should include the pursuit and production of beauty, as well as the accumulation of wealth, and we must always be aware that culture and the society that sustains it are fragile. But that, in so many ways, makes its preservation even more necessary.

Secondary Sources:

Alan Bullock, *The Humanist Tradition in the West.*

Supplementary Reading:
Daniel J. Boorstin, *The Discoverers: A History of Man's Search to Know His World and Himself.*

Questions to Consider:
1. Is there a place for Humanism in the 21st century?
2. Are science and Humanism mutually exclusive?

Lecture Thirty-Six—Transcript
Echoes of the Renaissance

Although the Italian Renaissance as a period of time has passed, its memory is still very much with us. It's still very much part of our collective unconscious and or mental geography. We carry it with us when we look at art and buildings. We carry it with us when we read literature, and it still forms some of the structure in the way that we interpret the world.

The ideals of 15th-century Italian art, for example, and the architecture that arose from the rediscovery of Vitruvius, and the application of classical vocabulary to Italian needs, provided the foundation of the western tradition in art and architecture until the early decades of the 20th century. Naturalism in art, with correct anatomy and linear perspective—these things lasted in academic painting and sculpture until very recently indeed, and they still are often found in the teachings of art schools. Reproducing what the eye sees is still an important western ideal—whether in painting, or now in photography. And the use of that classical modeling in architecture, based upon the Greek and Roman examples that so clearly flowed from the recovery of ancient knowledge, was fundamental in building until the end of the beaux-arts period in the 1920s.

Also, certain principles that we can see being traced from Petrarch through the 16th century remain important elements of our collective characters, at least in the west. The primacy of individual experience is central, as is the belief that we've got the capacity to create ourselves according to a set of principles that we choose to follow.

Each individual, then, has got the responsibility to choose who he or she is to be. We create ourselves according to a set of ideals that we adopt willingly. We choose examples from literature, from the practice of others. We look at what we ourselves can be, and we work hard in order to achieve that. It's not just personal ambition; it's really something that Petrarch began—the idea that we are all created, constructed personalities, and the important thing is to ensure that that construction conforms to ideals and principles that are good.

It means, then, that we have a responsibility to our community, and our community to us. These ideas are formed not just in literary works, or in philosophy, but in the very practice and structure of the Florentine Republic of the 15th century—how government as a sense of community, and how the community acting collectively as government, came together in order to create a world in which genius could flourish, and in which the individual ambitions of citizens could be turned to the benefit of the whole.

Participatory government is one of the foundations of our society today. This, too, is something we can see as coming from those republican models in Florence, and even Venice. And quality is best assured through competition, whether in the arts or in ideas. We have to have competition to make sure that we know what is out there, what's the best. How do we know that we are actually getting the best we can from our investment, whether it's time or money? And speech—not just the creation of words, but the art of communicating—this is a good index of the appropriateness of an individual for public office.

We listen to politicians speak to us. We make judgments about what they say and how they say it, and we choose, then, to send them out to speak with others so that they can benefit the community at large. For this to work and for the community to benefit, speech must be free. It must be untrammeled. It must be allowed to operate in such a way that ideas can rise, and that those ideas can be challenged, and then they can be identified as good or bad. And if good, they should be enshrined. And if bad, they should be rejected.

These are the principles in which governments like Florence functioned. It was the basis of the Renaissance dialogue as a literary form. The idea, then, is that a world is created in which the individual functions not only individually, but also jointly; in which the individual personality is brought to bear for the benefit of the community; and the creation of a set of ideas that supersedes that individual, and often supersedes the community, that evolves into the production of a kind of goal or ideal—something that we all can work towards and not achieve necessarily in one generation or even two, but something that gives us a value to work with.

It was a set of Renaissance humanist principles that dominated elite education well past the 19th-century rise of science. It was believed, as the humanists believed, that education is a preparation for citizenship. Why is it we learn what we do? Is it just instrumental to be good lawyers or plumbers? Well, of course. We need good lawyers and plumbers. But, at the same time, learning should also have some element that provides some measure of character. We should build character. We should establish values, and education can do this by providing the model of others.

We learn from history. We learn from poetry. We learn from rhetoric. We learn from all of those elements that determine the nature of the human condition. And we apply them to ourselves and to others. This is what the humanists taught. This is one of the purposes of their educational regimen.

It also is to provide us with a useful leisure. What is it that we do when our time is not structured? The humanists said it was extremely important to have an engaged and active mind. You don't turn off because you're not in school or at work. How are you going to spend your free time? For it to be useful to yourself and others, it should then accord also with certain values. So the very act of pleasure, in seeking pleasure, should also be the act of seeking knowledge and understanding. The humanists believed this. I think we should too.

Physical training—the sound mind in a sound body was something that they took from the ancients, and it was something that they practiced. We are seeing effects of ignoring the body now, and we realize that it's eventually going to have an effect on our collective mind. There is, indeed, a responsibility for the community to take its health as a responsibility.

We realize that not just the health of the mind, but the health of the body is something that we have to recognize. And here, too, our humanists are our models. They, with their recognition of that Juvenalian tag of *mens sana in corpore sano* ["a sound mind in a sound body"] were saying not just a moment of ancient knowledge recovered, but also something of profound importance to us all. They, of course, believed something that we have largely lost—that is, knowledge of the Greek and Latin languages would be sufficient to provide guidance in almost every element of life—whether you're going to be a physician, or whether you're going to be a scientist, or a politician, or a taxi driver, knowledge of ancient literature can provide both that useful leisure through the reading of poetry and philosophy, and then also examples from history of moral virtue and goodness.

We, of course, live in a far more complex time. There are other things that we need to know. But, nevertheless, we have perhaps lost some of the beauty in the world in not being able to access the literature of Greece and Rome in the original languages. I just hope that we, at least, read these in translation.

The Renaissance invention of the individual has remained a powerful force in our self-definition. In fact, some thinkers have said that the greatest contribution of the Renaissance was the reinvention and the definition of the concept of the autonomous individual who is able to create himself or herself according to principles recognized as good. In fact, we see this in every aspect of our life.

We see it in the trajectory of our love. It's not an accident that we read Petrarch, and Petrarch is still one of the most read of all of the Renaissance authors because he wrote so much about love. And, in fact, what we often read of Petrarch is the *Canzoniere*. We read his poetry because his poetry is about the sense of human emotion that is most effectively described in the love of one for another. When we use the vocabulary of love, we often, if we know the *Canzoniere* well, see that we are using Petrarch's vocabulary. When we set our beloved on a pedestal and worship from afar, we're, in fact, doing not just the recurring theme of situation comedies, we're also seeing, in fact, that idea that love doesn't necessarily have to be consummated in order to be effective, and good, and useful.

Platonic ideals of love find resonance in our even debased moments because we still believe, despite evidence to the contrary, we still believe in the uplifting power of love and the link between beauty, goodness, and truth; that there must be a connection amongst these things. It's not just a Platonic truism; it's not just a reflection of the Renaissance mind; it's something that, even if not true, we want to believe it to be true because it adds a great deal of dignity to our lives, and to the actions that we take on a daily basis. The search for beauty, the search for truth, the search for love, in many ways should be the same. To a Renaissance mind, this is natural. It's reasonable. The evidence is there. To us, it's more of a stretch, but one I think worth making.

All forms of human experience, then, are valid. All forms of human experience are instructive. When we learn from evil, or badness, or failure, we're still learning. When we learn from goodness and from moral rectitude, we learn. And we, in turn, can take these and apply their lessons to our lives, and be examples ourselves.

The forms of literature developed during the Renaissance remain important and, again, part of our world today. The psychological autobiography, resurrected by Petrarch after more than a thousand years of neglect, is one of the most common forms of personal memoir. You can't pick any book from the section of the library that's dedicated to biography without coming across the psychological autobiography of someone who thinks that his or her life is worth recording.

Now, of course, autobiography has become a subgenre fiction—but, to some extent, it doesn't matter because we believe in the constructed life. We believe that we make ourselves the people that we want to be. And even by writing that fictional autobiography, that desire to prove that everything we've done is good or true, or all of the evil that we have committed wasn't for a higher good, becomes instructive.

Petrarch was quite honest about himself. And, indeed, it's the responsibility of anyone writing an autobiography to share that honesty. And, to some extent, it matters not whether it's true, but whether it can serve as an exemplum and a model, and whether we can learn from it.

The sonnet sequence—again, invented by Petrarch—is something that we see develop right through the Renaissance, up until the 19th century. When we think of Shakespeare, of Sidney, of Spenser, right through to Elizabeth Barrett Browning and the sonnets from the Portuguese in the 19th century, we see that same genre—that collection of poems designed to analyze the emotional life of the poet, and the relation of the poet to the beloved, as something that works. We read these because they still matter to us. And often, we just don't recognize sufficiently that Petrarch invented this genre in order to achieve something very, very personal and particular to describe his relationship with the unattainable Laura.

The primary genre of Renaissance prose is the dialogue, and it remains an important instrument of reflecting the complexity of ideas and the multiple perspectives of human discourse to this day. We live in a complex world. Should there just be one voice, or should there be many voices? Does the dialogue in many ways not reflect the complexity that we have to deal with? Isn't the dialogue a way of trying to determine how to identify what is true and good from the many, many, many examples that will be put before us?

The Renaissance dialogue, then, knew this. It recognized it. And it put it not just in the shape of the dramatic dialogue, but ultimately into one of the great contributions of the Renaissance mind to our world—and that is theater. Renaissance theater is not just the reflection of a single civilization long gone; it's a reflection of the human condition, which is absolute. There is not a single school system at any level, anywhere in the west, in which Shakespeare is not taught. The reason being is that Shakespeare still speaks to us and still talks to us about things that we all share purely by virtue of being human.

So, Renaissance theater is more than just an antiquarian interest in a genre of the past; it's a statement about our continuing and shared humanity, despite the dramatic differences in our contexts. Shakespeare still speaks to us because Shakespeare speaks the language of the Renaissance mind—and, ultimately, that is the mind that we still exercise. It's the foundation of our principles and ideals—and is very, very much part of our daily lives, although so subsumed by later accretions that it's often hard to find.

Ideals of the Renaissance, things that galvanized and energized an entire civilization, are still with us—free will, with the concept of human agency as the cause of the events in the world. We find this in every Renaissance historian, beginning with Leonardo Bruni and his history of Florence. We see it through Guicciardini, that great historian who recognized that human self-interest was the motive power of historical change.

That very sense, then, that we are responsible for the world in which we live is an extremely important recognition. It's something that we have to accept because it gives us both the power to change the world in certain ways and the power to accept responsibility as individuals. It's easy now to try and avoid responsibility. But our humanist friends and the histories they wrote indicated to us clearly that you ultimately can't. Your actions have consequences, and those consequences themselves reverberate and ripple through an entire community. So we must know it. We must recognize, and we must live with it. We're not necessarily going to change, but we should at least know that what we do really matters and really affects others.

Concepts closely associated with this idea of human agency, close to the concept of the dignity of man, are still very much there. We still, essentially, believe in human dignity. Almost all of our legal systems, all of the principles that we say we collectively support, assume as the foundation the dignity of the individual person.

It's difficult after the past century, a terrible century in which human dignity was trampled by awful regimes, and regimes that committed crimes against humanity on a scale that had previously been unknown—in fact, unimagined. But, nevertheless, from it, even from that terrible suffering and from that period of historical chaos, there still survives the idea of human dignity. We can't escape it. We see it every time we deal with the legal system that provides for the freedom of the individual person—the recognition of innocence until proven guilty, the idea that each voice must be heard.

These, then, are principles that we can still accept and we still see acting, fundamentally, in the Renaissance in a secular way. These are principles that are not altogether separate from the religious idea of the individual soul and spirit and the idea of some form of divine creation. But we do live a secular life in a secular world. In the Renaissance, especially in cities like Florence, where the secular became the communal and the shared, then we see that we can sustain these regardless of the difference of our belief systems, or the difference of our experience. Maybe there is an absolute, and perhaps our Renaissance friends help identify that absolute, which has to do with the nature of the human condition—the ability to reason, and the ability to speak, which gives us a kind of dignity and authority that no other creature enjoys.

Context still matters a great deal to us, and principles are determined by context. The Renaissance realized that all things shift according to the circumstances in which the individual finds himself or herself. There are, of course, absolutes, such as human dignity, that we should not take away. But, nevertheless, there's also recognition that we live in a community, and that we have that responsibility to one another that I've already mentioned. This means that context does become important. It becomes important for us to know that as times change and circumstances alter, then we must as well.

I suggested in the last lecture that one of the tragedies of the end of the Renaissance was the Italians' failure of will. Having developed these complex principles, having created a sense of ideals that could drive and animate an entire civilization, they ultimately became overwhelmed by failure, by humiliation, and by fear—and so they gave up. This is an object lesson for us too. Should we give up regardless of the challenges we face? Well, no, we shouldn't, because the Italians may have been able to sustain some elements of their civilization in another way. Who's to say? It's a parlor game. It isn't history. It didn't happen.

But we have the example before us, history being one of the primary elements of those humanist subjects taught to every student. Because without knowledge of history, we can, in fact, make the same mistake they did. We can't have a failure of will because now, in our world, the stakes are simply too high.

I noted at the beginning of this series that there was, in the revolt of the medievalists, a strong assault on the Renaissance in the name of science. Those Renaissance scholars who simply say that science wasn't really the Renaissance mentality weren't interested in it. I think they're making a mistake because Renaissance science was different. It was connected with philosophy, and magic, and the syncretic religion in many ways. But, nevertheless, I think it's unfair to simply yield the field to those historians of science who say that the Renaissance was, in fact, a decline from the Middle Ages, when science was much more respected and practiced in a much more professional way.

There's no doubt that the Aristotelian model of empirical observation, and Aristotelianism being the great medieval intellectual structure, contributed profoundly to an understanding of nature before the Renaissance. But, Aristotle wasn't forgotten. Aristotle was still a great classical author whose respect and association with Plato were well known. So, the primacy of Aristotle in antiquity was something that would give the Renaissance mind some measure of pause. Aristotle wasn't rejected altogether; scholasticism was, but

Aristotle wasn't. He was still there as a classical philosopher and author, and his great works on the natural world were extremely well known.

Similarly, Galenic medicine practiced during the Renaissance accorded with medieval medical knowledge and the knowledge of the ancient world. There was a sense, then, that there was an inheritance from antiquity in science. But, like so many other things in the Renaissance, it was a heritage that needed to be challenged, and, ultimately, after applying it, in effect, to the degree possible, it should be superseded.

Classical sources, then, did tend to be the final arbiter of knowledge, but the recovery of certain scientific texts, especially the geographers and the mathematicians, did greatly affect, and influence, and drive the progress of science. Not everything was based on Pliny's *Historia naturalis*. It was an important text, but there were others as well.

There are other elements of the Renaissance mind that we carry with us and we need to address: the artistic obsession with perspective and reproducing what the eye sees, and the replication of observation. These things, in some ways, made modern science possible. The whole idea of the experimental model—in which an observer trusts his ability to observe and record, and then reproduce that experience—is something that the Renaissance developed, often in the context of art; but, nevertheless, it was something that they, in fact, perfected. And with the advent of printing, it was something that they could then share using mechanical devices. So that an animal or a plant found in one place can be tested against animals and plants found elsewhere, provided that the ability of the observer to reproduce that image is sufficiently developed. And, of course, with the rise of naturalism, with correct anatomy, with the ability to reproduce what the eye sees, this was a foregone conclusion. It was assumed.

Similarly, the idea of the voyages of discovery, the ability to place spots on a globe, plots on a map, at great distance from one another in some kind of reasonable way so that they could be understood in relation to one another, so the distances could be seen as constant, so, in fact, they could be charted—this was not just the application of linear perspective. This, in fact, is the creation of the ability to understand the immensity of the world and to chart it, to map it, to allow distant objects to be put in relation to one another in some form that could be easily understood by any observer. Others could then follow, and—in some ways—the voyages of discovery could be made possible.

There are a few examples I also want to give of those contributions at the very end of the Renaissance, the consequence of much scholarship and much learning that came to fruition in a single book or a single moment—things that built upon a century of previous work and that appeared in that critical time, the time that I identified with the end of the Renaissance—that is, the 1540s.

The first is the 1542 publication of Nicholas Copernicus's *De Revolutionibus* (*On the Orbits of the Heavenly Bodies*). It was a truly, truly remarkable book. Copernicus, a Polish priest working largely in Italy, observed the movements of the planets and created a series of tables. The only way these tables made sense was if the sun was the center of the universe, and not the earth. He was thereby rejecting not only Scripture, but also the learning of the ancients, the Ptolemaic system of that Alexandrian geographer.

He was, then, saying that his personal observation, and the correct recording of those observations and their consistency, resulted in his being able to make an individual judgment, and drawing an individual conclusion that was quite separate from, and distant from, the teachings of both Church and antiquity.

Copernicus did, in some ways, revolutionize the world, but not immediately. It was a book for specialists that came out at a time of crisis. The irony, of course, is that after the world had shifted, when the *Index of Prohibited Books* acted most dramatically, and when the Inquisition was at its greatest extent, Galileo Galilee took Copernicus's ideas and then reproduced them himself in his dialogue on the two great world systems, proving that Copernicus was right.

Copernicus died in his bed honoured and respected. Galileo was brought before the Inquisition, found to be a contumacious heretic, and only escaped death by burning by openly saying that he was wrong. Copernicus's truth, then, became Galileo's fate. And we see, then, the difference between these two moments: Copernicus, at the end of this Renaissance period of inquiry; Galileo in the midst of that closure of the mind that would not allow truth to come forward, even if clearly proved.

The other is Andrea Vesalius. Vesalius, in 1543, had printed one of the great books of anatomy ever, his *De Fabrica humani corporis*, on the structure of the human body. Richly illustrated and anatomically correct, it provided a complete and correct description of how the human body worked. This was the result of generations of Paduan physicians secretly taking cadavers and dissecting them.

There was the allowance for a certain amount of dissection by the Church, but not much. It was necessary, if you wanted to really discover how the body worked, to work almost outside the restrictions of the law. This was possible because Venice and Padua were amongst the most liberal places on the peninsula. The Church was really an extension of the state. The Inquisition was a branch of the state. So, it could happen; it could happen more easily. And Vesalius, then, could work in an environment that was supportive.

Also, at that same school, at almost exactly the same time, the first botanical garden in Europe was laid out in order to produce medicinal plants for the pharmacopoeia; again, based upon ancient models. But, at the same time, in order to make a contribution to the world, the Renaissance did see science as necessary, and did see the human condition as being part of the natural world. We can see, then, in these two moments and these two great experiences how the Renaissance can reach a sense of fulfilment and leave us with a sense of due respect in every area of human endeavour. There are concrete examples, but there is more and there are greater things that I think that we need to look at.

Baldassare Castiglione very abstractly in his *Book of the Courtier* at a time of terrible, terrible dislocation in Italy argued that there are shards that we must collect against our ruin; that we must, in fact, sustain civilization. We have to keep ideas alive, and, ultimately, it's the individual that sustains that; that we have to keep truth and beauty alive in ourselves—even in a world that suppresses them, we must sustain them. This is, again, a model of the Renaissance that I think we need to follow and always keep. Anything that we have within ourselves—our learning, our knowledge, our experience—can never be taken away from us. We're then able to impart them to others, so they'll never die.

This is part of our humanity. And, to some extent, I would like to leave you, then, with this Renaissance idea: Renaissance humanists often asked themselves this question in their elegant Latin: *Quam sit humaniter vivendum* (How might I live my life more humanely)? How might I live my life more humanely—that is, in consonance with my human dignity? The answer, of course, is that each of us must choose; that our human dignity varies with our knowledge, and our experiences, and our lives, our own creation.

I give my students the same assignment at the end of every year in my Renaissance course, and I am going to give it to you. The assignment is to turn your life into a work of art—not just a thing of beauty carefully crafted and well developed, but also something that can be polished and used as a model for others, and as an example for others.

The idea, then, of creating ourselves to be of benefit for our community, and to be models or beacons of understanding in an increasingly dark world, is something that we owe to the Renaissance and the Renaissance mentality. It's something that we can sustain. Ideas have their own lives, but if planted in our own experience, and then taken by us and expended, and expanded to others through our action and our speech, we can then share a set of principles, a concept of beauty and truth, an idea of responsibility, and an idea of individuality that can withstand anything. This, I think, is the real gift of the Renaissance.

Timeline

1478	Baldassare Castiglione born
1482	Federigo da Montefeltro dies
1482	Guidobaldo da Montefeltro becomes duke of Urbino
1483	Raphael born
c. 1485	Sandro Botticelli paints *The Birth of Venus*
c. 1486	Sandro Botticelli paints *La Primavera*
1492	Lorenzo de'Medici, "the Magnificent," dies
1492	Pope Innocent VIII dies
1492	Pope Alexander VI crowned (Rodrigo Borgia)
1494	Angelo Poliziano dies
1494	Pico della Mirandola dies
1494	Charles VIII of France invades Italy
1494	King Ferrante (Naples) dies
1495	Savonarola's constitution proclaimed in Florence
1495	Charles VIII captures Naples
1495	The League of Venice created
1496	Pope Alexander VI excommunicates Savonarola
1498	Savonarola executed
1498	Machiavelli becomes secretary of the Ten of War
1499	Marsilio Ficino dies
1500	France conquers Milan
1502	Piero Soderini elected *gonfaloniere* for life in Florence
1503	Naples under the Spanish viceroy

Visconti Family Tree

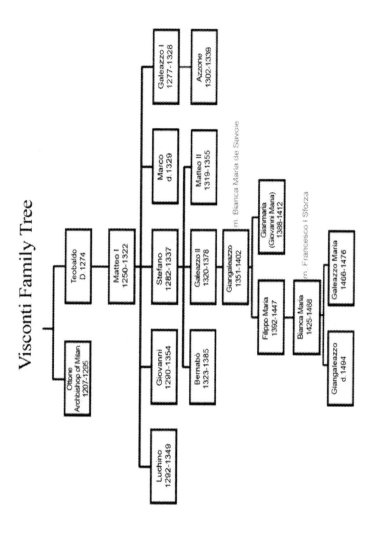

Medici Family Tree

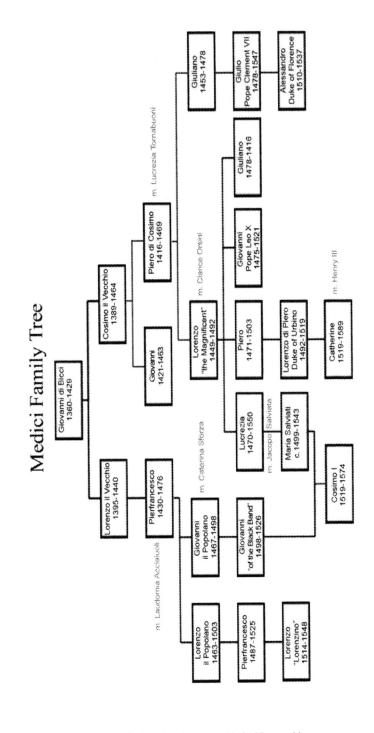

©2005 The Teaching Company Limited Partnership

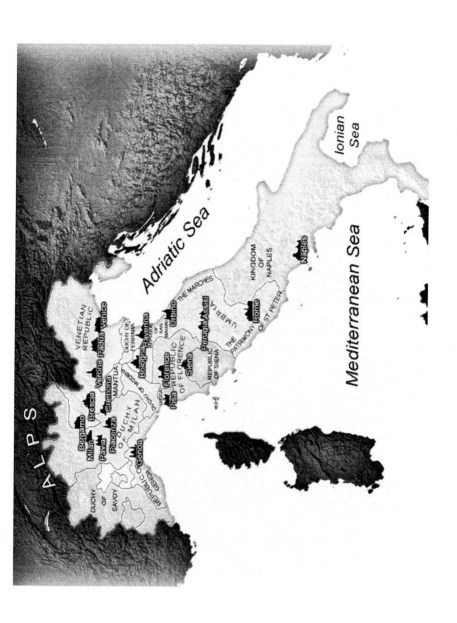

Glossary

Accoppiatori: Commissioners for elections in the Florentine Republic.

Arrabbiati: The anti-Savonarolan faction in Florence (literally, "hotheads").

Bands of Hope: Youths pledged by their parents to Savonarola.

Camera: The papal finance ministry.

Caput mundi: "The head of the world"; a description of Rome from classical times.

Catasto: Florentine income and wealth tax of 1427.

Ciompi: Poor, oppressed Florentine wool workers.

Citadini Originari: Wealthy citizens of Venice who did not have noble status.

Conciliarism: The doctrine that sovereignty in the Church resides in a general council rather than the person of the pope.

Condottiere: A mercenary captain.

Cortegiane oneste: High-class courtesans.

Doge: The Venetian word for "duke."

Gonfalioniere: Standard Bearer of Justice; one of the nine priors in Florence charged with enforcing the Ordinances of Justice.

Grandi: Wealthy old families originally of merchant stock but closely connected to the nobility in Florence.

Guild: A voluntary organization in a trade, industry, or profession for regulating prices, skills, admission, and other business practices. Matriculation in a guild was required for entry into Florentine political life in the republic.

Magnates: Landed aristocrats.

Monte: Florentine-funded public debt.

Monte delle doti: Florentine state dowry fund.

Monte di pietà: Florentine communal lending body for the poor.

Mundualdus: Male representative of a woman in court.

Palle: Medici rallying cry; the Italian word for "balls," referring to the five (later, six) balls on the Medici coat of arms.

Parlamento: The gathering of all heads of households to approve or reject a basic law.

Piagnoni: The pro-Savonarolan faction (literally "snivelers").

Podestà: Foreign military commander under annual contract with Florence.

Quadrivium: Four of the seven liberal arts of the Middle Ages: arithmetic, geometry, astronomy, and music.

Roman *campagna*: The rural territory outside Rome.

Rota: The central church court in Rome.

Sacred College: The College of Cardinals in Rome.

Scuola: A lay service organization or confraternity in Venice.

Serrata: The closing of the Venetian Great Council in 1297.

Studia humanitatis* or *litterae humaniores: The Renaissance liberal arts, usually including poetry, philosophy, ethics, history, and rhetoric.

Terraferma: Venetian mainland territory.

Biographical Notes

Alexander VI, pope (b. 1431; papacy, 1492–1503). As the nephew of Pope Calixtus III, Roderigo Borgia rose quickly through the ranks of the Church. He became a cardinal in 1456, vice-chancellor in 1457, and ultimately, pope in 1492. Alexander's papacy is best known for its nepotism, because he worked to secure high-level appointments and strategic marital alliances for his four illegitimate children fathered with his mistress Vanozza Catanei. His eldest, Juan, was destined to serve the Church as military commander but was murdered before he could fill this position. The role went to his next son, Cesare, known for his ruthless behavior. Alexander arranged several marriages for his daughter Lucrezia in an attempt to secure various political alliances. In spite of this focus on his family and his attempts to develop a Borgia kingdom, Alexander was a skilled administrator who worked to strengthen Rome's authority. Perhaps his greatest failure was his inability to recognize the threat that Charles VIII's invasion in 1494 would pose for Italy.

Borgia, Cesare (1475–1507). Cesare was one of four illegitimate children born to Rodrigo Borgia (Pope Alexander VI) and his mistress Vanozza Catanei. His career in the Church was launched by his father's election to the papacy in 1492, after which he was given many prominent appointments, including that of cardinal of Valencia and duke of Valentinois, and charged with various diplomatic missions. Cesare had a reputation for being ruthless and violent and is believed to have murdered his older brother. He led a series of campaigns in Emilia and Romagna, conquering the local princes in order to carve out his own principality. As he was turning his attention toward Florence, his father died (1503), and with the election of Giuliano della Rovere (Julius II), a bitter enemy of the Borgias, he was rendered powerless.

Bruni, Leonardo (1370–1444). Italian Humanist Leonardo Bruni's skill in Latin and Greek earned him a position in the papal court of Innocent VIII and enabled him to translate works by Aristotle and Plato. By 1415, he had taken a position in the Florentine government, rising to chancellor in 1427, where he used his influence to help spread Humanism. For Bruni, who viewed the ancient Roman Republic as a model state and praised Cicero's political activity and civic spirit, Humanism was closely associated with an active lay life. This interest in Civic Humanism is reflected in his *History of the Florentine People*, a work modeled on the historical writings of Livy and one that influenced the development of history as a discipline.

Clement VII, pope (b. 1478; papacy, 1523–1534). Giulio de'Medici was educated by his uncle Lorenzo the Magnificent and made a cardinal in 1513 by his cousin Pope Leo X. Like his two predecessors, he was a great patron of the arts, commissioning works by Cellini. His inability to make decisions led to the sack of Rome by the French in 1527, resulting in a seven-month period that saw the city ravaged and its art and culture destroyed. During this period, Clement sought refuge in Castel Sant' Angelo.

d'Este, Isabella (1474–1539). Born in 1474 to the duke of Ferrara, Ercole I, and his wife, Eleanora of Aragon, Isabella d'Este and her sister, Beatrice, were raised in the court culture of Ferrara, surrounded by poets, painters, and intellectuals. They each received a Humanist education, uncommon for women of the period, and Isabella was known to be a talented dancer, singer, and musician, who also excelled at hunting and riding. In 1490, Isabella married soldier and marquis Francesco Gonzaga (1466–1519) at the age of 16. As marchioness, Isabella had a great impact on both court life and in the political sphere. She was an avid reader and collector of art, books, tapestries, and antiquities. She was a patron of Leonardo da' Vinci, Titian, and Perugino and brought to Mantua great intellectuals of the period, including Pietro Bembo and Castiglione. Isabella was also a skilled ruler and gained a reputation for justice, diplomacy, and tenacity when governing Mantua for her husband during his absences on military campaigns, when he was briefly imprisoned in Venice, and after his death.

de'Medici, Cosimo, il Vecchio (1389–1464). Cosimo, the son of the wealthiest banker in Italy, Giovanni di Averrado de'Medici, was a follower of Humanism, a patron of the arts, and the founder of the Platonic Academy in Florence. He used his wealth to commission works by such artists as Lorenzo Ghiberti and Benozzo Gozzoli, to subsidize the search for classical texts by such Humanists as Niccolo Niccoli and Poggio Bracciolini, to rebuild San Lorenzo and the convent of the Badia at Fiesole, and to construct the Palazzo Medici. His political contributions are equally impressive. By 1433, the Medici were the most prominent and most influential family in

Florence. As a result, they had many opponents, including the Albizzi and Peruzzi families, who collaborated to run Cosimo out of town. In 1434, Cosimo returned to Florence with the help of the Popular Party and effectively "ruled" Florence until his death in 1464. Although never officially elected into Florentine government, Cosimo used his connections and influence to ensure the promotion of his policies and the election of those who supported his interests. In 1454, Cosimo helped to negotiate the Peace of Lodi with Milan, which established a balance of power in Italy.

de'Medici, Lorenzo, "il Magnifico" (1449–1492). Son of Piero de'Medici and grandson of Cosimo, Lorenzo took control of Florence at the age of 20 following his father's death. He was an active member of the Platonic Academy, a patron of the arts, and a beloved citizen of Florence. He was trained in the Humanist tradition and was surrounded by the leading intellectuals and artists of the day, including Pico della Mirandola, Angelo Poliziano, Marsilio Ficino, Michelangelo, and Botticelli. Politically, he was very astute and successfully strengthened and held together the republic during his rule (1469–1492). In 1478, he survived an attempt on his life by his detractors, the Pazzi family, in a plot that involved Pope Sixtus IV. This incident sparked a war between Naples and the papacy, which was ended through Lorenzo's efforts.

de'Medici, Piero, "il Sfortunato" (1471–1503). The eldest son of Lorenzo the Magnificent, Piero de'Medici ("the Unfortunate") succeeded his father in 1492 as ruler of Florence but proved to be lacking his father's diplomacy and his ability to rule effectively. During the French invasion of 1494, the Medici were expelled from Florence by their fellow citizens. All of Piero's attempts to regain his position in Florence failed, and he drowned while serving in the French army at the Battle of Garigliano.

Ferdinand of Aragon and Naples (1452–1516). With the marriage of Ferdinand, king of Sicily (1468–1516), Castile and Leon (1474–1504), Aragon (1479–1516), and Naples (1504–1516), to Isabella of Castile in 1469, Spain was united. Their rule focused on strengthening royal authority and curbing noble power. As a result of their efforts to maintain the purity of the Christian faith (through the establishment of the Inquisition in 1478 and the expulsion of the Jews in 1492), they were given the title of "Catholic Kings" by Pope Alexander VI in 1494. From 1479 to 1516, Ferdinand was involved on some level in almost every international conflict and negotiation, including a struggle with France for control of Italy during the Italian Wars (1494–1559).

Ficino, Marsilio (1433–1499). Ficino was an Italian philosopher, physician, and philologist and the most influential Renaissance Neoplatonist. Educated in Greek, Latin, and medicine, Ficino is best known for introducing Platonic philosophy to Europe. Much of his life's work focused on Plato and included translating Plato's texts into Latin; acting as the first president of the Florentine Platonic Academy; teaching Plato at the Academy, which attracted the leading citizens, thinkers, and artists of Florence; and publishing such works as the *Introduction to the Philosophy of Plato* and the *Platonic Theology* (1482). He further contributed to the growing body of ancient Greek literature with translations of Homer, Plotinus, and Dionysius the Areopagite.

Julius II, pope (b. 1443; papacy, 1503–1513). Giuliano della Rovere was educated by his uncle, Francesco della Rovere (Pope Sixtus IV) and, like him, was a member of the Franciscan Order. In 1471, he was made a cardinal by his uncle and held a number of episcopal sees and papal appointments before being elected pope in 1503. Julius's papacy is marked by significant artistic and military achievements. Under his patronage, Michelangelo painted the Sistine Chapel ceiling, Raphael painted rooms in the Vatican Palace, and Bramante began to rebuild St. Peter's (to be completed in 1612). Julius, who assumed personal command of an army, is often referred to as the "warrior pope" for his active role in the efforts to defend the Church and extend its temporal power. He is recognized for his efforts to free the papal court of abuses and for attempts to reestablish the pontifical estates and free Italy from control by foreign powers.

Leo X, pope (b. 1475; papacy, 1513–1521). Giovanni de'Medici, the second son of Lorenzo the Magnificent, was destined for a career in the Church, from an early age serving as an abbot and a cardinal before becoming the first Medici pope in 1513. As a young man, he received a Humanist education, taught by both Andrea Poliziano and Marsilio Ficino. He was known to be good-natured and well spoken, and his election to the papacy was met with high hopes from politicians, artists, and scholars. However, although viewed as a great diplomat, Leo was unsuccessful in political and religious affairs and paid little attention to the dangers threatening the papacy. In particular, he reacted too slowly when dealing with both the French invasion of 1516 and the developing Protestant Reformation. He was a great lover of entertainment, particularly banquets, and the arts, including music, theatre, and poetry, and Rome became the center of the literary world under Leo. In addition to great artistic commissions, Leo donated funds to convents, hospitals, pilgrims, and the sick. With his generosity and his spending habits, Leo managed to run through the papal coffers extremely quickly and, as a result, created new offices, announced jubilees, and expanded indulgences to raise money for the bankrupted treasury.

Montefeltro, Guidobaldo da (1472–1508). Guidobaldo was the son of Federigo da Montefeltro and Battista Sforza, duke and duchess of Urbino. He followed his father to become duke in 1482, serving until his death in 1508. Like his parents before him, Guidobaldo and his wife, Elisabetta Gonzaga (1471–1526), actively supported the arts and culture of Urbino. The unique court culture established here attracted young men from all over Europe and encouraged the participation of women. The great painter Raphael was raised in the court culture of Urbino during Guidolbaldo's reign, and Baldassare Castiglione served under him. Castiglione's work *The Courtier* is set in Urbino and relates a discussion among members of Italy's leading families at the palace of Guidobaldo and his wife. Guidobaldo is the absent character in this work, confined to bed, with Elisabetta acting as host.

Nicholas V, pope (b. 1397; papacy, 1447–1455). As a young man, Tommaso Parentucelli studied theology and worked as a tutor for the Strozzi and Albizzi families in Florence, where he came into contact with leading Humanist scholars. He was in the service of Niccolo Albergati, bishop of Bologna for 20 years, and was involved in diplomatic missions in Italy and Germany at the request of Pope Eugene, for which he was awarded the position of cardinal in 1446. The following year, 1447, he was elected pope. Nicholas V's primary goal at the outset of his papacy was to restore Rome—its monuments, churches, fortifications, streets, and aqueducts. He was particularly interested in rebuilding the Vatican Palace, St. Peter's, and the Leonine City. Nicholas was a patron of the arts, literature in particular, and he welcomed leading Humanists of the day into the papal court. In addition, he established the Vatican Library, bringing in more than 5,000 volumes during his papacy. On the political front, Nicholas supported the Peace of Lodi (1454) and entered the Italian League in 1455, which helped to secure the Papal States from further attacks.

Pico della Mirandola, Giovanni (1463–1494). Pico della Mirandola was an Italian philosopher, scholar, and Neoplatonist who devoted his life to study. He began his education at the age of 14 in Bologna studying canon law, but his quest for complete wisdom led him to study a wide range of disciplines, including languages (Greek, Latin, Arabic, Hebrew, Syriac), theology, philosophy (including Hebrew philosophy), the Cabala, occult lore, mathematics, music, and physics. At the age of 24, he traveled to Rome to post his 900 theses on a range of topics, prefaced in his *Oration on the Dignity of Man*, with a challenge to other scholars to join him in debate. Thirteen of his theses were condemned as heretical by Pope Innocent VII and Pico fled to France. He settled in Florence after being absolved by Pope Alexander VI, became a member of the Platonic Academy, and devoted his life to defending Christianity.

Raphael of Urbino (1483–1520). Born the son of a court painter and poet from Urbino, Raffaelo Sanzio would become one of the most skilled and prolific painters of the High Renaissance. He first studied painting in Urbino before moving to Perugia in 1500 to study under Pietro Perugino, then to Florence four years later to study with Leonardo da Vinci. In 1508, he was invited by Pope Julius II to paint rooms in the Vatican Palace, where he completed the *School of Athens*, the *Dispute of the Sacrament*, and *Parnassus*. His most well-known works also include portraits of Popes Leo X, Julius II, various cardinals, and Baldassare Castiglione. Raphael died at the age of 37 from pneumonia.

Salutati, Coluccio (1330–1406). Trained as a notary, Coluccio Salutati went on to hold various public offices, including the chancellorships of Todi (1367–1368), Lucca (1370), and Florence (1375–1406). A friend and correspondent of Petrarch, Salutati was a Humanist scholar with an interest in classical literature, culture, and history who actively contributed to the revival, rediscovery, and translation of ancient texts. During his term as chancellor, Humanism was institutionalized in the Florentine Republic, with Salutati hiring scholars trained in this tradition for positions in civic government. As a result, Florence became the leading center of Humanism in Europe.

Sforza, Francesco (1401–1466). As a *condottiere* employed by the duke of Milan, Francesco Sforza led a number of successful campaigns on Rome. Hoping to retain some of these captured lands for himself, he attempted to persuade Duke Filippo Maria Visconti to provide him with an independent principality in Lombardy as a dowry for marrying his daughter. The duke refused and Sforza turned against him, joining the Florentine and Venetian alliance. When the duke died in 1447, Sforza set in motion his plan to seize power. After defeating the Venetian army at Caravaggio, he marched on Milan and conquered the city in 1450, taking the title of duke. He proceeded to persuade Cosimo de'Medici to withdraw from the Venetian alliance to form a new Milanese-Florentine alliance, a move that brought the wars to an end with the signing of the Peace of Lodi in 1454.

Sforza, Lodovico, "il Moro" (1451/52–1508). Known as "il Moro" for his swarthy complexion, Lodovico Sforza, son of Francesco, served as the duke of Milan from 1494–1499. In order to protect Milan, he entered into an alliance with Charles VIII before the 1494 invasion of Italy but had turned against the French by 1495. He was eventually expelled from Milan in 1499 by Louis XII, who had a hereditary claim to the duchy of Milan. Overall, Lodovico was not a particularly competent ruler, showing much more interest in the social and cultural pursuits of his court. During his short marriage to Beatrice d'Este (who died in childbirth in 1497), the Milanese court flourished with the arrival of Leonardo da Vinci as military engineer and court painter.

Sixtus IV, pope (b.1414; papacy, 1471–1484). Born Francesco della Rovere to a poor family, the future pope studied theology and philosophy at the University of Pavia. He served as procurator in Rome and was made cardinal in 1467. Once elected pope, Sixtus launched a crusade against the Turks and attempted to reunite the Eastern Church with Rome but was not particularly successful in either endeavor. The last decade of his papacy was dominated by rather unscrupulous behavior, including nepotism and involvement in an attempt in 1478 to overthrow the Medici in Florence (resulting in an assassination attempt on Lorenzo). Following this event, Sixtus embarked upon a two-year war with Florence that was eventually resolved because of his inability to garner support from other Italian states. There were some bright spots during his reign. Sixtus was a great patron of the arts who commissioned the construction of the Sistine Chapel and the Sistine bridge across the Tiber, redesigned the Capitoline Museum, and added a collection of ancient statuary to the complex. He also strengthened the Vatican Library and made major improvements to the city of Rome

Visconti, Giangaleazzo (d. 1402). After murdering his uncle Bernabò, Visconti seized power in Milan in 1385 and, 10 years later, was recognized as duke by the emperor. During his reign, Visconti united the territories of Milan, supported the armament and silk industries, built hospitals and the Milan cathedral, and tried to enrich the culture of his city. He also led numerous campaigns to expand his territories and purchased or conquered cities around Milan, such as Pisa. Successfully taking over much of Lombardy, he set his sights on Umbria and Tuscany, including Florence, the only city that refused to surrender to Visconti. With his sudden death in 1402, Florence was saved and his efforts to carve out a northern Italian kingdom were dissolved; however, Italy was sent into chaos as struggles to regain conquered territories developed.

Bibliography

Acton, Harold. *The Pazzi Conspiracy: The Plot Against the Medici*. London: Thames and Hudson, 1979. ISBN 0 500 250642. An engaging discussion on the attempt on the life of Lorenzo the Magnificent and the murder of Giuliano de'Medici in 1478.

Aston, Margaret, ed. *The Panorama of the Renaissance: The Renaissance in the Perspective of History*. New York: Harry N. Abrams, 1996. ISBN 0 8109 3704 2. A beautifully illustrated, comprehensive survey of Renaissance Europe.

Atiya, Aziz S. *Crusade, Commerce and Culture*. Bloomington, IN: Indiana University Press, 1962. A discussion of the interrelation between the Crusades and commercial and cultural contact with non-Christian communities around the Mediterranean.

Barkan, Leonard. *Unearthing the Past: Archaeology and Aesthetics in the Making of Renaissance Culture*. New Haven, CT: Yale University, 1999. ISBN 0 300 07677 0. An investigation of the earliest archaeological discoveries undertaken by Renaissance Humanists and the influence the materials discovered had on the formation of the Renaissance mentality.

Baron, Hans. *Crisis of the Early Italian Renaissance*. Princeton, NJ: Princeton University Press, 1966. ISBN: 0 691 00752 7. A detailed study of the development of Civic Humanism in Florence as a consequence of the republic's struggle against the despotisms of Milan and Naples.

Bartlett, Kenneth R. *The Civilization of the Italian Renaissance*. Sources in Modern History. Lexington, MA: D.C. Heath, 1992. ISBN 0669 20900 7. A collection of primary source readings with introductions discussing many aspects of Italian Renaissance civilization.

Becker, Marvin B. *Medieval Italy: Constraints and Creativity*. Bloomington, IN: Indiana University Press, 1981. ISBN 0 253 15294 1. A history of Italy in the Middle Ages looking at the conditions that permitted the development of the Renaissance.

Benedetti, Alessandro. *Diaria de Bello Carolino* (*Diary of the Caroline War*). Edited and translated by Dorothy M. Schullian. Renaissance Text Series. New York: Frederick Ungar Publishing

Co., 1967. A firsthand account of the invasions of Charles VIII in 1494, written by an Italian physician.

Bertelli, Sergio. *Italian Renaissance Courts*. London: Sidgwick and Jackson, 1986. ISBN 0 283 99378 2. A beautifully illustrated survey of the court culture of the Italian Renaissance.

Black, Chris F. *Church, Religion and Society in Early Modern Italy*. London: Palgrave MacMillan, 2004. ISBN 0 333 61845 9. A modern but accessible study of post-Tridentine Italian culture illustrating the new role of the Church in education, art, and society.

———, et al. *Cultural Atlas of the Renaissance*. New York: Prentice Hall, 1993. ISBN 0 671 86523 4. A comprehensive survey of major centers in the European Renaissance from the point of view of their cultural achievement.

Black, Robert. *Humanism and Education in Medieval and Renaissance Italy: Tradition and Innovation in Latin Schools from the Twelfth to the Fifteenth Century*. Cambridge: Cambridge University Press, 2001. ISBN 0 521 401925. A detailed academic study of education in medieval and Renaissance Italy.

Boorstin, Daniel. J. *The Discoverers: A History of Man's Search to Know His World and Himself*. New York: Random House, 1983. ISBN 0 394 40229 4. An investigation of how new knowledge drives cultural and intellectual innovation.

Bouwsma, William. *The Waning of the Renaissance, 1550–1640*. New Haven, CT: Yale University Press, 2002. ISBN 0 300 097174. An investigation of the last years of the Renaissance reflecting the pessimism that accompanied the decline of Italian intellectual and political freedom.

Bracciolini, Poggio. *Two Renaissance Book Hunters: The Letters of Poggius Bracciolini to Nicolaus de Niccolis*. Translation and annotations by Phyllis Walter Goodhart Gordan. New York: Columbia University Press, 1974. ISBN 0 231 03777 5. A selection of letters between Poggio Bracciolini and Niccolò Niccoli describing their various discoveries of long-lost classical texts.

Brown, Alison. *The Medici in Florence: The Exercise and Language of Power*. Florence: Olschki, 1992. ISBN 88 222 3999 7. A study of the various instruments the Medici used to maintain their grip on power.

Brown, Judith C., and Robert C. Davis, eds. *Gender and Society in Renaissance Italy*. New York: Addison Wesley Longman Ltd., 1998. ISBN 0 582 29326 X. A diverse collection of essays on the subject of gender relations in the Italian Renaissance.

Brown, Patricia Fortini. *Art and Life in Renaissance Venice*. Princeton, NJ: Princeton University Press, 1998. ISBN 0 13 618455 3. A study of the relationship between art and society in the Republic of Venice during the period of the Renaissance.

Brucker, Gene A. *Renaissance Florence*. Berkeley, CA: UCLA Press, 1983. ISBN 0 520 04695 1. Still the best short, comprehensive survey of Florentine history during the period of the Renaissance.

———. *Giovanni and Lusanna: Love and Marriage in Renaissance Florence*. Berkeley, CA: University of California Press, 1986. ISBN 0 520 05655 8. A gripping story of love, betrayal, and a woman's search for justice in Renaissance Florence.

Bruni, Leonardo. *The Humanism of Leonardo Bruni: Selected Texts*. Translations and introductions by Gordon Griffiths, James Hankins, and David Thomson. Medieval and Renaissance Texts and Studies in conjunction with the Renaissance Society of America. Binghamton, NY: Center for Medieval and Early Renaissance Studies, State University of New York at Binghamton, 1987. ISBN 0 86698 029 6. A collection of primary source texts illustrating the broad Humanistic interests of the great Florentine chancellor.

Bullock, Alan. *The Humanist Tradition in the West*. London: W.W. Norton, 1985. ISBN 0 393 02237 4. An insightful study of the role of Humanism and human concerns in the complex history of the West.

Burckhardt, Jacob. *The Civilization of the Renaissance in Italy*. Vol. I: *The State as a Work of Art, The Development of the Individual, The Revival of Antiquity*. New York: Harper & Row Publishers, 1975. ISBN 0 06 090459 3.

———. *The Civilization of the Renaissance in Italy*. Vol. II: *The Discovery of the World and of Man, Society and Festivals, Morality and Religion*. New York: Harper & Row Publishers, 1975. ISBN 0 06 090460 7. Together, these two volumes comprise the foundation of Renaissance studies. First printed in 1860, they introduced the model of cultural history in the study of Renaissance Italy.

Burke, Peter. *The Italian Renaissance: Culture and Society in Italy.* Princeton, NJ: Princeton University Press, 1986. ISBN 0 691 02838 9. A dynamic survey of the relationship between Italian Renaissance culture and the society that produced it over the course of the Renaissance.

Cardini, Franco, introduction. *The Medici Women.* 2nd English ed. Florence: Arnaud Ed. S.r.l., 1997. ISBN 88 8015 034 0. A collection of biographies of women in the Medici family, written by various scholars and reflecting the times in which these women lived.

Castiglione, Baldesar. *The Book of the Courtier.* Translation by Charles S. Singleton. New York: Doubleday and Company, 1959. ISBN 0 385 09421 3. Still the best translation of Castiglione's fundamental dialogue reflecting the values of late Renaissance Italy.

Cellini, Benvenuto. *The Autobiography of Benvenuto Cellini.* Edited and translated by George Bull. Harmonsdworth, Middlesex: Penguin, 2004. ISBN 0140447180. Cellini was a master sculptor and goldsmith who recorded the events of his extraordinary life in an autobiography. Like many autobiographies, it contains not only a great deal of self aggrandizement and fiction, but also a personal insight into the remarkable times in which he lived, as well as the personalities of the kings, popes, princes, and artists he knew.

Chamberlin, E. R. *The Count of Virtue: Giangaleazzo Visconti.* London: Eyre and Spottiswoode, 1965. A popular biography of the first duke of Milan.

Chambers, D. S. *The Imperial Age of Venice, 1380–1580.* London: Thames and Hudson, 1970. ISBN 0 500 33020 4. An excellent illustrated survey of Venetian politics, society, and culture during the Renaissance.

Chambers, D., and B. Pullan, eds. *Venice: A Documentary History, 1450 to 1630.* Toronto: University of Toronto Press, 2001. ISBN 0802 08424 9. A collection of primary source documents illustrating many aspects of Venetian commerce, politics, culture, and society.

Chastel, André. *The Sack of Rome, 1527.* Translated from the French by Beth Archer. The A.W. Mellon Lectures in the Fine Arts, 1977. Bollingen Series XXXV.26. Princeton, NJ: Princeton University Press, 1983. ISBN 0 691 09947 2. An illustrated discussion of the impact the sack of Rome had on art and propagandistic illustration in Europe.

Clark, Kenneth. *The Art of Humanism*. New York: Harper and Row, 1983. ISBN 0 06 430861 8. A collection of essays discussing the influence of Humanist culture on some of the most important artists of the Renaissance.

Cochrane, Eric, ed. *The Late Italian Renaissance, 1525–1630*. Stratum Series. General editor J. R. Hale. London: Macmillan and Co., Ltd., 1970. ISBN 0333111257. A comprehensive collection of essays studying various aspects of late Renaissance Italy.

———. *Florence in the Forgotten Centuries, 1527–1800*. Chicago: University of Chicago Press, 1973. ISBN 0 226 11150 4. Still the best, if eccentric, history of Florence from the collapse of the republic until the period of the Napoleonic wars.

———. *Historians and Historiography in the Italian Renaissance*. Chicago: University of Chicago Press, 1981. ISBN 0 226 11152 0. An invaluable survey of historical writing during the Italian Renaissance.

Cohen, Elizabeth S., and Thomas V. Cohen. *Daily Life in Renaissance Italy*. Westport, CT: Greenwood Press, 2001. ISBN 0 313 30426 2. A wide and engaging survey of the daily life of all classes of society throughout the Italian peninsula.

Cole, Alison. *Virtue and Magnificence: Art of the Italian Renaissance Courts*. New York: Harry N. Abrams, 1995. ISBN 0 8109 2733 0. A series of studies of Italian Renaissance court patronage—beautifully illustrated.

Della Casa, Giovanni. *Il Galateo*. Translated by K. Bartlett and K. Eisenbichler. Ottawa: Dovehouse Press, 1990. A modern English translation of Della Casa's celebrated 16th-century treatise on manners.

Dennistoun, James. *Memoirs of the Dukes of Urbino*. New York: John Lane Company, 1909. A huge antiquarian survey of materials relating to the court of Urbino. Still the most comprehensive collection of information available in English about the duchy.

Ferguson, Wallace K. *The Renaissance in Historical Thought: Five Centuries of Interpretation*. Cambridge: Houghton Mifflin Company, 1948. An important, if dated, survey of the historiography on the Renaissance.

Field, Arthur M. *The Origins of the Platonic Academy of Florence*. Princeton, NJ: Princeton University Press, 1988. ISBN 0691055335.

A detailed study of the role of Neoplatonism in Florence at the time of the Medici.

Finlay, Robert. *Politics in Renaissance Venice*. New Brunswick, NJ: Rutgers University Press, 1980. ISBN 0 8135 0888 6. An excellent study of the complexities of political life in the Renaissance Republic of Venice.

Fragnito, Gigliola. *Church, Censorship and Culture in Early Modern Italy*. Cambridge: Cambridge University Press, 2001. ISBN 0521 66172 2. A collection of essays regarding the Church's attempt to control culture and ideas in 16th-century Italy.

Gilbert, Felix. *Machiavelli and Guicciardini: Politics and History in Sixteenth-Century Florence*. New York: W.W. Norton and Co., 1984. ISBN 0 393 30123 0. A superb comparative study of Machiavelli and Guicciardini as historians and practicing politicians.

Goldthwaite, Richard A. *The Building of Renaissance Florence: An Economic and Social History*. Baltimore, MD: Johns Hopkins University Press, 1980. ISBN 0 8018 2977 1. A study of palace construction in Florence during the period of the Renaissance.

————. *Wealth and the Demand for Art in Italy, 1300–1600*. Baltimore, MD: John Hopkins University Press, 1993. ISBN 0 8018 4612 9. An economic investigation of art as a commodity in the Italian Renaissance.

Grendler, Paul F. *Schooling in Renaissance Italy: Literacy and Learning, 1300–1600*. Baltimore, MD: Johns Hopkins University Press, 1989. ISBN 0 8018 4229 8. An excellent comprehensive survey of pre-university education in the Italian peninsula.

Guicciardini, Francesco. *The History of Italy*. Translated by Sidney Alexander. New York: Macmillan, 1969. Still the best translation of this important historical work written by one of the main actors in 16th-century Italian history.

Gundersheimer, Werner L. *Ferrara: The Style of a Renaissance Despotism*. Princeton, NJ: Princeton University Press, 1973. ISBN 0 691 05210 7. A thorough analysis of the rule of the Este family in Ferrara.

Hale, J. R. *Florence and the Medici: The Pattern of Control*. New York: Thames and Hudson, 1977. ISBN 0 500 27301 4. A nicely illustrated, accessible history of the Medici family in the context of their control of the city of Florence.

Hankins, James. *Plato in the Italian Renaissance*. New York: E.J. Brill, 1991. ISBN 90 04 09552 7. A specialist investigation of the knowledge of Plato in the Renaissance and the role this philosopher's works played in the development of Italian thought.

Hanlon, Gregory, *Early Modern Italy, 1550–1800*. London: Macmillan, 2000. ISBN 033362002X. An excellent, broad survey of Italian history from the late Renaissance until the time of Napoleon.

Hay, Denys, ed. *The Renaissance Debate*. European Problem Studies. New York: Holt, Rinehart and Winston, 1965. A collection of short excerpts from contemporary historians discussing the Renaissance as a historical period.

———, and John Law. *Italy in the Age of the Renaissance, 1380–1530*. Longman History of Italy. Essex: Longman Group UK Ltd., 1989. ISBN 0582 48359 X. A broad survey of peninsular history throughout the entire sweep of the Renaissance.

Hibbert, Christopher. *The House of Medici: Its Rise and Fall*. New York: HarperCollins, 1982. ISBN 0688053394. A popular discussion of the various members of the Medici family.

Holmes, George. *Dante*. Oxford: Oxford University Press, 1980. ISBN 0 19 287504 3. An excellent, short introduction to the life and works of Dante.

Hook, Judith. *Lorenzo de'Medici: An Historical Biography*. London: H. Hamilton, 1984. The best modern biography of Lorenzo, il Magnifico.

———. *The Sack of Rome*. London: Palgrave Macmillan, 2004. ISBN 1403917698. The complex situation in Europe that led to the terrible events of the 1527 sack and the effect that the sack had on the continent are brilliantly described in this classic account of one of history's most violent moments.

Kent, Dale. *The Rise of the Medici: Faction in Florence, 1426–1434*. Oxford: Oxford University Press, 1978. ISBN 0 19 822520 2. A specialist analysis of how Cosimo de'Medici and his faction achieved power in Florence in 1434.

King, Margaret. *Venetian Humanism in an Age of Patrician Dominance*. Princeton, NJ: Princeton University Press, 1986. ISBN 0691054657. A brilliant study of Venetian Humanism and its relation to the republic's patriciate.

Kohl, Benjamin G., and Alison Andrews Smith, eds. *Major Problems in the History of the Italian Renaissance*. Lexington, MA: D.C. Heath, 1995. ISBN 0 669 28002 X. A collection of essays surveying the central historiographical issues of the Renaissance.

———, and Ronald G. Witt, eds. *The Earthly Republic: Italian Humanists on Government and Society*. Pennsylvania: University of Pennsylvania Press, 1978. ISBN 0 81221097 2. A collection of primary source documents with introductions by several scholars focusing on Humanist perspectives on the relationship between the individual and the community.

Lane, Frederic. *Andrea Barbarigo, Merchant of Venice, 1418–1449*. New Haven, CT: Yale University Press, 1976. A fascinating study of one Venetian merchant's career as a reflection of the interpenetration of politics and mercantile activity.

Larner, John. *Italy in the Age of Dante and Petrarch, 1216–1380*. A Longman History of Italy. Vol. 2. New York: Longman Group Ltd., 1980. ISBN 0 582 49149 5. Perhaps the best survey available of late medieval and early Renaissance Italy.

———. *The Lords of Romagna: Romagnol Society and the Origins of the Signorie*. Ithaca, NY: Cornell University Press, 1965. A study of the petty despotisms of the province of the Romagna and the Papal States during the late Middle Ages and early Renaissance.

Levey, Michael. *Painting at Court*. The Wrightsman Lectures. London: Weidenfeld and Nicolson, 1971. ISBN 297 07 3494. A selection of studies of court patronage in which art glorified the person of the prince.

Lopez, Robert S., and Irving W. Raymond, trans. *Medieval Trade in the Mediterranean World*. New York: W.W. Norton & Co. ISBN 0 393 09720 X. An economic history of long-distance trade in the Mediterranean in the Middle Ages.

Loyola, Ignatius. *The Spiritual Exercises of Saint Ignatius*. Translated by Anthony Mottola. New York: Random House, 1964. ISBN 0385024363. St. Ignatius's document of spiritual discipline that informs the entire Jesuit order.

Lubkin, Gregory. *A Renaissance Court: Milan Under Galeazzo Maria Sforza*. Berkeley, CA: University of California Press, 1994. ISBN 0 520 08146 3. A detailed and comprehensive study of the court of Milan during the short rule of one of its less attractive dukes.

Machiavelli, Niccolò. *The Prince*. Translated and edited by Robert M. Adams. New York: Norton, 1977. ISBN 0 393 09149 X. The celebrated short text that has engaged political thinkers from the time of its first printing in 1532.

Mallett, Michael. *The Borgias: The Rise and Fall of a Renaissance Dynasty*. Chicago: Academy Chicago Publishers, 1987. ISBN 0 89733 238 5. A popular history of this infamous family, elegantly written by an excellent professional historian.

Martines, Lauro. *April Blood: Florence and the Plot Against the Medici*. Oxford: Oxford University Press, 2003. ISBN 0 19 515295 6. A compelling relation of the Pazzi Conspiracy of 1478 that resulted in the death of Giuliano de'Medici.

———. *Power and Imagination: City-States in Renaissance Italy*. New York: Alfred A. Knopf, 1979. ISBN 0 394 50112 8. A survey of the various states of Italy during the Italian Renaissance.

Mollat, Guillaume. *The Popes at Avignon, 1305–1378*. London: Thomas Nelson & Sons, 1963. Still the standard history of the Babylonian Captivity.

Najemy, John M. *Corporatism and Consensus in Florentine Electoral Politics, 1280–1400*. Chapel Hill: University of North Carolina Press, 1982. ISBN 0807815063. A specialist's study of guild and factional interaction during the early years of the Florentine Republic.

Norwich, John Julius. *A History of Venice*. New York: Alfred A. Knopf, 1982. ISBN 0 394 52410 1 A wonderful, broad survey of the entire history of Venice, from the beginning until the end of the republic.

O'Malley, J. W. *The First Jesuits*. Cambridge, MA: Harvard University Press, 1993. ISBN 0 674 303 12 1. A study of the first decades of the Jesuit order written by a leading Jesuit scholar of the 20th century.

Origo, Iris. *The Merchant of Prato*. Harmondsworth, Middlesex: Penguin Books, 1963. An engaging, detailed, popular narrative of the life of a 14th-century Tuscan merchant derived from his own correspondence.

Panofsky, Erwin. *Renaissance and Renascences in Western Art*. Icon Editions. New York: Harper & Row Publishers, 1972. ISBN 06

430026 9. The seminal study of the spirit that animated Renaissance culture in the context of what had come before.

Partner, Peter. *Renaissance Rome, 1500–1559: A Portrait of a Society.* Berkley, CA: University of California Press, 1976. ISBN 0 520 03945 9. The most accessible study of the city and the papacy in the first half of the 16th century.

Partridge, Loren. *The Art of Renaissance Rome, 1400–1600.* New York: Harry N. Abrams, 1996. ISBN 0 8109 2718 7. A beautifully illustrated and important study of the development of a distinctive Roman Renaissance culture.

Petrarch, Francesco. *The Secret.* Edited and with an introduction by Carol E. Quillen. Boston: Bedford/St. Martin's, 2003. ISBN 0 312 15438 0. The first psychological autobiography written in Europe since antiquity.

———. *Selected Sonnets, Odes and Letters.* Edited by Thomas Goddard Bergin. Crofts Classics. Northbrook, IL: AHM Publishing Corporation, 1966. ISBN 0 88295 066 5. A selection of writings by Petrarch that reflects the extensive interests of this first Renaissance man.

———. *Book Without a Name (Liber Sine Nomine).* Translation by Norman P. Zacour. Medieval Sources in Translation: 11. Toronto: Pontifical Institute of Medieval Studies, 1973. ISBN 0 88844 260 2. A collection of letters written by Petrarch describing the depravity of the Avignonese papal court.

Phillips, Mark. *Francesco Guicciardini: The Historian's Craft.* Toronto: University of Toronto Press, 1977. ISBN 0 8020 5371 8. The best modern study of Guicciardini as a historian.

———. *The Memoirs of Marco Parenti: A Life in Medici Florence.* Princeton, NJ: Princeton University Press, 1987. ISBN 0 691 00833 7. A narrative of an individual patrician's life during the period of Piero and Lorenzo de'Medici.

Polizzotto, Lorenzo. *The Elect Nation: The Savonarolan Movement in Florence, 1494–1545.* Oxford-Warburg Studies. Oxford: Clarendon Press, 1994. ISBN 0 199 20600 7. The best study of Savonarola and his influence in Florence, as well as the continuation of his theocratic ideas in the city until their suppression by Cosimo I.

Portoghesi, Paolo. *Rome of the Renaissance*. London: Phaidon, 1972. ISBN 07148 1419 9. A beautifully illustrated study of Renaissance architecture in Rome.

Robb, Nesca A. *Neoplatonism of the Italian Renaissance*. London: George Allen & Unwin Ltd., 1969. ISBN 0 04 940026 6. The most accessible and clearest formulation of Florentine Neoplatonism available.

Robin, Diana. *Filelfo in Milan: Writings, 1451–77*. Princeton, NJ: Princeton University Press, 1991. ISBN 0 69 103185 1. A collection of materials written by the artist Filelfo during the period of his residence with the Sforza rulers of Milan.

Sapori, Armando. *The Italian Merchant in the Middle Ages*. Translated by Patricia Ann Kennen. New York: Norton, 1970. ISBN 0 393 0995 6 3. Still a necessary study by a leading Italian economic historian of mercantile activity in the medieval Mediterranean.

Simon, Kate. *Renaissance Tapestry: The Gonzaga of Mantua*. New York: Harper and Row, 1988. ISBN 0060158476. An accessible survey of the Gonzaga rulers of Mantua during the Renaissance.

Skinner, Quentin. *Machiavelli*. Oxford: Oxford University Press, 1981. ISBN 0 19 287516 7. An excellent, short discussion of Machiavelli and his work, written by a leading political philosopher.

Stephens, J. N. *The Fall of the Florentine Republic, 1512–1530*. Oxford: Clarendon Press, 1983. ISBN 0 19 822599 7. A specialist study of Florence from the return of the Medici until the suppression of the last republic.

Stinger, Charles. L. *The Renaissance in Rome*. Bloomington, IN: Indiana University Press, 1998. ISBN 0 253 21208 1. The best comprehensive survey of the city of Rome during the sweep of the Renaissance.

Tabacco, Giovanni. *The Struggle for Power in Medieval Italy: Structures of Political Rule*. Cambridge Medieval Textbooks. Cambridge: Cambridge University Press, 1989. ISBN 0 521 33680 5. Still a central analysis of medieval Italy, written by a leading Italian historian.

Tafuri, Manfredo. *Venice and the Renaissance*. Translated by Jessica Levine. Massachusetts: Massachusetts Institute of Technology, 1989. ISBN 0 262 20072 4. A series of insights into Venetian culture and society during the Renaissance, written by an eminent Italian scholar.

Vespasiano da Bisticci. *The Vespasiano Memoirs: Lives of Illustrious Men of the XVth Century*. Renaissance Society of America Reprint Texts 7. Translated by William George and Emily Waters. Introduction by Myron P. Gilmore. Toronto: University of Toronto Press in association with the Renaissance Society of America, 1997. ISBN 0 8020 7968 7. A wonderful collection of biographies of the clients of the 15th-century Florentine bookseller Vespasiano da Bisticci, rich in personal anecdotes.

Viroli, Maurizio. *Niccolò's Smile: A Biography of Machiavelli*. Translated by Anthony Shugaar. New York: Farrar, Straus and Giroux, 2000. ISBN 0 374 22187 1. The most recent and intriguing of the great many biographies of the Renaissance statesman and historian.

Walker, Paul Robert. *The Feud That Sparked the Renaissance: How Brunelleschi and Ghiberti Changed the Art World*. New York: Harper Collins, 2002. ISBN 0 380 97787 7. An engaging study of the competition over the commission for the Cathedral of Florence.

Weinstein, Donald. *Savonarola and Florence: Prophesy and Patriotism in the Renaissance*. Princeton, NJ: Princeton University Press, 1970. An important discussion of Savonarola and the role his prophetic sermons played in the millenarian traditions and Humanistic vision of Florence.

Weiss, Roberto. *The Renaissance Discovery of Classical Antiquity*. New York: Humanities Press, 1973. ISBN 0631116907. A short, easily digestible discussion of the contributions Renaissance Humanists made to the recovery of ancient texts.

Welch, Evelyn. *Art and Society in Italy, 1350–1500*. Oxford History of Art. Oxford: Oxford University Press, 1997. ISBN 0 19 284203 X. An excellent, illustrated survey of the relationship between art and social structure during the Renaissance.

Westfall, C. W. *In This Most Perfect Paradise: Alberti, Nicholas V, and the Invention of Conscious Urban Planning in Rome, 1447–1455*. University Park, PA, and London: Pennsylvania University Press, 1974. ISBN 0 271 01175 0. A fascinating illustrated study of Pope Nicholas V's ambitious plans for rebuilding the city of Rome and his use of Leon Battista Alberti as his architect and urban planner.

Wilkins, Ernest Hatch. *Life of Petrarch.* Phoenix Books. Chicago: University of Chicago Press, 1961. Still the most readable and comprehensive short biography of Petrarch, written by one of the greatest contemporary Petrarch scholars.

———. *Petrarch's Eight Years in Milan.* The Medieval Academy of America Publication No. 69. Cambridge, MA: Medieval Academy of America, 1958. A detailed, concentrated discussion of the years Petrarch spent in Milan at the court of Giovanni Visconti.

Woodward, William Harrison. *Vittorino da Feltre and Other Humanist Educators.* Classics in Education No. 18. New York: Bureau of Publications, Teachers College, Columbia University, 1963. A collection of Humanist treatises on education, written by the leading teachers of the age.